A Dynamic Theory of Taxation

To Xenda and Ishbel

Anthony J. Laramie gratefully acknowledges the support of the Jerome Levy Economics Institute of Bard College.

A Dynamic Theory of Taxation

Integrating Kalecki into Modern Public Finance

Anthony J. Laramie

Professor of Economics, Merrimack College, MA., US

and

Douglas Mair

Professor of Economics, Heriot–Watt University, UK

Edward Elgar

Cheltenham, UK • Northampton, MA, USA

© Anthony J. Laramie and Douglas Mair 2000

Published by
Edward Elgar Publishing Limited
Glensanda House
Montpellier Parade
Cheltenham
Glos GL50 1UA
UK

Edward Elgar Publishing, Inc.
136 West Street
Suite 202
Northampton
Massachusetts 01060
USA

A catalogue record for this book is available from the British Library

Library of Congress Cataloguing in Publication Data
Laramie, Anthony J., 1956–
    A dynamic theory of taxation : integrating Kalecki into modern public finance/
Anthony J. Laramie and Douglas Mair.
    Includes bibliographical references.
    1. Taxation. 2. Finance, Public. 3. Kalecki, Michal. I. Mair, Douglas. II. Title.

HJ2305.L36 2000
336.2—dc21

99–059156

ISBN 1 85898 668 0

Printed and bound in Great Britain by Bookcraft (Bath) Ltd.

Contents

Contents

List of tables

1. The rationale for Kaleckian tax analysis

1 INTRODUCTION

Kalecki had the profound insight as early as 1937 that a consequence of the publication of Keynes's *General Theory* was that the theory of the incidence of taxation had to be rethought. He set out his ideas in a paper in the *Economic Journal* (Kalecki, 1937) in which he analysed the short-period effects of the taxation of commodities, incomes and capital on employment, national income and its distribution with capital equipment and money wages given. As anyone who has read Kalecki will be aware, he was not the man to make extravagant claims about the significance of his work. It was, therefore, surprisingly uncharacteristic of him to claim that the conclusions he reached in his 1937 paper were 'unexpected ... and of practical importance' (Kalecki, 1937, p. 444).

This gives rise to a puzzle. While Kalecki made a number of important theoretical contributions, particularly in the area of business cycles, his approach was always a practical one. His work is characterized by empirical examples where he uses data to support or illustrate his theoretical ideas. Having concluded that he had arrived at 'unexpected' results of 'practical importance', we might have expected Kalecki to develop his early ideas on taxation into his later work on investment and business cycles. This he never did.

In the literature on Kalecki and post Keynesian economics that has emerged in recent years, there is no discussion of a distinctly Kaleckian approach to taxation or fiscal policy (Sawyer, 1985; Reynolds, 1987; Arestis, 1992; Lavoie, 1992; King, 1996). In the post Keynesian literature, the discussion of fiscal policy is Keynesian (Davidson, 1994). In his chapter in Eichner's *A Guide to Post Keynesian Economics* (1979), Asimakopulos (1979) recognizes that while post Keynesian theory has developed principally from Keynes and Kalecki, in the theory of tax incidence the influence of Kalecki is the more important. But, having made that critical distinction, Asimakopulos then proceeds to discuss an essentially Keynesian model of tax incidence he developed with Burbidge (Asimakopulos and Burbidge, 1974).

Both Asimakopulos and Paladini (1989) agree that Kalecki's 1937 article on taxation has not received the attention it deserves. Asimakopulos offers no explanation for this neglect. Paladini (1989, p. 226) recognizes that a 'baffling

1

situation' has arisen. While Kalecki was fully aware of the 'surprising results' he had obtained, according to Paladini 'a veil of silence has nevertheless been spread over them'. He offers as possible explanations: 1) that Kalecki's work on taxation came too early; 2) that Kalecki's choice of title for his 1937 paper was not particularly illuminating; 3) that Kalecki has been regarded mainly as a business cycle theorist; or 4) that Kalecki's hypotheses were too 'Kaleckian' and had a deterring effect on faint-hearted economists of a nervous (non-Kaleckian) disposition. Be that as it may, there has been only limited recognition of Kalecki's ideas on taxation within post Keynesian circles, amounting at best to a token obeisance in the direction of his 1937 paper. Outside post Keynesian circles, ignorance of Kalecki on taxation is almost absolute.

This creates a number of dilemmas for us. The first is a consequence of the lack of a fully articulated Kaleckian theory of taxation. Our major purpose in this book is to develop such a theory by weaving the various strands of Kaleckian theory of taxation, theory of income determination, theory of income distribution, theory of investment, theory of the business cycle, theory of growth, theory of the political business cycle into an integrated, dynamic macroeconomic theory of tax incidence. In developing such a theory, we have the problem of deciding how faithful we should be to Kalecki's original formulation of these various elements. One (perhaps presumptuous) approach would be for us to attempt to present a theory of tax incidence very much as Kalecki himself might have written it. This 'pure' Kalecki approach would have the merit of theoretical integrity and would seek to establish Kalecki's own personal claim to recognition in the realm of public finance. The difficulty of this line of approach is that it is open to a number of the criticisms that are laid against Kaleckian theory in general – that it is excessively mechanical, incomplete in certain key respects and wrong in others.

In this book we more or less reject the 'Kalecki right or wrong' approach and we have therefore introduced into our analysis a number of important refinements and extensions to Kalecki's original formulations. We recognize that Kalecki's work has been critically evaluated by a host of others (for a good literature review see Courvisanos, 1996), and that a number of other extensions, refinements and corrections to Kalecki have been developed. Nevertheless, many of Kalecki's basic insights, for example, his theories of distribution and profits, remain at the core of these developments. Furthermore, we recognize that there is a diversity of competing and complementary models within the post Keynesian tradition, and we understand that Kalecki's theory of taxation could be introduced into those models, but, ultimately, such an introduction represents a modification to Kalecki's core theory. So, in order to make life easy for ourselves, although not necessarily for the reader, we show how Kalecki's core theories of profits, pricing, income determination, investment, the business cycle, and economic growth are modified by the introduction of taxation. In addition, we consider the implications of Kalecki's theory of taxation for such questions as the incidence of the corporation income tax and the effects of state and local taxation.

In developing Kalecki's theory of taxation into the core of his other theories, we introduce three major extensions. First, we introduce the theory of tax incidence into Kalecki's theory of pricing and distribution. By doing so, we are able to consider the political economy of taxation (see Chapter 2). Second, we modify Kalecki's theories of investment and of the business cycle and the trend to account explicitly for the role of taxation. Kalecki himself was not satisfied with the state in which he left these theories at the time of his death. He identified certain lines of inquiry along which he thought that future research into understanding the determination of investment and growth should proceed (Kalecki, 1971, p. 183). These include the contribution to profits from investment in new equipment, the rate at which existing equipment is replaced by new equipment and the share of profits in national income. Third, we extend Kalecki's theory of growth. Here again, on his own admission, Kalecki was not altogether happy with the state in which he had left his theory at the time of his death. Kalecki's theory has been corrected by Gomulka et al. (1990). The effect of their correction has been to transform Kalecki's original version from a stagnationist, under-consumptionist theory into a balanced theory encompassing both 'rash' and 'cautious' capitalism. Gomulka et al. achieve this by formulating what they call Kalecki's Growth Proposition that 'technological innovation is good for employment'. The effect of this reformulation, in their opinion, is to bring Kalecki much closer to Schumpeter and take him much further away from Marx. This reformulation of Kalecki's growth theory is consistent with Courvisanos's behavioural reformulation, an important element of which is the Schumpeter-inspired neo-institutionalist theory of innovation. We show in Chapter 5 how taxation can be introduced into this revised version of Kalecki's growth theory. As we demonstrate in Chapters 3 and 4, we have gone a considerable way to incorporating Kalecki's suggestions into our analysis of the effects of taxation on the cyclical behaviour of investment, and we consider the public policy implications for economic stability, economic growth, income distribution and unemployment.

However, we recognize that our extensions do not overcome other limitations in Kalecki's formulations of his theories of investment and growth. Courvisanos has published a substantial revision to Kalecki's theory of investment by integrating into it the idea of the 'susceptibility cycle'. Courvisanos links the works of Kalecki, Minsky, Steindl and others to show how profits, capacity utilization, financial constraints and expectations influence the investment cycle for different type of firms. In doing so, Courvisanos links two critical aspects of the investment process – the 'character of investment' and the 'psychological attitudes' of decision-makers – into a 'susceptibility cycle' to provide an integrated endogenous investment cycle. Courvisanos (1996, p. 116) defines susceptibility as 'the psychological tension felt by entrepreneurs in relation to their fragile confidence about a particular investment decision, given the level of investment decisions already committed'. Our extensions consider the effects of taxation on the character of investment, the amplitude of the business cycle and the trajectory of the trend, without focusing on the impact of taxation on the psychological attitudes or for that matter capacity utilization. Kalecki did have something to say about each of these,[1] but he abstracted from these determinants in developing his 'automatic' business cycle equations. We return to these issues in the concluding chapter.

By nailing our colours to the Kaleckian mast, we create another dilemma for ourselves, namely, how do we deal with Keynes? The short answer is that we don't. Within the post Keynesian school, there are two principal streams. There are those who argue that post Keynesian economics is (should be?) based on Keynes's ideas with the clear intent to extend them to their logical full development (Arestis, 1992, p. ix). Thus, post Keynesian economics purports to complete the aborted Keynesian revolution. This brand of post Keynesian economists views the 'grand neoclassical synthesis' as fundamentally neoclassical theory supplemented by a 'Keynesian' macroeconomics. This is very different from Keynes's own intentions. This 'grand neoclassical synthesis' has been the dominant system of thought within the world of academic economics and has had a major influence on the development of economic policy in most western societies.

The other principal strand of post Keynesian economics is identified as comprising those economists who are seeking to extend and generalize the seminal ideas of the unorthodox Cambridge economists of the 1950s, most notably Joan Robinson, Richard Kahn and Nicholas Kaldor (Lavoie, 1992, p. 1). While initially drawing its inspiration from Keynes, this strand of post Keynesian economics has over time progressively aligned itself with Kalecki as a preferable starting point for an alternative to neoclassical economics.

There may be difficulties in finding an accommodation between these two strands of post Keynesianism. Bhaduri (1986, p. ix) is of the opinion that the

---

1. Kalecki abstracted from the role of varying capacity utilization as a determinant of investment because he assumed excess capacity throughout the business cycle. As Courvisanos (1996, p. 21) notes, Steindl introduced planned excess capacity into the investment decision, and, therefore, modifies Kalecki. Kalecki also considered the effects of taxation on capitalists' consumption, but argued with all taxation being used to finance state expenditure on doles for the unemployed or on the wages of government employees, where workers spend all their wages, then a change in taxation would have no impact on the actual level of capitalists' income (profits), and, therefore, would not change capitalists' propensity to spend. Kalecki and Keynes debated this issue, and Moggridge (1983, p. 791) characterizes this debate as anticipating the advent of rational expectations.

very success of Keynesianism in the 1950s and 1960s contained its own seed of destruction. He writes:

> Unfortunately, the initial success of conventional Keynesianism blinded most of its exponents and practitioners to the inherently radical content of that theory. One has to learn this from Kalecki rather than from Keynes. Taking his clues from Marx, Kalecki not only independently discovered most of the central propositions of the Keynesian theory, but he also set it out with striking clarity to point to a set of problems which conventional Keynesianism had preferred to avoid. Conventional Keynesians remained content with the idea that capitalism could be managed by the State. And, they propagated a view of state-managed capitalism based on co-operation rather than conflict among the contending economic classes. In Kalecki's writings there was no such wishful thinking. He recognized that a view of co-operative capitalism was bound to run into problems in the longer run, as economic conflict among the classes begins to surface. He forewarned us about it in his theory of political business cycles.

The lost radicalism of Keynesian economics can only be recovered, according to Bhaduri, by concentrating on the common macroeconomic tradition of Marx, Kalecki and Keynes. Kaldor (1983, p. 15) is quite clear that Kalecki provides a better starting point than Keynes:

> Kalecki's original model of unemployment equilibrium, which takes monopolistic competition as its starting point, is clearly superior to Keynes's.

Joan Robinson (1977, pp. 14–15) was to become a great admirer of Kalecki:

> Kalecki was free from remnants of old-fashioned theory which Keynes had failed to throw off ... [he was better able] to weave together the analysis of imperfect competition and of effective demand and it was this that opened up the way for what goes under the name of post Keynesian theory.

We do not wish to become embroiled in a debate with our fellow post Keynesians as to whether the way ahead for post Keynesian economics is: 1) a 'fundamentalist' return to 'pure' Keynes; or 2) a synthesis of Marxist, Kaleckian, Keynesian and Kaldorian economics, as Bhaduri and Lavoie suggest; or 3) an unequivocal recognition of the superiority of either Kalecki or Keynes as the founding figure of post Keynesian economics. Instead, we prefer an eclectic approach that encompasses Kalecki, Keynes and others.

However, in the area of tax incidence theory, which is the central concern of this book, it is clear to us that Kalecki is the appropriate starting point. We have already cited Asimakopulos above as one authority for our claim. Eatwell (1976, pp. 165–6) identifies the fundamental incompatibility of neoclassical theory and the basic principles of the Keynesian theory of effective demand (of which more below). He demonstrated how a general Kaleckian theory of the determination of the level and distribution of income can be used to analyse real fiscal incidence.

In this chapter, we consider the critical issues that need to be addressed in tax incidence theory and how tax incidence theory poses a macro/micro conflict or tension within neoclassical economics. We contrast Kalecki and orthodox analysis, and, given that tax incidence theory is applied income distribution theory, consider the limitations of the marginal productivity theory of income distribution. We develop Kalecki's 'degree of monopoly' theory of income distribution as a useful alternative to the neoclassical approach and show how this theory can be used to reconcile the tensions between micro and macro theory. We show that in Kalecki's framework both micro and macro foundations are present. We summarize Kalecki's (1937) theory of taxation and discuss some extensions. Finally, we conclude the chapter by offering the Kaleckian approach as a viable alternative to understanding the incidence and effects of taxation.

2   CRITICAL ISSUES OF TAX INCIDENCE THEORY

We are reminded of the story of the Scottish professor of divinity who, having completely perplexed his students and himself over some obscure aspect of Old Testament theology, finally confessed, 'Gentlemen, we have here a problem of considerable difficulty. Let us look it squarely in the face and pass on'. In recent years, a number of distinguished economists have found themselves in the same predicament as the Scottish divine. The issue causing their problem has been the dichotomy between the micro and macroeconomic aspects of tax incidence theory and fiscal policy. At the macroeconomic level, economists have long recognized the role of taxation in affecting aggregate demand. At the microeconomic level, economists have analysed the effects and incidence of taxation by focusing on supply-side determinants, ignoring the demand effects (and interdependent tax-shifting factors). No bridge has been built between the two levels of analysis, and the notion that tax-induced changes in aggregate demand matter seems to have withered on the vine.

From our perspective, one of the critical issues facing modern tax incidence theory is the almost complete neglect given to the effects of taxation on the distribution of income and the level of demand. In other words, modern theory of tax incidence and its effects is relegated to a world where aggregate demand does not matter. In our opinion, the notion that aggregate demand does not matter is simply too strong an assumption. Our intent in this book is to bring aggregate demand analysis back into the analysis of the effects and incidence of taxation. Kalecki's 1937 seminal paper serves as the foundation for reintroducing aggregate demand analysis. We recognize that this neglect is the result of the macro/micro dichotomy in orthodox economics.

Atkinson and Stiglitz (1980, p. 222) recognize the dilemma between micro and macroeconomic approaches to taxation when they write:

> The general equilibrium analysis of tax incidence has to date been undertaken largely independently of the literature on macroeconomics. Thus, competitive equilibrium models, with all markets clearing, have been used to investigate the incidence of different taxes, whereas a quite separate literature, using aggregate demand/monetary models, has examined the implications of taxes for the level of employment and the rate of inflation. In other areas of economics, this gap has been narrowed, a notable example being the integration of relative price effects and income-expenditure determination in international economics; but in public finance this separation has persisted much longer.

Then, in a footnote, Atkinson and Stiglitz observe:

> However, note should be made of work in the Keynesian tradition. An early example is Kalecki (1937).

But making this note is as far as Atkinson and Stiglitz go. However, the problem they identify, the dichotomy between the microeconomic and macroeconomic dimensions of public finance, remains unresolved.

Another highly regarded graduate text in public economics is Auerbach and Feldstein, *Handbook of Public Economics* (1987) in which the chapter on tax incidence is contributed by Kotlikoff and Summers. They rightly recognize that the incidence of taxes is a fundamental question in public economics that has attracted the attention of economic theorists at least since Ricardo. Kotlikoff and Summers make no reference to Kalecki in their extensive discussion of the literature on tax incidence. But they, too, are driven to the same conclusion as Atkinson and Stiglitz. In terms of the importance and excitement that Kotlikoff and Summers attach to new theoretical developments in tax incidence theory there is a strong resonance with the sentiments that Kalecki had expressed fifty years earlier. They write (Kotlikoff and Summers, 1987, p. 1088):

> Economics is at its best when it offers important insights that contradict initial, casual impressions. The theory of tax incidence provides a rich assortment of such insights ... The study of tax incidence is both fun, because it offers such surprising findings, and very important, because of its implications about the impacts of government policies. Much of the current tax incidence literature considers settings of certainty, perfect information, and market clearing. As more sophisticated models relax these assumptions, the theory of tax incidence will be enriched and, with all probability, provide even more surprising and exciting insights.

Kotlikoff and Summers (pp. 1043–4) recognize that tax incidence is part of a broad study of how exogenous interventions affect the economy and is necessarily predicated on a theory of economic equilibrium. This means that the conclusions are heavily dependent on which theory of economic equilibrium is chosen. They admit to following, *faute de mieux,* the main thrust of the literature and studying the effects of taxes in competitive economies in which markets clear and are constrained by the supply side. They do so, not because they necessarily believe in the realism of such conditions but because of the lack of a widely accepted and fully articulated alternative to the competitive paradigm. Our principal purpose in this book is to take the first steps towards presenting such an alternative paradigm.

Professor Richard Musgrave is widely regarded as the doyen of modern public finance theorists. He has recently drawn attention to the continuing tensions between the micro and macro aspects of fiscal policy and has posed the basic question as to whether the distinction between them is a valid one (Musgrave, 1997). The issues raised by Musgrave are important and central to the theme of this book. For that reason, we present them at some length.

He expresses the problem in the following terms (Musgrave, 1997, p. 13):

> More basically, is the distinction between the micro and macro issues [of public finance] a valid one? ... The role of fiscal policy and indeed the consequences of fiscal behaviour depend on the macro as well as on the micro functioning of the economy. But where micro analysis has moved along a steady path, macro models have remained in a state of flux, as have perceptions of the macro role of fiscal policy and the interplay of micro and macro concerns.

Fiscal policy has both micro and macro objectives, but how these interact remains an issue of debate. To use Musgrave's own terminology, what are the interactions and conflicts between the allocation, distribution and stabilization branches of public finance? Even in a context of market clearing, is it appropriate to regard macroeconomic behaviour simply as the aggregation of microeconomic behaviour? Musgrave thinks not. While Musgrave appears to be satisfied with the microeconomic aspects of public finance theory, he recognizes that macroeconomic models remain in a state of flux, as do perceptions of the macroeconomic role of fiscal policy and the interplay between microeconomic and macroeconomic issues.

The pre-Keynesian classical view saw fiscal policy in the microeconomic context of efficient resource use and distributional equity. The macroeconomic concerns for the effects of fiscal policy on savings and capital formation were subordinated to microeconomic concerns over incentives and were not seen as a means of maintaining an efficient level of economic activity. The advent of the Keynesian model switched the macroeconomic emphasis from one of market clearing to one of what Musgrave calls market jamming. Fiscal policy, either by increasing government expenditure or by cutting taxes, was seen as the macroeconomic solution to the failure of markets to clear. But increasing concerns over the possibility of ever growing burdens of public debt and the emergence of stagflation brought about the demise of the Keynesian model.

The 'neoclassical synthesis' of the 1960s reinstated monetary policy as an effective device to be used in conjunction with fiscal policy to achieve the correct policy balance. The return of growth theory to the classical vision of market clearing has resulted in equilibrium growth models identifying the effect of the state of the government's budgetary balance to be on the overall rate of saving and consequently on capital formation.

Musgrave (1997, p. 16) poses a set of questions emanating from the equilibrium growth model approach. He does not consider that any of them have been answered satisfactorily. Our intention in this book is either to attempt to answer them or, if we cannot do so, at least to provide a theoretical framework within which they can be answered.

1. Are the short-run microeconomic premises (based on market failure) consistent with the long-run premises (based on market clearing)?
2. Can both versions offer policy guidance at the same time?
3. Are the short- and long-run models alternatives each analytically consistent, but based on incompatible assumptions?
4. Can their incompatibility be resolved by replacing full employment as a policy target by the natural rate of unemployment?
5. Will their incompatibility wash out in the long run by a tendency of the economy to fluctuate around a full-employment level?
6. Will monetary policy be sufficiently powerful to implement short-run stabilization and allow fiscal policy to operate as in the classical system?
7. What should be the reliance on public investment as a means of securing growth if private sector investment is lagging?

Failure to answer these questions leaves macro policy, and within it the role of fiscal policy, in limbo between the Scylla of the short-run constraints of the neoclassical model and the Charybdis of the long-run logic of the classical model. Nor is the problem resolved by recourse to the new classical model which argues that rational expectations will render stabilization policy ineffective.

Musgrave (1997, pp. 20–21) argues that at a normative level, the conflicts between the microeconomic and macroeconomic dimensions of fiscal policy can be resolved. In practice, however, a number of problems arise. Current orthodox public finance thinking sets a great deal of store by the discipline of a balanced budget. In such a situation, any fiscal action to expand the economy by combining increases in expenditure and taxation has to be matched by simultaneous action to reduce taxation and expenditure. As a consequence, the multiplier effects of fiscal action are largely lost and the burden of stabilization has to lie primarily with monetary policy. Any advantages to be had from the combined use of fiscal and monetary instruments are largely dissipated.

Musgrave and the public finance orthodoxy are sceptical of the use of tax structures as a means of achieving fiscal objectives. Musgrave's (1997, pp. 22–3) opinion is that conflicts will arise when trying to use a single tax structure. His view is that the use of a single tax system to alter the level of aggregate demand via changes in the overall level of taxation will have possibly unwelcome distributional effects. As he correctly recognizes, the problem is not simply one of choosing the level of taxation, but also of choosing among taxes. For reasons that will become apparent later in this book, we disagree fundamentally with Musgrave on the economic feasibility of using tax structures as the means of achieving macro objectives although we do recognize the existence of political constraints. Recognizing the connection between the distribution and level of incomes, we argue, is the principal means by which the circle of the incompatibility of the microeconomic and macroeconomic aspects of fiscal policy may be squared.

The microeconomic foundations of public finance theory to which Musgrave refers are those of orthodox neoclassical economics. Economic agents are rational utility/profit maximizers, operating in a world of certainty under competitive market conditions. The distribution of income is determined in accordance with marginal revenue productivities. The normative criteria derive from Paretian welfare economics and the theory of the state derives from Downs (1957), Buchanan and Tullock (1971), Niskanen et al. (1971). The macroeconomic foundations are Keynesian or some variant thereof.

3   CONTRASTS BETWEEN KALECKIAN AND ORTHODOX ANALYSIS

In this book we avoid the microeconomic, macroeconomic and normative foundations of conventional public finance theory. As Sawyer (1985, p. 8) observes, reading Kalecki can come as something of a shock and present difficulties for those steeped in neoclassical economics. Sawyer (1985, pp. 8–12) identifies three broad aspects of Kalecki's work which contrast with neoclassical orthodoxy.

First, Kalecki consistently viewed capitalist economies as 'semi-monopolistic and monopolistic'. He regarded perfect competition 'as a most unrealistic assumption' which 'when its actual status of a handy model is forgotten becomes a dangerous myth' (Kalecki, 1971, p. 158). Second, Kalecki made little use of, and indeed was hostile to, the concept of equilibrium analysis.[2] He regarded equilibrium positions as hypothetical ones that would not be reached. There was a danger, he thought, in confusing possible equilibrium positions with what actually happens. Kalecki was concerned with the evolution of economic systems through time without imposing the view that they would reach some ultimate position of equilibrium or that they would grow at some balanced equilibrium rate of growth. Third, Kalecki made virtually no use of the standard tools of neoclassical economics, the utility function and the production function.[3] He never used the concept of utility at all and made only limited use of something that might be described as a production function and then only in the context of a socialist economy. Fourth, Kalecki used historical time instead of the logical time. Thus, Kalecki referred to the short period, where investment was fixed by past decisions, or the long period, where investment was a variable. In the orthodox approaches time is referred to in runs which logically represent the variability of inputs – in the short run some inputs are fixed and others are variable, in the long run, the planning horizon, all inputs are variable. The orthodox approach of using the logical time creates a situation where the short run does not matter in influencing the long run. In contrast, Kalecki sees the long period made up of and dependent upon the short period. In Kalecki's approach history matters.

Kalecki operated in the Ricardo–Marx tradition that stresses the importance of the conflicts of interest between social classes. In the atomistic world of neoclassical economics, the starting point of analysis is the utility/profit maximizing individual. Kalecki's use of the social classes of workers and capitalists ignored the orthodox Paretian welfare criteria.

These differences between Kaleckian and orthodox approaches have implications for the analysis of the effects and incidence of taxation. First, from a Kaleckian perspective the incidence and effects of taxation has to be understood in the context of the legitimation and accumulation functions of the state. We show in Chapter 2 that redistributive tax policies need not pose any economic contradiction between these functions and that the contradictions are more likely to political in nature. We also show that objectives of full employment, stability, equity and growth can be achieved through fiscal policy. Some redistributive tax policies can be Pareto optimal – in the sense that it is possible, depending upon the conditions, to improve one social class's wellbeing (e.g.

2. We recognize that Kalecki (1954) developed his famous profit equation using the national income and product identity that GDP in terms of expenditures equals GDP in terms of income, and in so doing he minimized the role of unplanned investment. He did so by assuming inventories to be a highly liquid asset.
3. However, by assuming constant unit labour costs, Kalecki implicitly assumes a constant labour to output ratio.

labour, the poor, the unemployed) without hurting another social class's welfare (e.g. capitalists). Second, we discuss the incidence and effects of taxation in terms of functional distributions – distributions in terms of wages and profits – as opposed to personal distributions.[4] Third, given Kalecki's use of historical time, profits taxes, as we show in subsequent chapters, can be shifted in the short period, depending on the government budget stance and other things. Tax shifting then has dynamic long-period effects on the economy through changes in investment. In the orthodox approach, assuming that marginal costs are unaffected by a profits tax in the short run and no tax-induced demand effects are present, the firm bears the full incidence of the profits tax. In the long run, the incidence of the profits tax depends on factor demand and supply conditions and the elasticities of substitution between factors of production (again assuming no tax-induced demand effects).

As we shall see later in this book, tax-induced changes in the distribution of income and the reactions thereby generated are extremely important. The orthodox economists (and Keynes implicitly) espouse the marginal productivity theory of income distribution.[5] In contrast, we employ Kalecki's 'degree of monopoly' theory of income distribution to provide one of the foundations for understanding the incidence and effects of taxation.

4   DEGREE OF MONOPOLY THEORY OF INCOME DISTRIBUTION

By adopting Kalecki's 'degree of monopoly' theory, we recognize that we lay ourselves open to criticism but we argue that if Kalecki's theory is interpreted properly then it is unquestionably a behavioural theory of income distribution. The version of Kalecki's theory we use is the one which appeared in *Theory of Economic Dynamics* (Kalecki, 1954). This provided an integrated treatment of the theories of income determination and income distribution, under which both microeconomic and macroeconomic forces act together. Direct labour's share of national income is determined by the process of firms marking up their direct costs of production (wages and materials) to obtain prices. The level of profits is determined by investment decisions taken in the past and 'the national output will be pushed up to the point where profits carved out of it in accordance with the "distribution factors" are equal to the sum of capitalists' consumption

4. Since most of family income is derived from wages and salaries, we suspect a close but not exact relationship between functional and personal distributions of income.
5. For a sample of the critiques of neoclassical theory, including the marginal productivity theory of income distribution, see Lavoie (1992), Lydall (1979), Braff (1988), Trussler (1982) and Garegnani (1978).

and investment' (Kalecki, 1954, p. 47). The essential feature of Kalecki's theory is that, unlike marginal productivity theory, it is consistent with an approach to economics under which income and employment are determined, at least in part, by effective demand and where persistent underemployment is possible.

For firms in the manufacturing sector of the economy, Kalecki argued that prices are determined by a markup over prime costs. 'In fixing its price the firm takes into account its average prime costs and the prices of other firms producing similar products' (Kalecki, 1954, p. 12). This is captured by the equation:

$$p = mu + np^*$$ (1.1)

where p = firm's own price; u = firm's average prime cost; p^* = average industry price. The coefficients m and n characterize the price-fixing policy of the firm and reflect what may be called the 'degree of monopoly' of the firm's position.

By aggregating across all firms in an industry, rearranging and defining $k = (m^*/1 - n^*)$ where m^* and n^* are appropriately weighted averages of m and n, we obtain:

$$p = ku$$ (1.2)

Thus, k is determined by the degree of monopoly.

In this context the term 'degree of monopoly' does not have the interpretation given to it by Lerner (1934). It is not merely the reciprocal of the elasticity of demand since 'in view of the uncertainties faced in the process of price fixing it will not be assumed that the firm attempts to maximise its profits in any precise sort of manner' (Kalecki, 1954, p. 12). Following Reynolds (1983), we prefer to think of the markup as reflecting the institutional and environmental influences on the firm. In this respect, Kalecki's is a behavioural theory of pricing. Firms are not assumed to maximize precisely either the level of profits in the short period or the rate of return on capital. The pricing behaviour indicated by equation (1.1) is consistent with a model in which firms aim to maximize profits in the long period, recognizing that the long-run trend is a slowly changing component of a chain of short-period situations.

In Kalecki (1954, p. 17) the main factors bringing about changes in the degree of monopoly are 'first and foremost the process of concentration in industry leading to the formation of giant corporations'; then 'the second major influence is the development of sales promotion through advertising, selling agents etc.'; and, finally, 'in addition to the above, two other factors must be considered: (a) the influence of changes in the level of overheads in relation to prime costs upon the degree of monopoly, and (b) the significance of the power of trade unions'.

Once the markup is established for a particular industry, direct labour's share of income for that industry is determined according to the relation:

$$\alpha = 1/[1 + (k - 1)(1 + j)] \tag{1.3}$$

where α is direct labour's share of value added, k is the markup and j is the ratio of wage costs to material costs.

Misinterpretation of Kalecki's 'degree of monopoly' has led to much unnecessary confusion and accusations that it is nothing more than a tautology. Following Reynolds (1983), we use the term 'degree of monopoly' to refer to those institutional and environmental influences which affect firms' pricing behaviour. On this interpretation, the ratio of price to prime cost is a *reflection* of the degree of monopoly rather than its *definition* and consequently the question of tautology does not arise.

Hahn (1972, p. 2) argues that distribution theory has got into a muddle in recent years. For his purposes, he defines a theory of distribution as neoclassical if it employs a model of perfect competition in permanent equilibrium, what he calls the production theory of distribution. This theory has nothing simply to offer to the question of why the shares of wages and profits are what they are. This is because the distribution of income between social classes is not an explanatory variable of neoclassical theory. Hahn (1972, p. 159) argues that the theory of distribution held by most economists has not altered significantly since the publication of Marshall's *Principles*. The only significant departure he sees from the main trend of thought is Kalecki's analysis of the degree of monopoly.

However, Hahn (1972, pp. 44–5) identifies a number of problems with Kalecki's theory. While it may be useful in analysing the distribution of income in a depression, Hahn considers it to be not proven on theoretical grounds to apply to stationary states with zero net investment or disinvestment. Other problematic aspects of Kalecki that Hahn identifies are: 1) the 'average degree of monopoly' is not a measure associated with any of the attributes normally associated with monopoly; a change in the degree of monopoly, therefore, need not imply a change in the degree of concentration of industry or any increase in any other index of monopoly power; 2) Kalecki's theory cannot deal adequately with oligopoly; 3) Kalecki stipulates a supply curve of entrepreneurship by speaking of 'normal' profit but says nothing about this curve; 4) Kalecki's theory is static and ignores all lags.

A reinterpretation of Kalecki substantially disposes of Hahn's criticisms. Defining the ratio of price to prime cost as the *reflection*, rather than the *definition* of the degree of monopoly, Reynolds (1996, p. 76–7) argues that it is possible to proceed in either of two ways. One is to follow the standard static structure–conduct–performance paradigm, extensively used in industrial economics, and regard the extent of industrial concentration, ratio of advertising to sales and other possible degree of monopoly influences as structural characteristics of an individual industry. This seems to us to be Hahn's interpretation.

An alternative interpretation, and the one we prefer, is to take an 'Austrian' approach and consider the 'degree of monopoly' as a set of factors which hinder or counter the process of competition. On this interpretation, the influence of competition may be better appreciated by understanding it as a process rather than as a structure. Thus, we would not expect the level of industrial concentration to be first and foremost among the influences on the markup (or the degree of monopoly). For example, a low degree of monopoly would be associated with very intensive competitive pressures and a high degree of monopoly would imply that the competitive process was relatively weak.

While Kalecki (1954, p. 17) did appear to imply a monotonic relationship between the degree of concentration and the markup, Reynolds (1996, pp. 76–7) argues that there are problems with this interpretation. For example, whether the process of competition is more intense in an industry with two firms than with three is an open question and depends on the responses (actual or anticipated) to changes (actual or anticipated) among the firms. These responses will be influenced by a number of historical, legal and other institutional influences. Thus, Reynolds concludes:

> There is more to the degree of monopoly than industrial structure. The latter is just one set of factors affecting the intensity of competition; the legal framework, affecting firms' propensity to collude is another. Firms' expectations about the future, the psychology of the decision-takers and the internal organization of the firm are all important in influencing how a firm responds to external circumstances, such as fluctuations in costs or demand. It is the sum total of these factors that we refer to as the 'degree of monopoly' and it is changes and variations in the degree of monopoly which lead to changes and variations in the mark up on prime costs.

Following Reynolds, Laramie, Mair, Miller and Reynolds (1998) have estimated the degree of monopoly in the 'spirit' of Kalecki for a sample of UK manufacturing industries for the period 1985–90 from the following equation:

$$k = f(CR5(1 - R1), A{:}S, [E\%(1 - R1)], [E(MCR)], R1, R4, SI, \hat{g}, \hat{w}, \mu)$$
(1.4)

where k = the industry markup over prime costs (ratio of gross output/wage plus material costs); $CR5(1 - R1)$ = 5 – firm concentration ratio multiplied by one minus the index of industry import penetration; $A{:}S$ = advertising sales ratio; $E\%(1 - R1)$ = percentage effect of scale economies (minimum efficient scale divided by net output) multiplied by one minus the index of industry import penetration; $E(MCR)$ = minimum capital requirement of scale economies (minimum efficient scale multiplied by the industry capital: output ratio); $R1$ = ratio of industry imports to UK manufacturers' sales plus imports minus exports; $R4$ = ratio of industry exports to UK manufacturers' sales plus imports; SI = index of industry specialization; $\hat{g}$ = annual real growth rate of industry output; $\hat{w}$ = annual real growth rate of industry earnings per head; μ = disturbance term.

The 'pure' Kaleckian arguments in the above equation are the 5-firm concentration ratio, the advertising:sales ratio, the annual real growth rate of industry output (a measure of the influence of changes in overhead costs in relation to prime costs) and the growth rate of earnings, (a measure of trade union influence). Other institutional influences operating on the markup in the 'spirit' of Kalecki are entry barriers, captured through the percentage effect of economies of scale, the minimum capital requirement, product differentiation (the advertising:sales ratio) and product diversification (the index of specialization). The effect on the markup of the degree of openness of markets is captured by the inclusion of the import and export penetration ratios ($R1$ and $R4$). OLS regression confirms entry barriers, the growth rate of industry output and the extent of industry openness as the principal determinants of the 'degree of monopoly', with an adjusted R^2 of 0.61 and a DW statistic of 2.07. Thus, k and its inverse, the share of wages in national income, can be estimated empirically from industry data.

In deciding to go with Kalecki's theory of income distribution, we are parting company with the generally held post Keynesian approach. Reynolds (1996, pp. 84–8) identifies this as a version of the model set out by Kaldor (1960) in which income shares are determined by the proportion of income invested and the relative savings propensities of capitalists and workers. In the simplified version of this model the profit share is given as:

$$\Pi/Y = (1/s_c)/(I/Y) \tag{1.5}$$

where Π = aggregate profits, Y = national income, s_c = capitalists' propensity to save and I = investment.

The basic problem with Kaldor's model is that it is under-determined, having only three equations to determine its four variables. The model can only be closed by assuming full employment. Thus, Reynolds sees the Kaldor model as consisting of the simple demand-side equations of 'bastard' Keynesianism, augmented by the neoclassical assumption that the economy, in the long run, will be at full employment. A change in any of the terms on the right-hand side of equation (1.5) will bring into play forces that will move the economy away from full employment, thereby violating one of the assumptions of Kaldor's distribution theory.

The important difference between Kaldor and Kalecki on income distribution is that in Kalecki the 'Keynesian' demand-side macroeconomic equations interact with the microeconomic conditions of price determination. The markups established by firms, in conjunction with their investment decisions, serve to determine both the level of income and its distribution. The Kaldor approach, as well as that of Pasinetti (1974), which relate the profit share to savings and the investment-output ratio, are seen by Reynolds as interesting expressions of the relationships which must hold between these magnitudes if an economy is to be on a particular steady-state growth path. However, they do not provide a theory of income distribution in that they do not explain the causes of changes in the distribution of income.

5 MICRO/MACRO RELATIONSHIP IN KALECKIAN THEORY

From the above discussion, it is clear that our approach in this book stands in marked contrast to mainstream public finance theory. In a sense, this behoves us to be like Caesar's wife. In particular, if we are to be critical of the failure of the mainstream approach to achieve a proper integration of its microeconomic and macroeconomic elements, then we have to demonstrate that our Kaleckian approach does not suffer from the same problem. Howitt (1987, pp. 273–5) recognizes that the lack of clear connection between micro and macroeconomics has long been a source of discontent among economists. He quotes Arrow's (1967) view that it is a 'major scandal' that neoclassical price theory cannot account for such macroeconomic phenomena as unemployment. The attempts by Clower (1965), Barro and Grossman (1971), Lucas (1972) and others to establish a *rapprochement* between neoclassical microeconomics and Keynesian macroeconomics do not concern us here.

Rather, we draw on Kriesler's (1996) discussion of the relationship between the microeconomic and macroeconomic elements of Kalecki's theories. We follow Kriesler by focusing at this stage on what he calls Kalecki's 'pure' model, that is, a model of a closed economy with no government and in which workers do not save, in order to highlight the underlying relations. When we introduce later in this book government, workers' savings and an open economy, the relationships become more complex.

Kalecki was concerned to keep his microeconomic and macroeconomic elements quite independent of each other. His theory of the determination of the shares of wages and profits in national income he derived, as we have seen above, from the pricing behaviour of individual firms and may be considered microeconomic. The macroeconomic aspect is the determination of gross profits by capitalists' spending. There would be a fallacy of composition if the behaviour of individual capitalists were simply aggregated to derive aggregate class behaviour. Kalecki was always at pains to attempt to remove the influence of industrial composition from his microeconomic analysis and the determination of the wage share.

The relationship between the microeconomic and macroeconomic elements of Kalecki's analysis is best understood from studying his three books which contained both, *Essays in the Theory of Economic Fluctuations* (Kalecki, 1939), *Studies in Economic Dynamics* (Kalecki, 1943) and *Theory of Economic Dynamics* (Kalecki, 1954). Kriesler (1996, p. 61) argues that the sequence in which Kalecki presented the themes in these books is significant in understanding his micro-macro relationship. They all begin with the microeconomic analysis of pricing in the manufacturing sector and the determination of the share of wages in national income. They then discuss the determination of macroeconomic variables such as aggregate profits, the level of national income, the rate of interest and investment. Finally, each discusses the business cycle. Thus, Kalecki's microeconomic analysis has to be understood in terms of its contribution to the analysis of the business cycle and, therefore, to Kalecki's macroeconomic analysis.

The link between Kalecki's micro and macro analysis is most clearly stated in *Studies in Economic Dynamics* (Kalecki, 1943, p. 50):

> These factors [i.e. those determining prices and the distribution of income] ... will not affect real profits but the real wage and salary bill and consequently the national output. If, for instance, the degree of market imperfection or oligopoly increases, and, as a result, so does the ratio of profits to wages, real profits do not change, but the real wage bill falls, first, because of the fall in real wage rates, and secondly, because of the consequent reduction in demand for wage goods, and thus of output and employment in the wage good industries ... [Markups] increase but the national output falls just so much that, as a result, the real total profits remain the same. However great the margin of profit on a unit of output, the capitalists cannot make more in total profits than they consume and invest.

As Kriesler (1996, p. 65) points out, this passage is very important in understanding the link between Kalecki's microeconomic and macroeconomic analysis. Real gross profits are determined by capitalists' consumption and investment decisions. In a three-sector model, if total profits, capitalists' consumption and investment are determined in real terms, then so too are the levels of output and employment in the capital goods sector (sector 1) and the capitalist-consumption goods sector (sector 2). Therefore, the microeconomic factors that determine the distribution of income will act through real wages and influence the level of output through their impact on the wage goods sector (sector 3). Changes in the degree of monopoly cannot affect gross profits but they will influence output and employment in the wage-good sector. An increase in the markup increases profits in the capital goods and capitalist-consumption sectors, while at the same time reducing wages in these sectors. This results in a fall in demand for wage goods, reducing output, employment and profits in that sector. This reduction in profits in the wage good sector is equal to the increased profits in the other two sectors so that total profit remains unchanged. The main function of Kalecki's macroeconomic analysis is to explain the determination of total profits, while the main function of his microeconomic analysis is to explain the wage share in national income. Together they determine the level of national income.

As Kriesler (1996, p. 66) observes, both microeconomic and macroeconomic analysis have a part to play in the determination of the level of income. They lie side by side, existing independently but on an equal footing. This does not imply that Kalecki regarded them as being of equal importance. His microeconomic analysis is a step towards the development of this theory of output and the business cycle.

6 KALECKI'S THEORY OF TAXATION

The introduction of taxation into Kalecki's theory does not fundamentally alter the micro:macro relationships. At the macroeconomic level, the aggregate spending flows in the economy determine the level of profits. At the microeconomic level, the degree of monopoly determines the distribution of income. Tax policy can affect the aggregate flows of spending and profits, but firms' pricing decisions, as reflected in their markups of price over prime cost determine the intra- and inter-industry and class distributions of income. Ultimately, the confluence of these factors determines the short-period incidence of taxes. It is this incidence, through its impact on firms' investment decisions that generates a long-period effect. Thus, there is a critical interdependence between the microeconomic and macroeconomic forces in Kaleckian theory in general, and in tax theory in particular, that we consider is missing from mainstream public finance theory.

In this book, we integrate Kalecki's theories of taxation, income distribution, national income determination, investment, the business cycle, and the trend to produce a dynamic macroeconomic theory of taxation. In so doing, we relax a number of the assumptions that Kalecki made in his original 1937 paper. The most important assumptions we dispense with are those of a closed economy and no workers' savings. This enables us to develop a better understanding of the macroeconomic effects of taxation and the regional effects of local taxation.

We now set out the principal features of Kalecki's 1937 paper. His opening sentence read (Kalecki, 1937, p. 444):

Mr Keynes's theory [the *General Theory*] gives us a new basis for the enquiry into the problems of taxation. The analysis of the influence of various types of taxes on effective demand leads, as we shall see, to quite unexpected results which may be of practical importance.

He analysed the effects of taxes on commodities, capitalists' income and capital on employment and the determination and distribution of national income in an economy with capital equipment and wages given. His simplifying assumptions were: 1) a closed system with a surplus of all types of labour and capital equipment; 2) workers spend all they receive as wages; and 3) a balanced government budget with all government expenditure financed by taxation.

He began by considering short-period equilibrium in an economy with no taxation and no government expenditure. He defined gross profits as the difference between the value of sales and prime costs (wages plus materials). National income is the sum of gross profits and the wage bill. It can also be defined as the sum of total consumption plus investment. As, by assumption, workers consume all they earn, total gross profits must be equal to the sum of capitalists' consumption (Cc) plus investment (I). If Cc plus I changes, employment will be pushed to the point at which gross profits will be equal to the changed $Cc + I$. Gross profits (P) are determined by investment (I) – which is equal to capitalists' savings – and by capitalists' propensity to consume (c_c).

Kalecki makes two assumptions about the determinants of gross profits: 1) the rate of investment (I) does not change immediately in response to some exogenous change as it is the result of previous investment decisions which require some finite length of time for completion; and 2) capitalists' propensity to consume is insensitive to expectations of changes in income. From these assumptions, it follows that $P = Cc + I$ with a certain, not very short, time lag. He then introduces into the system taxation that pays for the salaries of officials or is disbursed as doles to the unemployed. He conducts the analysis in terms of the macroeconomic effects of three categories of taxes, commodities, on capitalists' income (profits) and on capital.

1   Tax on Commodities

Kalecki first considers the funding of government expenditure from a constant-rate *ad valorem* tax, Tw, on all kinds of wage goods. This tax constitutes a new category of prime cost. National income now equals gross profits (P) plus wages (W) plus the tax on wage goods (Tw). Workers' wages are spent entirely on wage goods. Total taxes (Tw) equal government expenditure that is spent on the consumption of wage goods. Thus, gross profits are again equal to $Cc + I$. In an economy with commodity taxation only, there is no change in the level of national income as there is no stimulus to capitalists' consumption or to investment. There has simply been a change in the distribution of income as a consequence of a shift in purchasing power from those in employment to the unemployed.

2 Tax on Capitalists' Income

Kalecki next introduces a tax on capitalists' income (Ti) levied at a constant percentage. This is not a prime cost but a part of gross profits (P) which are now equal to $Cc + I + Ti$, and the part received by capitalists is $Cc + I$. If Ti is increased from, say 15 per cent to 25 per cent, nothing will happen to investment or to capitalists' consumption in the period immediately following the increase in Ti. The immediate effect is a rise in P because of the rise in Ti. Employment will be 'pushed' to the point at which P increases by the amount of Ti.

The increase in Ti must raise the rate of interest, otherwise the net reward to lending will fall. The rise in the rate of interest will not diminish the willingness of lenders to lend but will exert downward pressure on the willingness of capitalists to invest.[6] However, this may not be the final result because, in the first period of the new tax regime, gross profits (P) rise by just the amount of the increase in Ti. If capitalists expect future returns to increase by the same amount as current returns, this will be just enough to counter the depressive effect of the increase in Ti on the incentive to invest. If that is so, then $Cc + I$ remains unchanged and, therefore, gross profits will rise by the amount of the increase in Ti and so, too, will employment. The principal result from the introduction of a tax on capitalists' income will be a rise in workers' consumption from the unemployed. This will raise both the price and the output of wage goods, reducing the consumption of already employed workers but increasing the consumption of newly employed workers.

3 Tax on Capital

Finally, Kalecki introduces capital taxation (Tc) levied at a uniform rate on all forms of owned capital. Again, Tc does not constitute a prime cost and gross profits (P) will be equal to $Cc + I + Ti + Tc$. The immediate effect of increasing Tc is to leave Cc and I unchanged, but employment rises as a response to the increase in P of the increase in Tc. Unlike Ti, Tc is not a cost of production in the long run and, therefore, does not affect the net profitability of investment. Whether or not a lender lends does not affect the amount of Tc he pays. Thus, the inducement to invest is not weakened by the rise in Tc if the expected returns were the same as before. Gross profits have risen by the increase in Tc

---

6. Kalecki does not offer any particular theory of the rate of interest in developing his 1937 article.

which improves the expectation of future returns and strengthens the inducement to invest. Tc not only increases gross profits by the increase in Tc but capitalists' income ($Cc + I$) also increases significantly. The increase in capitalists' after-tax income via the real wage bill is higher than in the case of Ti because of the stronger rise in employment induced by Tc.

7 EXTENSIONS OF KALECKI'S THEORY

This is as far as Kalecki took his analysis and he never formally returned to the theory of taxation in his later writings. Despite his demonstration of the short-period macroeconomic effects of different taxes, a number of important extensions and developments of his model are clearly required. The first attempt to extend Kalecki's model was by Asimakopulos and Burbidge (1974). They continued to operate within a short-period framework in which investment is taking place but in which changes in productive capacity can be ignored because these are small relative to the total stock of capital. They distinguished between the propensities to save out of wages and out of profits and retained the Kaleckian assumption of a zero propensity to save out of wage income. Retaining also Kalecki's assumptions that exports and imports and the government's budget are in balance, an economy will be in short-period equilibrium when the predetermined investment is realized and is equal to what capitalists have chosen to save, given their incomes. Asimakopulos and Burbidge showed that this equilibrium condition and the supporting assumptions are sufficient to determine post-tax profits in real terms as a function of the savings propensities and rate of investment in real terms. If the government announces and implements a higher rate of profits tax at the beginning of the short period, and spends the extra revenue it obtains from this increase, then post-tax profits in this period will be unaffected by the tax if short-period equilibrium is re-established.

Asimakopulos and Burbidge showed that their conclusion holds for competitive as well as for non-competitive market conditions, because government expenditures, even when financed by an equal increase in taxes, have an expansionary impact on the economy through the balanced budget multiplier effect. The decrease in private expenditure due to the imposition of the tax is less than the balancing increase in government expenditure because the tax increase is partly absorbed by a reduction in capitalist saving. With competitive markets, the expansion due to the balanced budget multiplier effect will be accompanied by lower real-wage rates because the increased demand leads to higher prices relative to wages and hence to higher costs. The resulting higher pre-tax profits make it possible for post-tax profits to remain unchanged, even though the rate of profits tax is higher.

In oligopolistic markets, the balanced budget multiplier effect will be reflected in a sharper increase in output and employment. The leading firms in these markets set prices by adding a markup to prime costs, calculated on the basis that assumed output is less than capacity output. Short-period variations in demand are accommodated by changes in output rather than in price. Asimakopulos and Burbidge make the important point that because of the changes in the distribution of income brought about by changes in government fiscal policy, the legal and economic incidence of taxes can differ even in a context of short-period adjustments.

As with Kalecki's 1937 paper, the Asimakopulos and Burbidge extension has made little impact in the public finance literature. In part, this may be due to the fact that it is still a short-period model and still retains most of Kalecki's initial rather restrictive assumptions. A more recent attempt to introduce dynamics in Kalecki's original model is Damania and Mair (1992). An essential weakness of the Asimakopulos and Burbidge approach was its failure to provide an explanation of the dynamic processes through which prices in non-competitive markets are determined or sustained over the business cycle. The Asimakopulos and Burbidge model assumed price leadership but this is only one of several possible alternatives.

An implication of the price leadership assumption is that prices are set in some unspecified way by price leaders and held unchanged over the business cycle. Changes in demand lead only to variations in output and the aggregate supply curve in the Asimakopulos and Burbidge model is assumed to be perfectly elastic. This did not seem to Damania and Mair to capture the spirit of Kalecki's insight that changes in the degree of monopoly 'can be reinforced by tacit agreement ... [and that] tacit agreements, in turn, may develop into a more or less formal cartel' (Kalecki, 1943, p. 50).

Drawing on the game theoretic ideas of trigger pricing, uncertainty and informational imperfections, Damania and Mair develop a model which demonstrates the possibility that tax policies which raise aggregate demand will tend to generate price wars in the transition to a new equilibrium. However, in this new equilibrium, the collusive power of oligopolistic firms will be restored and they will be able to shift the burden of increased taxes through higher prices.

However, Damania and Mair realized that instead of producing a correction to an important limitation of the Asimakopulos and Burbidge model short-period model of tax incidence, what they have done instead is to produce an explanation of the determination of the real wage over the business cycle. This is because in the Asimakopulos and Burbidge model, profits are determined independently of the markup. This underlines the necessity of having a Kaleckian model in which capitalists' consumption and workers' savings are both non-zero. In this case, a change in the markup will bring about a change in the income share of wages. This will cause a change in the incomes of workers that in turn will bring about a change in the difference between capitalists' consumption and workers' savings and, thus, the level of profits. If the wage share does not change in response to the effects of changes in taxation, there will be no macroeconomic implications from tax changes. In this case, Kaleckian tax incidence theory becomes essentially a question of the determination of the real wage.

This finding by Damania and Mair underlines the importance of the interdependence of the microeconomic and macroeconomic elements of Kaleckian economics. If there are no microeconomic effects of tax changes, i.e. no changes in income distribution via changes in the degree of monopoly, then there will be no macroeconomic effects. But if the degree of monopoly changes and there are microeconomic effects, these will give rise to macroeconomic effects. This contrasts with the neoclassical position on tax incidence where, by assumption, microeconomic effects are precluded and, consequently, there are no macroeconomic effects, only relative price effects. In the analysis that follows in the remainder of this book, tax-induced changes in the distribution of income through the operation of the degree of monopoly are of central importance.

Mott and Slattery (1994) address the issue of the effects of tax shifting. They recognize that neither neoclassical tax incidence theory generally nor Kaleckian tax incidence theory up to the time they wrote their paper had linked macroeconomic concerns about changes in the levels of output and employment with microeconomic concerns of how individual agents respond to taxes. In this respect, Mott and Slattery pick up on the earlier recognition by Laramie (1991) that firms may treat business taxes as part of prime costs rather than as overhead costs. Mair and Laramie (1992) and Laramie and Mair (1993) (see Chapter 3) have tested empirically the treatment of business property taxes by firms in the manufacturing sector of the UK, whether as a prime or an overhead cost and whether shifted or not. Laramie and Mair (1996) (see Chapter 4) have also demonstrated that quite different effects on the business cycle follow if wage or profits taxes are shifted as compared with what happens if no tax shifting occurs.

Mott and Slattery are correct to identify the issue of tax shifting as an important aspect of Kaleckian tax theory. They postulate four price equations in which: 1) taxes are added to the prices of output; 2) taxes are added to the markup; 3) taxes are treated as a prime cost; or 4) taxes are not treated in the pricing decision at all. Their analysis indicates that the story of the macroeconomic effects that follow the imposition of taxes is more than just what taxes are imposed and how firms treat taxes. The outcomes are also critically influenced by the relative magnitudes of the propensities to save out of wage and profit income and by the propensity to invest out of profit income. We agree entirely with Mott and Slattery (1994, p. 394) that adding a government sector with taxation to Kalecki's theory of investment allows the analysis of the macroeconomic effects and incidence of taxation to proceed beyond Kalecki's original analysis in a way that is vitally relevant to current tax policy questions.

8   LIFTING THE VEIL OF SILENCE

We referred above to the 'veil of silence' that Paladini claims has surrounded Kalecki's work on taxation. We hope that in this book we may begin to lift this veil. We show how Kalecki's 1937 theory can be integrated with his later theories of income distribution, income determination, investment and then with Kalecki's own version of his business cycle theory. By so doing, we hope that we have developed a theory of taxation in which the important interactions between the microeconomic and macroeconomic elements have been fully taken into account. To the extent that we have been successful, we argue that a Kaleckian approach fills the void that has been recognized by orthodox economists.

Our purpose in this book is to develop from a Kaleckian perspective a theory of the effects and incidence of taxation which avoids the difficulties of conventional theory and which may properly be considered dynamic. This requires us to consider the following issues: theory of the state; theory of taxation; theory of income determination; theory of income distribution; and theory of investment, the business cycle and the trend. We show how these elements can be combined into a dynamic Kaleckian theory of taxation in which the unhelpful dichotomy between the microeconomics and the macroeconomics of conventional theory is replaced with a fully integrated relationship between the two.

Our findings have as far-reaching implications for Kaleckian and post-Keynesian economists as they do for orthodox economists. We describe later in this book a number of ways in which a Kaleckian model may be used to examine the macroeconomic effects of taxes and fiscal policy. Thus, even at an a comparatively early stage of its development, a Kaleckian dynamic theory of taxation can open up important new insights into the macroeconomic dynamics of fiscal policy. A potentially significant feature of this book is that it provides a challenge to the supply-side fiscal shibboleth that economic growth can only be stimulated by cutting government spending and taxation as asserted by Knoester (1991) in his advocacy of the inverted Haavelmo effect (see Chapter 9). The question of the existence of the Haavelmo effect, whether in upright or in inverted form, underlines, in our opinion, the need to distinguish clearly in post Keynesian analysis between the orthodox Keynesian and the Kaleckian approaches. As we have pointed out, Kalecki appreciated as soon as the *General Theory* was published the need to develop a new approach to the theory of taxation. But this far-reaching insight has never been recognized by post Keynesians nor, must it be said, by the majority of Kaleckians either. Therefore, orthodox Keynesian fiscal analysis has never been able to defend itself against supply-side criticisms of the Knoester type. What we hope to demonstrate is that by adopting the Kaleckian theoretical model set out in this book, post Keynesian economists may be in a position to engage in more constructive debate on issues of fiscal policy.

REFERENCES

Arestis, P. (1992), *The Post Keynesian Approach to Economics*, Aldershot, Edward Elgar.

Arrow, K.J. (1967), 'Samuelson collected', *Journal of Political Economy*, **75**, 730–37.

Asimakopulos, A. and Burbidge, J. (1974), 'The short-period incidence of taxation', *Economic Journal*, **84**, 267–88.

Asimakopulos, A. (1979), 'Tax incidence', in Eichner, A.S. (ed.), *A Guide to Post Keynesian Economics*, New York, M.E. Sharpe.

Atkinson, A. and Stiglitz, J.E. (1980), *Lectures on Public Economics*, London, McGraw-Hill.

Auerbach, A.J. and Feldstein, M.J. (1987), *Handbook of Public Economics, Vols. I and II*, Amsterdam, North Holland.

Barro, R.J. and Grossman, H.I. (1971), 'A general disequilibrium model of income and employment', *American Economic Review*, **61**, 82–93.

Bhaduri, A. (1986) *Macro-Economics: The Dynamics of Commodity Production*, Armonk, M.E. Sharpe.

Braff, A.J. (1988), 'Distribution: neo-classical' in Asimakopulos, A. (ed.), *Theories of Income Distribution*, Boston, Kluwer.

Buchanan, J.M. and Tullock, G. (1971), *The Calculus of Consent*, Ann Arbor, University of Michigan Press.

Clower, R.W. (1965), 'The Keynesian counter-revolution: a theoretical appraisal', in Hahn, F.H. and Brechling, F.P.R. (eds), *The Theory of Interest Rates*, London, Macmillan.

Courvisanos, J. (1996), *Investment Cycles in Capitalist Economies*, Cheltenham, UK, Edward Elgar.

Damania, D. and Mair, D. (1992), 'The short-period incidence of taxation revisited', *Cambridge Journal of Economics*, **16**, 195–206.

Damania, D. and Mair, D. (1993), 'A post Keynesian approach to the incidence of taxation' in Arestis, P. and Chick, V. (eds), *Recent Developments in Post Keynesian Economics*, Aldershot, Edward Elgar.

Davidson, P. (1994), *Post Keynesian Macroeconomic Theory*, Aldershot, Edward Elgar.

Downs, A. (1957), *An Economic Theory of Democracy*, New York, Harper and Row.

Eichner, A.S. (1978), *A Guide to Post Keynesian Economics*, New York, M.E. Sharpe.

Eatwell, J. (1976), 'A simple framework for the analysis of taxation, distribution and effective demand', mimeo, Department of Economics, University of Cambridge.

Garegnani, P (1978), 'Notes on consumption, investment and effective demand: II', *Cambridge Journal of Economics*, **2**, (4), 335–53.

Gomulka, S., Ostaszewski, A. and Davies, R.O. (1990), 'The innovation rate and Kalecki's theory of the trend, unemployment and the business cycle', *Economica*, **57**, 525–40.

Hahn, F.H. (1972), *The Share of Wages in the National Income'*, London, Weidenfeld and Nicolson.

Harberger, A.C. (1962), 'The incidence of the corporation income tax', *Journal of Political Economy*, **70**, 215–40.

Harris, D.J. (1978), *Capital Accumulation and Income Distribution*, London, Routledge and Kegan Paul.

Howitt, P. (1987), 'Macroeconomics: relations with microeconomics' in Eatwell, J., Milgate, M. and Newman, P. (eds), *The New Palgrave, Vol. III*, London, Macmillan.

Kaldor, N. (1960), *Essays on Value and Distribution*, London, Duckworth and Co.

Kaldor, N. (1983), 'Keynesian economics after 50 years', in Worswick, D. and Trevithick, J. (eds), *Keynes and the Modern World*, Cambridge, Cambridge University Press.

Kalecki, M. (1937), 'A theory of commodity, income and capital taxation', *Economic Journal*, **47**, 444–50.

Kalecki, M. (1939), *Essays in the Theory of Economic Fluctuations*, London, Allen and Unwin.

Kalecki, M. (1943), *Studies in Economic Dynamics*, London, Allen and Unwin.

Kalecki, M. (1954), *Theory of Economic Dynamics*, London, Unwin University Books.

Kalecki, M. (1971), *Selected Essays on the Dynamics of the Capitalist Economy*, Cambridge, Cambridge University Press.

King, J.E. (1996), *An Alternative Macroeconomic Theory: The Kaleckian Model and Post-Keynesian Economics*, Boston, Kluwer.

Knoester, A. (1991), 'Supply-side economics and the inverted Haavelmo effect', in Phelps, E.S. (ed.), *Recent Developments in Macroeconomics, Vol. II*, International Library of Critical Writings in Economics series, Aldershot, Edward Elgar.

Kotlikoff, L. and Summers, L. (1987), 'Tax incidence' in Auerbach, A.J. and Feldstein, M.J. (eds), *Handbook of Public Economics, Vol. II*, Amsterdam, North Holland.

Kriesler, P. (1996), 'Microfoundations: a Kaleckian perspective', in King, J.E. (ed.), *An Alternative Economic Theory: The Kaleckian Model and Post Keynesian Economics*, Boston, Kluwer.

Laramie, A.J. (1991), 'Taxation and Kalecki's distribution factors', *Journal of Post Keynesian Economics*, **13**, (4) 583–94.

Laramie, A.J. and Mair, D. (1993), 'The incidence of business rates: a post Keynesian approach', *Review of Political Economy*, **5**, (1) 55–72.

Laramie, A.J. and Mair, D. (1996), 'Taxation and Kalecki's theory of the business cycle', *Cambridge Journal of Economics*, **20**, (4) 451–64.

Laramie, A.J., Miller, A.G., Mair, D. and Reynolds, P.J. (1998), 'An empirical estimate of the degree of monopoly in the spirit of Kalecki', mimeo, Department of Economics, Heriot-Watt University.

Lavoie, M. (1992), *Foundations of Post-Keynesian Economic Analysis*, Aldershot, Edward Elgar.

Lerner, A.P. (1934), 'The concept of monopoly and the measurement of monopoly power', *Review of Economic Studies* **1**, 24–35.

Lucas, R.E., (1972), 'Expectations and the neutrality of money', *Journal of Economic Theory*, **4**, 103–24.

Lydall, H. (1979), *A Theory of Income Distribution*, Oxford, Clarendon Press.

Mair, D. and Laramie, A.J. (1992), 'The incidence of business rates on manufacturing industry in Scotland and the rest of the UK', *Scottish Journal of Political Economy*, **39** (1), 76–94.

A dynamic theory of taxation

Mieszkowski, P.M. (1969), 'Tax incidence theory: the effects of taxation on the distri-bution of income', *Journal of Economic Literature*, **7**, 1103–24.
Moggridge, D. (1983), *The Collected Writings of John Maynard Keynes, Vol. XII*, London, Macmillan, Cambridge University Press.
Mott, T. and Slattery E. (1994), 'Tax incidence and macroeconomic effects in a Kaleckian model when profits finance affects investment and prices may respond to taxes', *Journal of Post Keynesian Economics*, **16** (3), 391–409.
Musgrave, R.A. (1997), 'Micro and macro aspects of fiscal policy', in Blejer, M.I. and Ter-Minassian, T. (eds), *Macroeconomic Dimensions of Public Finance*, London, Routledge.
Niskanen, W.A. (1971), *Bureaucracy and Representative Government*, Chicago, Aldine-Atherton.
Paladini, R. (1989), 'Kalecki and fiscal policy', in Sebastiani, M. (ed.), *Kalecki's Relevance Today*, London, Macmillan.
Pasinetti, L. (1974), *Growth and Income Distribution: Essays in Economic Theory*, Cambridge, Cambridge University Press.
Reynolds, P.J. (1983), 'An empirical analysis of the degree of monopoly theory of income distribution', *Bulletin of Economic Research*, **36**, 59–84.
Reynolds, P.J. (1987), *Political Economy: A Synthesis of Kaleckian and Post Keynesian Economics*, Brighton, Wheatsheaf.
Reynolds, P.J. (1996) 'Kalecki's theory of prices and distribution' in King, J.E. (ed.), *An Alternative Economic Theory: The Kaleckian Model and Post Keynesian Economics*, Boston, Kluwer.
Robinson, J. (1977), 'Michal Kalecki on the economics of capitalism', *Oxford Bulletin of Economics and Statistics*, **39**, (1), 7–17.
Rothschild, K.W. (1961), 'Some recent contributions to a macroeconomic theory of income distribution', *Scottish Journal of Political Economy*, 173–99.
Sawyer, M.C. (1985), *The Economics of Michal Kalecki*, London, Macmillan.
Trussler, S. (1982), 'Regional and inter-regional fiscal incidence: theory, methodology and applications', unpublished PhD thesis, University of Cambridge.

2. Integrating Kalecki's theories of taxation and income determination[1]

1 INTRODUCTION

This chapter integrates Kalecki's (1937) theory of taxation and Kalecki's (1968) theory of income determination. We review briefly Kalecki's views on the incidence and effects of taxation. We then present Kalecki's theory of income distribution and illustrate the impact of the tax system on aggregate pre-tax and post-tax profits, the wage bill and national income. Next, we consider the impact of the structure of taxation on the post-tax distribution of income at the industry and macroeconomic levels, and discuss some of the macroeconomic policy implications. We show the incidence and effects of taxation under different pricing behaviours and analyse the impact of business property taxes on UK manufacturing industry. Finally, we present briefly the political economy of taxation.

2 KALECKI'S THEORY OF TAXATION

As we saw in the previous chapter, Kalecki (1937) analysed the effects of commodity, income and capital taxation on employment, national income and its distribution. He assumed that the economic system is closed; that the system operates with surplus labour and capacity; that workers' savings equal zero; that the government budget is in balance, that all government expenditures are financed by taxation; that any increase in taxation is spent for officials' salaries or is distributed as doles to the unemployed; that investment is determined prior to the period under consideration; that capitalists' marginal propensity to consume is fixed and insensitive to expectations of changes in their incomes; that the money supply is perfectly elastic; and that the money wage rate is fixed. Under these assumptions, an increase in the tax rate, *ad valorem*, on wage goods does not affect the level of gross profits (the difference between sales and prime costs). The tax on wage goods represents a new type of prime costs. When this tax increases, prime costs and the value of sales increase, leaving gross profits and national income unchanged but reducing workers' real wage rate.

---

1. This Chapter is a revised version of Laramie (1991) and Laramie (1994).

The introduction of an income tax on capitalists' income, where the tax is not part of prime costs, increases gross profits by the amount of the income tax and leaves unaffected the part of gross profits received by capitalists. This increase in gross profits leaves unaffected the expected profitability of investment, increases employment, while the effect on real wages is uncertain. On the assumption that interest receipts constitute one element of capitalists' incomes, then an increase in the taxation of capitalists' income must increase the rate of interest in order to maintain the net (after tax) reward for lending. The increase in the rate of interest reduces the net rate of return to entrepreneurs and, thus, diminishes their willingness to invest. However, the higher level of gross profits, via the increase in the taxation of capitalists' income, increases expected sales and thus just offsets the negative effect on expected sales of the increase in the rate of interest. The impact of the tax increase on real wages depends on whether the increase in demand for wage goods increases the price of wage goods for a given wage rate.

Finally, Kalecki introduces a capital tax levied on every type of owned capital. Gross profits again increase by the amount of the tax, and, in the short-run, the portion of gross profits going to capitalists remains constant, but the expected profitability of investment increases, and thus increases future profits and employment. An increase in the tax on capital does not result in an increase in the rate of interest, as in the case of a tax on capitalists' incomes. This is because if a person lends, or if a person borrows in order to invest, or if a person invests his/her own capital, that person still pays the same amount of tax as if he/she had not lent, borrowed or invested. Kalecki saw a tax on capital as providing the same stimulus to output and employment as debt financing but with none of the costs. However, he recognized that the strength of the vested interests supporting private property under capitalism would render such a tax politically impossible.[2]

3   KALECKI'S THEORIES OF INCOME DISTRIBUTION AND NATIONAL INCOME DETERMINATION

There is an extensive literature on Kalecki's theory of income distribution. For example, Sawyer (1985), Asimakopulos (1975), Weintraub (1981), and Reynolds (1984, 1996) have all examined various elements of Kalecki's theory. His theory is rooted in the pricing behaviour of firms. He assumed that firms in the manufacturing sector operate at a 'standard' rate of capacity that lies below full capacity. Prices of manufactured goods, he assumed, are cost

2. Asimakopulos and Burbidge (1974) duplicate and extend Kalecki's conclusions (Asimakopulos (1975, p. 328, fn. 31).

determined, whereby firms set prices by applying a markup over prime (wage and material) unit costs. These prime unit costs are assumed to be constant over the relevant ranges of production, and the markup is determined by environmental/institutional factors, exogenous to the firm, such as the degree of industrial concentration, product differentiation, trade union activity and the level of overheads.[3] Initially, Kalecki assumed all taxes to be zero.

Under these assumptions, value added for industry i is given as:

$$Y_i = (k_i - 1)(W_i + M_i) + W_i \qquad (2.1)$$

and pre-tax profits plus overheads is written as:

$$\Pi_i + O_i = (k_i - 1)(W_i + M_i) \qquad (2.2)$$

The distribution of value-added can be expressed as:

$$\Pi_i/Y_i = [(k_i - 1)(1 + j) - O_i/W_i]/[(k_i - 1)(1 + j_i) + 1] \qquad (2.3)$$

$$W_i/Y_i = 1/[(k_i - 1)(1 + j_i) + 1] \qquad (2.4)$$

$$\frac{O_i}{Y_i} = [O_i / W_i]/[(k_i - 1)(1 + j_i) + 1] \qquad (2.5)$$

where Π_i = pre-tax profits plus overheads, Y = value-added, k = the markup, j = ratio of material costs to the wage bill, O = overheads, and W = the wage bill.

Kalecki and Kaleckians claim that the above expressions of income shares are not simply definitional, but have theoretical content. The factors that determine the price/prime costs markup are reflected in the 'degree of monopoly' and are influenced by such things as the degree of industry concentration, the sales to advertising ratio, and the extent of trade unionization (Kalecki (1954), Reynolds, (1996)).

Kalecki assumed that offsetting changes in k and j would result in the wage share remaining constant over the business cycle, and salaries are fixed over the business cycle. This enabled Kalecki (1968) to express the wage and salary shares of gross private sector income as:

$$V/Y = \beta/Y + \alpha \qquad (2.6)$$

where V = wage and salary income, β = salaries, a part of overheads, and α = wages' share of value-added.

---

3. See Reynolds (1996). For an example of the literature concerning the precise determinants of the markup see Chapter 1, Kalecki (1954) (1971), Asimakopulos (1975) and Block (1980).

Sawyer (1985, p. 80) equates α with the right-hand side of equation (2.4) and uses this term to derive the basic Kaleckian multiplier, $1/(1 - \alpha)$. This is illustrated by noting that $V = Y - \Pi$ and then solving for Y which yields:

$$Y = (\beta + \Pi)(1 - \alpha) \qquad (2.7)$$

Equation (2.7) demonstrates how the 'distribution factors', α and β, influence the level of private sector income. Kalecki (1968, p. 61) states: 'Gross income ... is pushed up to a point at which profits out of it are determined by the "distribution factors".'

The level of national income can be expressed as a function of expenditures by finding an expression for after-tax profits. Kalecki (1954, p. 49) used the income and expenditure identity in the national income and product accounts to show that aggregate after-tax profits, P, can be expressed as:

$$P = I + G - Tw - Tp + X - M + Cc - \Omega - Ws \qquad (2.8)$$

or:

$$\Pi = P + Tp = I + G - Tw + X - M + Cc + \Omega - Ws \qquad (2.9)$$

where I = gross investment,[4] G = government purchases, Tw = wage taxes, Tp = profits tax, X = exports, M = imports, Cc = capitalists' consumption, Ω = government transfer payments (assumed to be completely consumed), and Ws = workers' savings.

As is well known among Kaleckians and post Keynesians, Kalecki believed equations (2.8) and (2.9) to be more than identities. He stated that capitalists cannot decide the level of profits they wish to earn but they can decide the level of investment they wish to undertake, and, therefore, profits are determined, *inter alia*, by investment (Kalecki, 1954). Referring to Kalecki's profit equation, with the government budget and trade both in balance, and assuming worker saving is zero, Robinson (1980) aphorized it as showing that 'capitalists earn what they spend and workers spend what they earn'.

4   TAXATION AND NATIONAL INCOME DETERMINATION

We now consider the role of taxation with and without balanced budget constraints. We assume that capitalists' consumption, workers' savings, profit taxes and wage taxes can be simply written as:

---

4. Gross investment includes unplanned inventory investment. Kalecki remarked on the liquid nature of inventories in including unplanned inventory investment in profits.

$$Cc = cc(\Pi - Tp) \tag{2.10}$$

$$Ws = sw(V - Tw) \tag{2.11}$$

$$Tp = tp(\Pi) \tag{2.12}$$

$$Tw = tw(V) \tag{2.13}$$

where cc is capitalists' propensity to consume, sw is workers' propensity to save, tp is the rate of profits tax and tw is the rate of wage tax.

Without a Balanced Budget Constraint

We now consider the effects of taxation on national income holding government expenditures, $Ge = G + \Omega$, constant. The effects of taxation on national income are formally presented in the Appendix. Given equations (2.10) to (2.13), and assuming that overhead salaries equal zero, equations (2.7) and (2.9) can be rewritten as:

$$\Pi = [I + Ge + X - M](1 - \alpha)/\{(1 - \alpha)[1 - cc(1 - tp)] + \alpha[tw + sw\,(1 - tw)]\} \tag{2.9'}$$

and:

$$Y = [I + Ge + X - M]/\{(1 - \alpha)[1 - cc(1 - tp)] + \alpha[tw + sw(1 - tw)]\} \tag{2.7'}$$

The impact of taxation on the level of pre-tax profits and national income is explicitly reflected in the terms tp, tw and Ge. An increase in the profits tax rate, holding government expenditures constant, reduces capitalists' consumption, the levels of pre-tax and post-tax profits, the level of national income and the pre-tax wage bill. An increase in the wage tax rate, holding government purchases constant, reduces workers' consumption relative to the wage bill and reduces pre-tax and post-tax profits and the level of national income.

So far, this analysis has abstracted from the impact of taxation on the distribution factor, α. As tax revenue changes, this distribution factor might change, depending on the method of taxation that is used. For example, an increase in wage taxes, if shifted, will result in lower business markups, causing α, the wage share, the Kaleckian income multiplier and national income to increase, thereby dampening the negative impact of the wage tax on national income. An increase in the taxation of profits, if shifted, will result in higher business markups, reducing the wage share, the Kaleckian income multiplier and national income, and, therefore, the shifting of the profits tax heightens the negative impact the profits tax has on national income.

Balanced Budget Constraint

The effects of a balanced budget change in taxation on national income are formally presented in the Appendix. If the change in government expenditures is constrained to be equal to any change in the level of taxation, the results are quite different. If capitalists do not consume ($cc = 0$) and workers do not save ($sw = 0$), then the impact of taxation on profits, national income and the wage bill is simply through changes in government expenditures. A change in the profits tax, accompanied by an increase in government expenditures, has no impact on post-tax profits, but increases pre-tax profits and national income and the wage bill (pre- or post-tax). If workers do save, the resulting increase in workers' savings (due to an increase in income) dampens the increase in pre-tax profits and causes post-tax profits to decrease.

If capitalists do not consume ($cc = 0$) and workers do not save ($sw = 0$), a change in the wage tax, accompanied by an increase in government expenditures, has no impact on pre-tax or post-tax profits, national income or the wage bill. If workers save, an increase in the wage tax results in an increase in pre-tax profits equal to the resulting decrease in workers' savings. Through the operation of the Kaleckian income multiplier, national income and the pre-tax wage bill both increase. We illustrate the effects of the various tax changes with a numerical example in Chapter 8.

The shifting of the profits tax through a higher markup and lower wage share dampens the positive effect of the profits tax on national income, although the shifting of the profits tax increases profits through a reduction in worker savings. The shifting of the wage tax through a lower markup and higher wage share increases the positive effect wage tax has on national income, when worker savings is nonzero. These results are shown in the Appendix.

5   THE METHOD OF RAISING TAX REVENUES AND THE POST TAX DISTRIBUTION OF VALUE ADDED

We now examine the impact of the method of raising tax revenues on the distribution factors, profits and national income. As we show above, the impact of taxation on the economy as a whole and on the distribution of income depends on the types of taxes levied, the way in which firms treat taxes (whether as prime costs or as overhead costs) and the impact of taxation on the markup. Above, we assumed that in formulating their pricing decisions, firms treat business taxes as part of overheads. However, the economic consequences of tax policy differ significantly depending on the pricing behaviour of firms. For example, let us suppose that firms practise full-cost pricing. The costs that are marked up are defined as:

$$u = W/Q + M/Q + tp(\Pi)/Q \qquad (2.14)$$

Given equation (2.14), firms' after-tax profits and value-added can be written as:

$$P = (k - 1)((W + M) + tp(\Pi)) \qquad (2.15)$$

and:

$$Y = (k - 1)((W + M) + tp(\Pi)) + W \qquad (2.16)$$

These expressions can be rewritten by noting that the profits tax, $tp(\Pi) = [tp/(1 - tp)](P)$, and, thus:

$$P = (k - 1)(1 - tp)(W + M)/(1 - tp(k)) \qquad (2.15')$$

and:

$$Y = [(k - 1)(1 - tp)(W + M)/(1 - tp(k))] + W \qquad (2.16')$$

Thus, the share of wages in value-added is expressed as:

$$W/Y = \alpha = (1 - tp(k))/[(k - 1)(1 + j) + 1 - tp(k)] \qquad (2.17)$$

When business taxes are included in firms' overhead costs, a £($) increase in these taxes causes a £($) reduction in profits. This reduces firms' after-tax share in value-added by £($)1/Y, increases the share of overhead costs in value-added by £($)1/Y, and leaves unaffected the share of wages in value-added. Value-added is simply redistributed from profits to overheads, holding the markup constant. However, when business taxes are included as prime costs, the results change significantly. The increase in business taxes increases direct costs which, when marked up, increase total profits. Since pre-tax wages and overhead costs remain unaffected, an increase in business taxes increases profits and the share of business taxes in value-added, and reduces the shares of wages and overhead costs in value-added.

6   IMPACT OF BUSINESS PROPERTY TAX ON UK MANUFACTURING INDUSTRY

We now consider whether or not UK manufacturing firms treat business property taxes as an overhead cost with markups invariant with respect to the tax, a prime cost, or an overhead cost with markups variable with respect to the tax (Laramie and Mair, 1993). The tax base of the British business property tax is the annual value of heritable buildings and plant and machinery. Roughly speaking, plant and machinery is deemed to be heritable if it cannot be removed without also removing all or part of the building in which it is housed. Normally, tax assessors use rental evidence to establish annual value. In the absence of rental evidence, they resort to a technique known as the Contractor's Principle under which they annualize their estimate of the replacement capital value of the heritable property. At the time of the Laramie and Mair study reported below, the tax rate, or rate poundage, was set by individual local authorities, which retained the accruing tax revenue. Since 1990, firms have paid business property taxes at a national uniform rate (the Uniform Business Rate) set by central government. The tax proceeds are then distributed to local authorities on a per capita basis.

The business property tax is a major business tax in the United Kingdom. The yield of the tax between 1990 and 1996 has been in the range £11 850m to £14 400m. In the early 1990s, British businesses were paying between £80 and £90 in property tax for every £100 they were paying in Corporation Tax, although this has fallen more recently to around £55 for every £100 of Corporation Tax. The property tax is obviously an important business tax about whose macro-economic effects virtually nothing is known. The economic impact of the business property tax will depend on two things: first whether firms treat the tax as a prime cost or as an overhead cost and, second, the impact of the tax on business markups. We examined the incidence of the business property tax on the manufacturing sector of the UK economy over the period 1979–86 under three assumptions. First, we assumed that firms treat the business property tax as an overhead cost and do not adjust their markups in response to changes in the tax. Second, we assumed that firms treat the property tax as a prime cost and again do not adjust their markups in response to a tax change. Third, we assumed that firms treat the tax as an overhead cost and shift it by means of a change in their markups.

Under the first assumption, the effect on profits of an increase in the business property tax will be to increase the income share of the tax, and reduce the income share of profits. The income shares of wages and salaries remain unchanged as does the level of profits, holding all other things constant. In this case, the effect of an increase in business property taxation is to produce a lower income share of profits and a higher income share of wages (Laramie and Mair, 1993, p. 59). The short-period macroeconomic effect will be expansionary, through the operation of the income multiplier.

Under the second assumption, an increase in the rate of business property taxation will increase the shares in value-added of profits and business property taxes and reduce the shares of wages and overhead costs. The macroeconomic implication that follows is that there will be falls in the share of wages, in the value of the multiplier, in national income and in the aggregate level of profits, holding other things constant. The overall effect will be contractionary (Laramie and Mair, 1993, p. 60).

Under the third assumption, where the property tax is treated as an overhead cost but the markup is allowed to vary, the results are basically the same as under the previous assumption. To the extent that firms' markups increase because of higher property taxes, the lower will be the value of the basic Kaleckian income multiplier, thus affecting the level of profits, national income and the distribution of income. The major difference between the results obtained under this assumption and those obtained under the second assumption is that the shifting of the tax is not automatic or spontaneous and will depend on the environmental/distributional factors governing the degree of monopoly.

We tested these three assumptions with data for 111 industries in the UK manufacturing sector over the period 1979 to 1986 (Laramie and Mair, 1993, pp. 61–8). The results suggest that our first assumption was the most consistent with the data, that is, that firms treat the business property tax as an overhead cost and do not adjust their markups in response to changes in the tax. If that is so, then the short-period effect of an increase in business property taxation on manufacturing industry is to increase the income share of the tax and reduce the income share of profits. Wage and salary shares are not affected by the tax, nor is the level of output.

If we are correct in this conclusion, then important policy implications follow. In the Budget of 1992, the Chancellor of the Exchequer announced a reduction in business property taxation of 3.25 per cent, equivalent to £480m. He justified the tax cut as a means of assisting the recovery of UK industry from recession with the intention of providing 'significant and early benefit to many thousands of businesses throughout the United Kingdom' (*Financial Times*, 11 March, 1992). The analysis we have presented above suggests that the short-period effect of this reduction in business property taxation will be to increase the share of profits and lower the share of taxation in a national income that will not otherwise change. The Chancellor also intimated that the central government would make up the consequential shortfall in the tax revenues of local authorities, so that there had to be a switch of the order of half a billion pounds from business property taxation onto other forms of taxation. Our analysis suggests that such a tax switch would be likely to have deflationary effects, so that the intended expansionary macroeconomic effects of the 1992 cut in business property taxation are unlikely to have occurred.

7 TAX TREATMENT AND MACROECONOMIC EFFECTS

The example we have given above of the UK business property tax illustrates the importance of establishing how firms treat taxes and whether or not they shift them. Three related macroeconomic implications follow. First, since an increase in profits taxes reduces the share of wages in value-added, this reduction will reduce the value of the basic Kaleckian income multiplier, $(1/(1-\alpha))$, and, therefore, will reduce national income and the wage bill, holding other things constant. Second, if the government's policy objective is to stimulate an increase in national income, a question then arises. Should firms' profits be taxed, if, in fact, the response by firms is to mark up business taxes? Instead of taxing firms' profits to achieve the government's policy objective, it would be clearly preferable to tax some other base not included as a prime cost. Taxation of some alternative base would not adversely affect the share of wages in value-added as this alternative base would be treated as part of firms' overhead costs. Third, the analysis provides a Kaleckian explanation for Hotson's (1976) conclusion that a counter-cyclical tax policy contributes to stagflation. The increase in business taxes increases prime unit costs and thus prices, and, ignoring other factors, reduces national income.

8 THE POLITICAL ECONOMY OF TAXATION

In this section, we briefly consider a radical perspective on taxation and consider the role of taxation in light of the accumulation and legitimation functions of the state. In radical economics, the functions of the capitalist state are accumulation and legitimation. It follows, therefore, that labour bears the burden of taxation, in the same manner as it bears the full burden of the creation of profits; and the capitalist state, through its powers of taxation, is a principal agency of exploitation. As a consequence, taxation may be thought of as epitomizing the contradiction between accumulation and legitimation. The state, in raising revenues to promote the accumulation of capital, raises class antagonisms. In attempting to legitimize class relations, by, for example, redistributing income through the tax system, the state undermines the accumulation process. The contradiction between accumulation and legitimation is considered in light of the following: 1) the expenses necessary to maintain a 'legitimate' tax system; and 2) the economic effects of redistributive taxation.

At the political level, as O'Connor (1973) so aptly describes, tax systems have been designed to conceal the distribution of the tax burden through a myriad of taxes and definitions of what is taxable. As such, tax systems, perceived to be progressive because of a progressive income tax rate structure, may actually be regressive because of the definition of taxable income (like excluding various profit-source incomes), and because of the existence of other tax bases (like taxes on wage goods). The cost of this obfuscation, in terms of a tax code that is both costly to administer and comply with, is one of the expenses of legitimation both incurred and imposed by the state.

These legitimation expenses incurred and imposed by the state are minimized by the extent to which tax ideologies are effective. Given the exploitative nature of taxation, tax ideologies are necessary to support the development of tax systems and compliance to them. These tax ideologies are represented in the methodological approach presented in mainstream public finance textbooks. In this methodology, the political and the economic are separated. The state is seen as an expression of individuals' wills or the outcome of a median voter process whose goal is to maximize social welfare subject to some constraints. The study and analysis of tax systems are, therefore, relegated to social welfare criteria where the existence of class domination and intra- and inter-class conflicts are ignored.

The failure of tax ideologies causes legitimation crises that pave the way for tax 'reforms'. However, the process of class domination (O'Connor 1973) causes anti-tax sentiments and movements to be co-opted and translated into the dominant interests within the state apparatus. For example, in the 1980s in the USA, a tax revolt led to an increased reliance on regressive forms of taxation under the guise of increasing economic efficiency, through 'trickle down' or supply-side effects. In Chapter 4, we provide evidence that regressive forms of taxation reduced the level of investment

The pervasiveness of commodity fetishism, tax ideologies and the complexity of the tax system may conceal the true distribution of tax burdens, but what impact does taxation have upon accumulation and what can be said about its impact on the relationship between accumulation and legitimation? Kalecki's model of income distribution and determination give us some insight.

To begin, the existence of the expenses of the state necessary to maintain the legitimacy of the tax system, whether borne publicly or privately, consumes capital necessary for the expansion of the capitalist mode of production. These legitimation expenses impose a trade-off between accumulation and legitimation. In contrast, in a world where markets do not continuously clear, and where aggregate demand matters in affecting production, employment and growth, redistributive tax policies impose no clear contradiction between accumulation and legitimation. As we showed earlier, and discuss in subsequent chapters, redistributive tax policies to promote legitimation, may, paradoxically, under some circumstances, have no impact on accumulation and, indeed, may actually promote it. The pursuit by the state of the accumulation function may undermine the conditions necessary for legitimation while having no impact on, or perhaps actually hindering accumulation. To illustrate this argument, we consider the economic effects of taxation from a radical perspective.

As implied above, the economic effects of taxation depend on: 1) the distribution of the tax burden; 2) the relationship between the level and type of tax revenue (wage taxes vs. profit taxes) and the level and direction of government spending; and 3) the power of economic classes to react to being taxed. We consider each of these briefly and then discuss the dynamic effects of taxation in light of the accumulation and legitimation functions.

The state derives and reports tax receipts from a variety of bases, such as personal income, business and personal property, corporate profits and sales. These tax bases represent sources of tax revenues derived from various economic classes – labour, capital, rentiers and the unemployed. The distribution of tax liabilities, within and between classes, is the outcome of political conflict and reflects the relative degree of power each class exercises within the state apparatus.

The inter-class distribution of taxation is important in determining the macroeconomic effects of taxation, given that different classes derive income from different sources, pay different average tax rates and have different propensities to spend. For example, increases in a profits tax used to subsidize the consumption of the unemployed or wage earners, if the unemployed or workers spend all that they earn, have no impact on the aggregate level of profits.[5] Under these conditions, the pursuit by the state of the legitimation function does not hinder accumulation. However, an increase in the wage tax, if financed totally out of a decrease in worker consumption, and redistributed to individual capitalists, results in no additional profits and undermines the conditions for legitimacy without promoting accumulation. As Kalecki (1971) suggests, opposition to the legitimation expenses through redistributive tax policies, are, therefore, political, although expressed in economic terms.

These conclusions are predicated on the standard Kaleckian assumptions that labour spends all its earnings, that business investment is fixed in the short period by past investment decisions, and that business price/cost markups are constant with respect to a change in the tax structure. The assumption that labour spends all its earnings can be relaxed while still maintaining much of the force of the argument. However, if the assumption that business price/cost markups do not change in response to changes in tax structures is relaxed, the

5. Even if workers do have a positive propensity to save, the state could counteract this dampening effect by generating a budget deficit, have a negative propensity to save.

state may be unable to carry out its legitimation function through redistributive tax policies. This complication is discussed further in following chapters.

Whether a change in the tax structure is regressive or progressive, it can be argued that the aggregate markup may vary with respect to changes in the functional distribution of tax liabilities. The extent to which this will happen will depend on the power to react of the various classes and the specific economic conditions underlying the determination of the markup. These reactions are likely to be asymmetrical as attempts will be made to shift tax increases but not tax decreases. Following an increase in taxation on labour income, workers may seek higher wages that may reduce business price/cost markups (Kalecki, 1971); or businesses may pass on a hike in profits tax through higher markups. Rentiers may react to an increase in taxation by attempting to shift the term structure of interest rates upwards. If successful, profits will be redistributed from debtors to rentiers. To offset this loss, businesses may attempt to raise markups. Thus, the rentier tax may be ultimately be shifted onto labour. If businesses and rentiers are able to shift taxes, these taxes become equivalent to a tax on wages. Assuming that businesses and rentiers are able to shift taxes onto labour, the state, in the absence of an incomes policy, is constrained in fulfilling the legitimation function through redistributive tax policies. In all likelihood, some degree of shifting will take place. The degree of tax shifting depends on the factors that determine the degree of monopoly (Kalecki, 1954) and how these are affected by the tax system. The extent to which shifting takes place and the dynamic process of tax shifting remains to be solved. We deal with tax shifting in subsequent chapters simply by introducing a tax-shift parameter into the markup function.

In addition to tax shifting effects on the markup, an intra-class income distribution effect should also be considered. This effect arises when the state redistributes income within economic classes. For example, if the government increases corporate profits taxes to finance purchases of public investment goods, the government is redistributing profits from some industries paying taxes but not receiving the benefits provided by the public investment goods. As O'Connor (1973) describes, industries receiving benefits may be able to 'bottle up' the gains provided by the state through adjusting markups relative to costs. The state, therefore, promotes accumulation within specific industries at the expense of other industries. The 'bottling up' of benefits compounds inter-class conflict with intra-class conflict, and, as a consequence, crises of legitimation may take on new dimensions resulting in the formation of inter-class alliances.

In moving to the long period, where in the Kaleckian system current profits determine future investment, we can consider circumstances where legitimation and accumulation come into conflict. As we show in Chapter 3, a balanced budget increase in a wage tax can increase national income and current profits and future investment, but reduce after-tax wage income, if workers pay for some of the tax increase by reducing their savings. Likewise, a balanced budget increase in a profits tax can result in higher national income, and higher pre-tax and post-tax wages, but lower after tax profits and lower future investment, if workers save some of their additional wage income. The solution to this conflict though is obvious. The government can alter its budget stance and increase its propensity to spend. As long as the government maintains a marginal propensity to spend at a sufficient level to counteract the effects of workers' marginal propensity to save, the conflict between accumulation and legitima-tion in the long period, at least as reflected in fiscal policy, need not exist!

However, Kalecki (1971, pp. 138–45) recognized that in the long run, political changes may result from the pursuit of full employment policies which may diminish the political power of business leaders and lead to a decline in their ability as a class to accumulate wealth. Thus, the contradiction between accumulation and legitimation is not economic, *per se*, but political with economic consequences. Given that Kalecki first published his ideas on taxation as long ago as 1937, we might have expected more interest in this topic. However, relatively little attention has been paid in the radical literature to the effects of taxation, in particular, to the dynamic effects. While the work by O'Connor referred to above has taken Kalecki's analysis out of a short-period framework, many issues remain unresolved.

To summarize, three problems arise in considering the impact of taxation on the relationship between accumulation and legitimation. First, the 'true' functional distribution of taxation and income is not known. Second, the nature of the dynamic processes, short-run and long-run, through which various economic classes will react to the imposition of new taxes is uncertain and not yet completely understood. Third, the redistributive impact of the state's budget on specific industry markups and on the aggregate markup is also not fully understood. Recognizing that these complications exist, we begin in Chapters 3 and 4 to consider the dynamic effects of taxation.

9   CONCLUSION

In this chapter, we have considered the role of taxation in the short period. We have assumed that taxes are levied on profits or wages. The macroeconomic impact of taxation on the economy depends on: 1) the relative marginal propen-sities to spend out of wages and profits; 2) whether compensating changes in government expenditures exist; 3) the degree to which a tax change is shifted through changes in business markups. Thus, the pricing behaviour of firms determines whether increases in profit taxes are marked up or not. The conclusions presented in this chapter have been developed in a short-period framework. We have retained the assumption that business investment expenditures are determined by investment decisions in some previous time period. In the next chapter we proceed to consider the role of taxation in the long period.

APPENDIX

The relationships between national income and taxation and national income investment without and with balanced budget constraints are presented formally in this Appendix.

The Relationship between National Income and Taxation without a Balanced Budget Constraint

Differentiating national income as given by equation (2.7') with respect to wage and profits tax rates, and by assuming that the wage share can simply be written as $\alpha = 1/k$, where $k = k(t_w, t_p)$ and $k_{tw} <$ or $= 0$ and $k_{tp} >$ or $= 0$ yields:

$$dY/dti = \partial Y/\partial ti + (\partial Y/\partial a)(\partial a/\partial k)(\partial k/\partial ti) \qquad (2.1A)$$

where $i = p$ and w, and $\partial k/\partial ti = k_{ti}$.

$$dY/dtp = -[I'/D^2]\{(1 - \alpha)cc + [1 - cc(1 - tp) - tw - sw(1 - tw)](\alpha^2)k_{tp}]\}$$
$$< 0 \text{ if } k_{tp} = \text{or} > 0 \qquad (2.2A)$$

$$dY/dtw = -[I'/D^2][-\alpha(1 - sw) + [1 - cc(1 - tp) - tw - sw(1 - tw)](\alpha^2)k_{tw}]$$
$$< 0 \text{ if } k_{tp} = 0$$
$$< \text{or} = \text{or} > 0 \text{ if } k_{tw} < 0 \qquad (2.3A)$$

where $D = (1 - \alpha)[1 - cc(1 - tp)] + \alpha[tw + sw(1 - tw)]$; $I' = I + Ge + X - M$ and assuming $[1 - cc(1 - tp) - tw - sw(1 - tw)] > 0$.

The Relationship between National Income and Taxation with a Balanced Budget Constraint

To illustrate the relationships between the profits tax and the wage tax and national income under a balance budget constraint, the expressions for national income equation (2.7') and pre-tax profits equation (2.9') are rewritten assuming that $Ge = Tw + Tp$; i.e.:

$$\Pi = [I''](1 - \alpha)/\{(1 - \alpha)(1 - tp)(1 - cc) + sw(\alpha)(1 - tw) \qquad (2.4A)$$

and:

$$Y = [I'']/\{(1 - \alpha)(1 - tp)(1 - cc) + sw(\alpha)(1 - tw)\} \qquad (2.5A)$$

where $I'' = I + X - M$.

Differentiating equation (2.5A) with respect to the profits and wage tax rates yields:

$$dY/dtp = [I''/D^2]\{(1 - \alpha)(1 - cc) -[(1 - cc)(1 - tp) - sw(1 - tw)](\alpha^2)k_{tp}]\}$$
$$> 0, \text{ if } k_{tp} = 0$$
$$> \text{ or } = \text{ or } < 0 \text{ if } k_{tp} > 0 \qquad (2.6A)$$

$$dY/dtw = [I''/D^2]\{sw(\alpha) - [(1 - cc)(1 - tp) - sw(1 - tw)](\alpha^2)k_{tw}]\} \qquad (2.7A)$$
$$> 0, \text{ if } k_{tw} = \text{ or } < 0$$

where $D' = (1 - \alpha)(1 - tp)(1 - cc) + sw(\alpha)(1 - tw)$ and assuming $(1 - cc)$ $(1 - tp) - sw(1 - tw) > 0$.

REFERENCES

Asimakopulos, A. (1975), 'A Kaleckian theory of income distribution', *Canadian Journal of Economics*, **8** (3), 313–33.

Asimakopulos, A. and Burbidge, J.B. (1974), 'The short-period incidence of taxation', *Economic Journal*, **84**, 267–88.

Block, H. (1980), 'Price leadership and the degree of monopoly', *Journal of Post Keynesian Economics*, **12**, 439–51.

Hotson, J.H. (1976), *Stagflation and the Bastard Keynesians*, Waterloo, University of Waterloo Press.

Kalecki, M. (1937), 'A theory of commodity, income and capital taxation', *Economic Journal*, **47**, 444–50.

Kalecki, M. (1954), *Theory of Economic Dynamics*, London, Unwin University Books.

Kalecki, M. (1968), 'Trend and business cycles reconsidered', *Economic Journal*, **78**, 263–76.

Kalecki, M. (1971), *Selected Essays on the Dynamics of the Capitalist Economy*, Cambridge, Cambridge University Press.

Laramie, A.J. (1991) 'Taxation and Kalecki's distribution factors', *Journal of Post Keynesian Economics*, **4**, 583–94.

Laramie, A.J. (1994), 'The incidence of the corporate profits tax revisited: a post Keynesian approach', *Jerome Levy Economics Institute*, Working Paper No. 109.

Laramie, A.J. and Mair, D. (1993), 'The incidence of business rates: a post Keynesian approach', *Review of Political Economy*, **5** (1), 55–72.

O'Connor, J. (1973), *The Fiscal Crisis of the State*, New York, St. Martin's Press.

Reynolds, P.J. (1984), 'An empirical analysis of the degree of monopoly theory of distribution', *Bulletin of Economic Research*, **36** (1), 59–84.

Reynolds, P.J. (1996), 'Kalecki's theory of prices and distribution', in King, J.E. (ed.), *An Alternative Economic Theory: The Kaleckian Model and Post-Keynesian Economics*, Boston, Kluwer.
Robinson, J. (1980), *What are the Questions and Other Essays*, Armonk, NY, M.E. Sharpe.
Sawyer, M.C. (1985), *The Economics of Michal Kalecki*, London, Macmillan.
Weintraub, S. (1981), 'An eclectic theory of income shares', *Journal of Post Keynesian Economics*, **4** (1), 10–24.

3. Taxation and Kalecki's theory of the business cycle[1]

1 INTRODUCTION

In studying the incidence of taxation, post Keynesians have found it convenient to break their analysis into two parts: 1) a study of short-period tax incidence; and 2) a study of long-period tax incidence. In the orthodox mainstream approach, the short period is defined in the classical sense as the time period during which the capital stock remains constant following a change in the corporation profits tax. With demand conditions unchanged and a constant capital stock and with no substitution of labour for capital, the conclusion of orthodox studies is that marginal cost, and, thus, price remain constant following a change in the rate of corporate profits tax.[2]

In contrast, post Keynesians, like Asimakopulos and Burbidge (1979), define the short period as the time period over which investment is fixed (by past decisions) and changes in aggregate demand are met by varying the rate of capacity utilization. Asimakopulos and Burbidge (1979, p. 71) argue that the short period, so defined, can be measured in 'calendar time, for example a quarter of a year, a half of a year or even a year.' The long period is the time period when capital stock and investment can vary, that is, where past investment decisions have an impact on the present.

In this chapter, we attempt to advance the theory of tax incidence into the long period by integrating Kalecki's (1937) theory of taxation and his theory of the business cycle (Kalecki, (1968/1971)). We show that wage and profits taxes have short-period effects on profits, and that the short-period-tax-profit effects have long-period effects on investment. These long-period effects of the wage and profit taxes can affect the amplitude of the business cycle and the investment trend. By introducing the tax system into Kalecki's theory of the business cycle, we are following Kalecki's (1968/1971) suggestion that further studies of growth be directed at the factors influencing the national income multiplier and the rate of depreciation.

---

1. This chapter is a revision of Laramie and Mair (1996).
2. This approach has caused others, like Musgrave and Musgrave (1989), to conclude that short-run shifting is the consequence of non profit maximizing behaviour.

We have considered elsewhere the effects of wage and profit taxes in other models (for example, Laramie and Mair (1991), and Laramie and Mair (1992)). In this chapter we specifically analyse the effects of wage and profit taxes in the context of Kalecki's (1968/1971) version III investment equation.[3] According to Courvisanos (1996, p. 18), version III's investment equation has the same structure as that of version II, but the means used to derive version III are quite novel. In version II, investment expenditures are positively related to profits and to the change in the level of profits, negatively related to the change in the capital stock, and technological change is included as exogenous factor. The level of profits provides internal funds to finance purchases of new equipment and structures. The change in the level of profits, via an accelerator effect, generates expectations of future profits. The change in the capital stock is inversely related to the rate of profits, and, therefore, is negatively related to new investment decisions. In version III, Kalecki (1968/1971, p. 171) incorporates these variables into his investment equation by assuming that investment decisions depend on 'two considerations: a) those concerning gross entrepreneurial savings [the savings of the firm's controlling group]; and b) those considering the prerequisite for their reinvestment'. Entrepreneurial savings are related to the aggregate level of profits, and whether or not investment decisions are greater than, less than, or equal to entrepreneurial savings depends on the firm's reaction to differences between the actual level of new investment and investment that yields the standard rate of profits. The standard rate of profit is the inverse of the payback period. If current investment is greater (less) than investment that yields the standard rate of profits, then Kalecki assumes that the rate of profit is below (above) the standard rate of profit. If investment is below (above) the level which yields the standard rate of profits, then investment decisions will be less than (greater than) entrepreneurial savings.

The novel aspect of this approach is that Kalecki explicitly considers the channels through which new investment captures new profits. First, because of ample unused capacity, new investment will capture only an increment of the new profits generated in a given period. Second, because new investment brings new technological innovations to the market, some existing equipment will lose profits to new investment. In other words, some new equipment gains profit at the expense of old equipment causing *real* economic depreciation of the old equipment. We can see from this novel approach that Kalecki again shows that investment decisions depend on the level of profits, through entrepreneurial savings, on the change in the level of profits (through the ability of new investment to capture market share as augmented by technological change), and on the change in the capital stock which provides a negative feedback

3. For a description of Kalecki's other investment equations, versions I and II, see Courvisanos (1996).

effect on investment. These latter two effects combine to give the marginal rate of profits and endogenous technological change a central role in the theory of investment, the business cycle and the trend.

The chapter is structured as follows. We begin by outlining Kalecki's theory of the business cycle, identifying the changes we make to the original in order to incorporate the tax system. We then consider the effects of taxation on the rate of depreciation, the level of profits and the structure of the business cycle and examine the consequences of shifting the wage and profit taxes. Finally, we present our conclusions. We keep the amount of mathematics in the body of the chapter to a minimum but show our derivations in a mathematical appendix.

2   KALECKIAN THEORY OF THE BUSINESS CYCLE AND THE TAX SYSTEM

In the previous chapter, we showed how taxation has an impact on the level of profits, national income and the wage bill under a number of assumptions, including a balanced budget constraint and non-zero marginal propensities to consume and save. It is possible to analyse the effects of taxation on the business cycle under a wide range of assumptions, possible stances of government budget balance and different directions of the trend rate of growth. Inevitably, the greater the number of assumptions, the greater the complexity of the mathematics and the greater the length of the chapter. Accordingly, we limit discussion to one budget stance where government purchases are constrained to equal tax receipts, and to an economy that is fluctuating around a zero trend. We are happy to provide a fuller analysis of other trend and budget scenarios on request.[4]

Like Keynes, Kalecki focused on private sector investment as the source of cyclical fluctuations. We modify Kalecki's (1968/1971) theory of the business cycle, in order to achieve greater simplicity and generality while losing none of Kalecki's essential arguments. Following Kalecki (1968/1971), we ignore the inventory investment component of the business cycle. We continue to assume for the present a closed economy, but now we explicitly introduce government purchases and taxation into the analysis. We present in Chapter 8 an open economy version of our model.

To illustrate the long-period effect of taxation, we drop the autonomous portion of capitalists' consumption from the analysis and also drop the assumption that workers do not save. Like Kalecki, we explicitly exclude overhead (salaried) labour from the analysis. Finally, we assume that the

4. The impact of taxation on investment for a non-zero trend is analysed in the Appendix.

aggregate markup is constant with respect to changes in tax rates, although we drop this assumption later.

Kalecki (1968/1971, p. 171) considered three determinants of new investment decisions: 1) entrepreneurial savings; 2) the prerequisites for the reinvestment of these savings; and 3) an innovation factor. Entrepreneurial savings, E, influence investment decisions because of capital market limits and increasing risk (Kalecki, 1968/1971, p. 172). Whether entrepreneurial savings are reinvested or not depends on the relationship between the actual level of investment, I, and the investment that generates the standard ('normal') rate of profit, $I(\pi)$, where the standard rate of profits, π, is the reciprocal of the payoff period. Entrepreneurs undertake investment in the expectation that it will pay itself back in some standard or 'normal' period. If, in fact, it pays itself back in less than the 'normal' period, this will act as an inducement to entrepreneurs to contemplate increasing investment and vice versa. The extent to which the difference between investment that generates the standard rate of profits, $I(\pi)$, and actual investment, I, has an impact on investment decisions depends on r, the 'intensity of the reaction of entrepreneurs' (Kalecki, 1968/1971, p. 172). To these determinants, Kalecki (1968/1971, p. 173) added innovations-induced investment decisions, $B(t)$. He represented this factor as a semi-autonomous function, depending on 'past economic, social and technological developments' (Kalecki, 1968/1971, p. 173), that are assumed to change slowly over time.

Accordingly, fixed investment decisions, D, can be written as:

$$D = E + r(I(\pi) - I) + B(t) \tag{3.1}$$

Kalecki rewrites equation (3.1) by finding expressions for entrepreneurial savings, E, and investment that generates the standard rate of profits, $I(\pi)$. He assumes (Kalecki 1968/1971, p. 172) that entrepreneurial savings are a fraction of gross savings, workers' savings being assumed to be zero. Given this assumption, we can write entrepreneurial savings as a fraction of total post-tax profits; thus:

$$E = \lambda(P) \tag{3.2}$$

where P = aggregate post-tax profits.

In order to find an expression for investment that generates the standard rate of profits, Kalecki (1968/1971, p. 170) assumes 'ample unused productive capacities' and that new investment that generates the standard rate of profits will capture only a portion, n, of the new 'real' profits generated, ΔP. This amount is augmented by the extent to which new investment results, through technological change, in productivity increases. These productivity increases associated with new investment increase the real costs of existing equipment, cause some shift in production from existing to new investment, reduce the real profits from existing equipment and increase profits from new equipment.

The loss in profits from existing equipment (or, the same thing, the gain in profits from new equipment) is assumed to be proportional to real costs. This is expressed as the difference between national income, Y, and post-tax profits, P, that is: $\omega(Y - P)$. The greater the rate of technical progress, the greater is the value of ω, and the greater is the gain in profits from new equipment. As a consequence, the profits generated by new investment, ρ, is $n\Delta P + \omega(Y - P)$, and if new investment is just sufficient to generate the standard rate of profits (i.e. if I is equal to $I(\pi)$), then by definition, $\rho = \pi$, thus

$$\pi = [n\Delta P + \omega(Y - P)]/I(\pi) \qquad (3.3)$$

where $I(\pi)$ = investment that yields the standard rate of profits, which by rearrangement yields:

$$I(\pi) = [n\Delta P + \omega(Y - P)]/(\pi) \qquad (3.4)$$

In turn, equation (3.4) can be rewritten by finding an expression for national income as a function of profits. To do this we rewrite equation (2.7), assuming overhead salaries, β, is zero, and by assuming that profit taxes can be written as $Tp = t_p(\Pi)$. Thus, we write (see the Appendix):

$$Y = P/(1 - t_p)(1 - \alpha) \qquad (3.5)$$

where t_p = the tax rate on profits; and α = the wage share.

Equation (3.5) is important because it shows that the tax system influences the relationship between aggregate profits (P) and national income (Y) directly through the impact of taxation on profits (t_p) and indirectly through the wage share, α.

By substituting equation (3.5) into equation (3.4), the level of investment fetching the standard rate of profit, $I(\pi)$, can be rewritten as:

$$I(\pi) = [n\Delta P + \delta P]/\alpha \qquad (3.6)$$

where:

$$\delta = \omega[\alpha + t_p(1 - \alpha)]/(1 - t_p)(1 - \alpha) \qquad (3.7)$$

where δ = the rate of depreciation in the sense that it represents the rate at which profits are lost to existing capital as the result of technical progress (Kalecki 1968/1971, p. 171, fn).

Following Kalecki, investment decisions taken in the time period t are translated into investment expenditures in $t + \tau$, so that $I_{t+\tau} = D_t$. Thus, by substituting equations (3.2) and (3.3) into equation (3.1), we can rewrite equation (3.1) as:

$$I_{t+\tau} = \lambda P_t + r(\{[n\Delta P + \delta P]/\pi\} - I_t) + B(t) \qquad (3.1')$$

From equation (3.1') we can summarize the determinants of investment expenditures. Current investment expenditures depend on the level and the change in the level of past profits, on the past level of investment expenditures and on an innovations factor, given the parameters λ, r, n, δ and π. For example, an increase in profits results in a rise in entrepreneurial savings and an increase in the profitability of new investment relative to actual investment. The rise in entrepreneurial savings reduces the risk associated with new investment and provides greater access to capital markets. The rise in profits and an increase in the rate of change in profits cause new investment to become more profitable. This makes more investment possible at the standard rate of profits, since the volume of profits captured by new investment increases, given n and δ. The rise in investment that yields the standard rate of profits relative to actual investment induces entrepreneurs to undertake investment expenditures in excess of entrepreneurial savings, given the intensity of entrepreneurs' reactions, r.

3   IMPACT OF TAXATION ON THE BUSINESS CYCLE AND TREND

We now proceed to use the investment function as specified in equation (3.1') to consider the impact of the tax system on the business cycle and the trend.

1   Taxation and Depreciation

The impact of the tax system on investment operates via the rate of depreciation and the level of profits. The impact of taxation on depreciation is by affecting the real tax bill associated with old equipment. Technical progress, through new investment, results in increases in the productivity of new equipment which, *ceteris paribus*, result in lower prices. This increases the real costs and lowers the real profits associated with existing equipment. The decline in real profits from existing equipment accelerates its obsolescence. Thus, an increase in the tax on profits will increase the rate of depreciation, given the rate of technical progress.

To consider how a change in the tax rates on wages or profits has an impact on the rate of depreciation, we recognize that a change in any of the parameters that increases national income relative to profits, given the rate of technical progress, increases the rate of depreciation. We consider here and in the next two sections how changes in the tax rates on wages and profits have an impact on depreciation for two cases: 1) no tax shifting; and 2) tax shifting.

In the no tax shifting case, the markup, k, is constant with respect to a change in the tax rates, t_w and t_p. In the tax shifting case, we assume an inverse relationship between the markup and the wage tax rate, t_w, and a positive relationship between the markup and the profits tax rate, t_p. By differentiating the rate of depreciation with respect to a change in either tax rate, we consider the impact of taxation on the rate of depreciation, i.e.:

$$d\delta/dt_i = \partial d/\partial t_i + (\partial d/\partial a)(\partial a/\partial k)(\partial k/\partial t_i)^5 \tag{3.8}$$

where $i = w$ and p.

With no tax shifting, an increase in the tax rate on wages, t_w, has no impact on the rate of depreciation (see the Appendix). When the wage tax shifting effect is considered, the fall in business markups, given profits, increases the wage bill and national income and, therefore, increases the rate of depreciation (see the Appendix).

With no tax shifting, an increase in the tax rate on profits, t_p, given post-tax profits, causes pre-tax profits to increase, thereby increasing national income, Y, relative to aggregate profits, P, and increases the rate of depreciation. With profits tax shifting, the increase in business markups reduces the wage bill, dampens the increases in both national income and in the rate of depreciation (see the Appendix). The significance of these results is discussed more fully below. Given that a change in the rate of depreciation affects the level of new investment, taxation will have an impact on the level of investment and the structure of the business cycle.

2   Taxation and the Level of Profits

Kalecki (1968) showed that aggregate profits, as measured by the difference between aggregate sales and prime costs (materials and wages), can be represented as the sum of gross private investment, the government budget

---

5. As shown in equation (2.7), the shifting effect is through a change in the impact of the markup on the wage share. Kalecki (1968/1971) argued that the markup and the ratio of materials costs to wage costs move counter-cyclically, see equation (2.4), causing the wage share to be relatively constant. Whether such a counter-cyclical movement exists with respect to a change in the tax rates is an empirical question and beyond the scope of this work.

deficit, the trade surplus and the difference between capitalists' consumption and workers' savings. Thus, assuming that the trade balance is zero, the level of profits is expressed as:

$$P = I + G - T + Cc - Ws \qquad (3.9)$$

where G = government purchases, T = tax receipts, Cc = capitalists' consumption and Ws = workers' savings.

Assuming a balanced budget constraint, $G = T$, and that $Cc = c_c(P)$ and $Ws = (1 - t_w)s_w(V)$, where c_c = the propensity to consume out of profits, and s_w = the propensity to save out of wages, the profit function can be written as:

$$P = I(1 - \alpha)(1 - t_p)/[(1 - t_p)(1 - \alpha)(1 - c_c) + s_w(1 - t_w)\alpha] \qquad (3.10)$$

As reflected in equation (3.10), aggregate profits are equal to investment, when workers do not save and capitalists do not consume, and the government budget is in balance. The impact of taxation on the level of profits can be formally represented by differentiating equation (3.10) with respect to a change in the rates of tax on wages and profits, i.e.:

$$dP/dt_i = (\partial P/\partial a)(\partial a/\partial k)(\partial k/\partial t_i) + (\partial P/\partial t_i) \qquad (3.11)$$

where $i = w$ and p.

As evidenced in equation (3.11), assuming a balanced budget constraint, the impact of taxation on the level of profits in the short period is directly through a change in the tax rates and indirectly through a change the wage share. In the no tax shifting case, a balanced budget increase in the wage tax causes a reduction in workers' savings which increases the level of post-tax profits. If the wage tax is shifted, then this positive impact on profits is reduced by the extent to which shifting increases the wage share, α, and the wage bill and workers' savings. If workers' savings are zero, then the balanced budget tax change has no impact on post-tax profits (see the Appendix).

By contrast, an unshifted balanced budget increase in the profits tax reduces after tax profits, because the rise in pre-tax profits increases national income, the wage bill and workers' savings. However, if the profits tax is shifted, the dampening effect of the increase in workers' savings is reduced. If workers do not save, the balanced budget increase in the profits tax has no effect on post-tax profits.

We have now shown that taxation has an impact on investment through two channels: 1) the rate of depreciation, and 2) the level of profits. In the next section, we proceed to analyse the impact of taxation on investment over different stages of the business cycle.

4   TAXATION AND THE CYCLE AND TREND COMPONENTS OF INVESTMENT

The cyclical component of investment is derived by differencing the profits function, equation (3.10), and then by substituting the profits function and its difference form into the investment equation, (3.1'). By subtracting the corresponding trend level, $y_t = 0$, from the investment equation and by assuming the cyclical variation in government purchases equals zero, the following expression for the business cycle is derived.[6]

$$I_{t+\tau} - y_{t+\tau} = (q - r)(I_t - y_t) + s[\Delta(I_t - y_t)] \qquad (3.12)$$

where y = the trend value of I, and where:

$$q = \{[[\lambda + (r/p)\delta](1 - \alpha)(1 - t_p)]/[(1 - t_p)(1 - \alpha)(1 - c_c) + s_w(1 - t_w)\alpha] \qquad (3.13)$$

$$s = (r/\pi)n(1 - \alpha)(1 - t_p)/[(1 - t_p)(1 - \alpha)(1 - c_c) + s_w(1 - t_w)\alpha] \qquad (3.14)$$

Since we are examining the special case where the trend level of investment equals zero, the investment equation can be rewritten as:

$$I_{t+\tau} = (q - r)(I_t - y_t) + s[\Delta(I_t - y_t)] \qquad (3.12')$$

The impact of taxation on future investment is channelled through q and s. Thus, the change in investment with respect to a change in the tax rates on wage or profits is given as:

$$d(I_{t+\tau})/dt_i = [\partial(I_{t+t})/\partial q[dq/dt_i] + [\partial(I_{t+\tau})/\partial s][ds/dt_i] \qquad (3.15)$$

where:

$$dq/dt_i = [\partial q/\partial \delta][d\delta/dt_i] + [\partial q/\partial a][\partial a/\partial k][\partial k/\partial t_i] + [\partial q/\partial t_i] \qquad (3.16)$$

$$ds/dt_i = [\partial s/\partial a][\partial a/\partial k][\partial k/\partial t_i] + [\partial s/\partial t_i] \qquad (3.17)$$

and where $i = w$ and p.

As evidenced in equations (3.15), (3.16) and (3.17), the impact of taxation on investment depends on: 1) the cyclical variation in investment,

---

6. Given the assumption of a balanced budget constraint, we are abstracting from the automatic stabilization feature implicit in the government budget.

$\partial(I_{t+\tau})/\partial q = (I_t - y_t) < = > 0;^7$ 2) the change in the cyclical variation in investment, $\partial(I_{t+\tau})/\partial s(1 - \alpha) = \Delta(I_t - y_t) >=< 0$; and 3) three parameter shift effects: a) a depreciation effect, the first term in equation (3.16); b) a distribution effect, the second and first terms in equations (3.16) and (3.17) respectively; and c) a profits effect, the last terms in equations (3.16) and (3.17). We consider these effects below in describing how changes in wage and profits taxes have an impact on investment and the structure of the business cycle.

To illustrate the impact of the taxation of wages on investment, we assume that the tax is not shifted. As we show above, a change in the wage tax rate has no impact on the rate of depreciation when no shifting is assumed. As a consequence, the wage tax rate alters investment and the structure of the business cycle through its effect on profits. As we show above, a balanced budget change in the wage tax pushes up the level of profits. If investment is in an upswing or at its peak, where current investment determines current profits, and current profits determine future investment, an increase (decrease) in the wage tax rate increases (reduces) the impact of current investment on current profits and future investment. Through the balanced budget effect, the impact of the change in the wage tax on profits is that the increase (decrease) in the wage tax rate heightens the upswing and increases the peak of the business cycle. The opposite occurs during the downswing and at the trough of the business cycle. As a consequence, an increase (decrease) in the wage tax rate heightens (dampens) the amplitude of the business cycle.

Still retaining the assumptions of no tax shifting, the effects of a change in the tax rate on profits are quite different. The impact of the profits tax rate on the structure of the business cycle is through a depreciation effect and a profits effect. An increase in the profits tax rate heightens the rate of depreciation while it reduces the level of profits (assuming non-zero workers' savings). These opposing forces cause the profits tax rate to have an indeterminate effect on investment. Assuming that the impact of the profits effect on the investment coefficient, q, is greater than the depreciation effect, we can reach some tentative conclusions. If investment is in an upswing or at its peak, where current investment determines current profits, and current profits determine future investment, an increase (decrease) in the profits tax rate decreases (increases) the impact of current investment and current profit on future investment. Thus, the decrease (increase) in the profits tax rate reduces (increases) investment during the upswing and at the peak of the business cycle. The opposite occurs during the downswing and at the trough of the business cycle. As a consequence,

---

7. As is shown in the Appendix, if a non-zero trend is assumed, this term contains a trend component. As a consequence, the impact of taxation on investment also depends on the value of the trend component.

A dynamic theory of taxation

an increase (decrease) in the profits tax rate dampens (heightens) the amplitude of the business cycle.

If the depreciation effect of a change in the impact of the profit tax rate on the investment coefficient, q, is greater than the profits effect, then: 1) an increase in the profits tax rate reduces investment during the first two stages of the recovery of the cycle; 2) has an indeterminate impact in the third stage of recovery; 3) increases the peak level of investment; 4) increases investment during the first and second stages recession; 5) has an indeterminate impact in the third stage of recession; and 6) lowers the trough level of investment. To sum up, the depreciation effect tends to heighten the amplitude of business cycle.

These results are formally presented in the Appendix and are summarized in Table 3.1 and depicted in Figure 3.1 below for eight different stages of the business cycle.

Table 3.1 The effects of taxation on investment at different stages of the business cycle, with no tax shifting and trend = 0

	$d(I_{t+1})/dt_w$	$d(I_{t+1})/dt_p$*	$d(I_{t+1})/dt_p$**
Stage I	?	?	–
Stage II	+	–	–
Stage III	+	–	?
Stage IV	+	–	+
Stage V	?	?	+
Stage VI	–	+	+
Stage VII	–	+	?
Stage VIII	–	+	–

Notes:
* Profit effect is greater than the depreciation effect.
** Depreciation effect is greater than the profit effect.

When tax shifting is considered, the results change significantly. For example, shifting of the wage tax, where the markup is inversely related to the wage tax, increases the rate of depreciation but lowers the level of profits (assuming workers' savings are non-zero). If the tax shifting effect on profits is greater than that on depreciation, the shifting of the wage tax will dampen the increasing amplitude of the business cycle. Similarly, the shifting of the profits tax rate has a positive impact on the level of profits (assuming workers' savings are non-zero) and negatively on the rate of depreciation. Thus, an increase in the profits tax rate, if shifted, assuming the profits effect is greater than the depreciation effect,

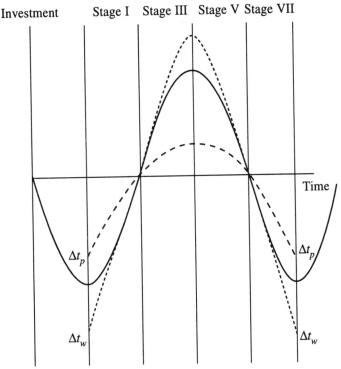

Investment   Stage I   Stage III   Stage V   Stage VII

Time

Δt_p

Δt_p

Δt_w

Δt_w

Stage II   Stage IV   Stage VI   StageVIII

Stage I: First stage of recovery: $(I_t - y_t) < 0$ and $\Delta(I_t - y_t) > 0$;
Stage II: Second stage of recovery: $(I_t - y_t) = 0$ and $\Delta(I_t - y_t) > 0$
Stage III: Third stage of recovery: $(I_t - y_t) > 0$ and $\Delta(I_t - y_t) > 0$;
Stage IV: Peak of the cycle: $(I_t - y_t) > 0$ and $\Delta(I_t - y_t) = 0$;
Stage V: First stage of recession: $(I_t - y_t) > 0$ and $\Delta(I_t - y_t) < 0$;
Stage VI: Second stage of recession: $(I_t - y_t) = 0$ and $\Delta(I_t - y_t) < 0$;
Stage VII: Third stage of recession: $(I_t - y_t) < 0$ and $\Delta(I_t - y_t) < 0$;
Stage VIII: Trough of the cycle: $(I_t - y_t) < 0$ and $\Delta(I_t - y_t) = 0$.

Figure 3.1   Impact of Δt_w and Δt_p on the amplitude of the business cycle with no tax shifting, assuming that the effect of a change in the profits tax rate on profits is greater than its effect on depreciation – – – Δtp; ... Δtw

dampens the falling amplitude of the business cycle. The consequence of introducing tax shifting is that the signs of the impact of taxation on investment all become indeterminate. The issue then becomes an empirical one.

To summarize: when considering the impact of taxation on the business cycle, it is important to know: 1) the stage of the cycle at which the economy happens to be; 2) the long-run trend of investment; 3) the direction of tax policy; and 4) the process and degree of tax shifting.

5 SOME POLICY IMPLICATIONS

The results presented in this chapter have as important policy implications for post Keynesians as for neoclassical economists. Until now, Kalecki's writings on fiscal theory and policy have never been properly integrated into the corpus of his work on the business cycle. Thus, Paladini (1989) concludes that while there is a fundamental role for fiscal policy in Kalecki's macroeconomics in the short period, there is no analogous role in the long period. However, we have demonstrated in this chapter that within the framework of Kalecki's business cycle theory, taxes do indeed have an impact on investment.

The opportunity now exists for post Keynesians to explore the long-period macroeconomic implications of taxation in the context of a paradigm that is not constrained by the limitations of neoclassical theory. Using the kind of analysis described in this chapter, Laramie et al. (1996), for example, have explored the effects of tax incentives on business fixed investment in the US in the 1980s and have found evidence to suggest that attempts to stimulate investment by traditional policy measures, such as reducing profits tax rates and increasing payroll or compensation taxes, are likely to be frustrated. These taxes reduce income to wage earners and cause a reduction in spending on wage goods relative to the wage bill, holding government spending constant. The result is a reduction in profits and business investment. We discuss these results in more detail in Chapter 6.

As we observe in Chapter 1, orthodox writers on public finance (e.g. Atkinson and Stiglitz, 1980) have recognized a need for a closer integration of the micro-economic and macroeconomic elements in the study of the effects of taxation and a relaxation of such conventional neoclassical assumptions as continuous market clearing. Tax incidence theory is, after all, applied income distribution theory and for neoclassicals income distribution theory is marginal productivity theory. Whether orthodox public finance economists are prepared to abandon such a major shibboleth of neoclassical theory is a question which only they can answer, but it seems to us that failure to do so could result in the perpetuation of tax policy prescriptions derived from contentious theoretical analysis.

We conclude this chapter by giving three examples of tax policy conclusions which follow from our approach, and which conflict diametrically with orthodox policy prescriptions, as illustrations of the need we perceive for a radical rethink of the analysis of taxation. First, the incidence of taxation needs to be explicitly considered when determining the effects of taxation on investment. Within the neoclassical framework, an increase in the wage tax rate is assumed to be partially shifted onto businesses, depending on the elasticity of the demand for labour. The increase in the wage tax rate increases the relative price of labour and causes an increase in the demand for capital. In other words, the increase in the wage tax rate results in new investment, assuming labour and capital are substitutes.

In contrast, by relaxing the balanced budget assumption, the conclusion of the model presented in this chapter suggests that an increase in the wage tax rate is more likely to reduce the flow of profits and depress investment. Traditional investment tax incentive policies like accelerated depreciation allowances or investment tax credits, may, therefore, be swamped by regressive income tax policies. In other words, the 'trickle down' policies advocated in supply-side economics may actually stifle investment.

A second conclusion we draw is that by comparison to the neoclassical standpoint, changes in average tax rates as opposed to marginal tax rates matter more in effecting changes in investment. This poses the interesting problem as to how to stimulate investment without providing windfall gains to the wealthy. A reduction in the profits tax rate may stimulate investment, if the profit effect is greater than the depreciation effect, but the likely result is an increase in the distribution of income towards the rich. Our results suggest that tax policies that have the objective of stimulating investment may not pose an equity/efficiency trade-off. Investment may actually be stimulated by equalizing the distribution of income through the tax system.

Finally, as suggested in Figure 3.1, the imposition of a balanced budget constraint over the business cycle neutralizes the long-run effects of taxation on investment when a zero trend is assumed. With a balanced budget constraint, taxation has an impact on investment over the long run, only if a non-zero trend is present. However, if we analyse the effects of taxation on the trend (see the Appendix), it is possible to show that any tax change that increases the investment coefficient, q, acts as a stimulus to long-period economic growth. Thus, assuming workers' savings are non-zero, a balanced budget increase in the profits tax reduces the trend level of investment (assuming the profits effect is greater than the depreciation effect); and a balanced budget increase in the wage tax increases the trend level of investment. Tax reductions independent of changes in government spending increase the investment coefficient, q, and the trend level of investment. This conclusion has obvious comforting implications for governments concerned with problems of deficit reduction and the maintenance of growth.

APPENDIX

1 National Income as a Function of Profits

Recall that the wage and salary share is given as:

$$V/Y = \beta/Y + \alpha \qquad (3.1A)$$

If, as Kalecki assumes, the salary bill is zero, then equation (3.1A) can be rewritten as:

$$V/Y = \alpha \qquad (3.1A')$$

Since the pre-tax wage bill equals national income (Y) minus aggregate pre-tax profits (P), the level of national income can be found by solving for Y in equation (3.1A'); thus:

$$Y = \Pi/(1 - \alpha) \qquad (3.2A)$$

where $\Pi = P + Tp$ and Tp = profit tax receipts.
Since:

$$Tp = t_p(\Pi) \qquad (3.3A)$$

$$P = P/(1 - t_p) \qquad (3.4A)$$

where t_p = the tax rate on profits.
As a result of equations (3.1A) to (3.4A), equation (3.4) is derived.

2 Wage Tax Rate and Depreciation

The impact of a change in the wage tax rate on the rate of depreciation can be formally written as:

$$d\delta/dt_w = -[\omega(1 - t_p)(1 + j)\alpha^2 k_{t_w}]/[(1 - t_p)(1 - \alpha)]^2 => 0, \text{ if } k_{t_w} <= 0 \qquad (3.5A)$$

where k_{t_w} = the change in the markup with respect to a change in the wage rate.

3 Profits Tax Rate and Depreciation

The impact of a change in the profits tax rate on the rate of depreciation is given as:

$$d\delta/dt_p = \{\omega(1 - t_p)/[(1 - t_p)(1 - \alpha)]^2\}\{1 - (1 + j)\alpha^2 k_{tp}\} > = < 0 \quad (3.6A)$$

where k_{tp} = the change in the markup with respect to a change in the tax rate on profits.

4 Wage Tax Rate and Aggregate Profits

The impact of a change in the wage tax rate on aggregate profits is given as:

$$dP/dt_w = \{I(s_w)(1 - t_p)/[(1 - t_p)(1 - \alpha)(1 - c_c) + s_w(1 - t_w)\alpha]^2\}$$
$$\{\alpha(1 - \alpha) + (1 + j)(1 - t_w)a^2 k_{tw}\} > = < 0 \quad (3.7A)$$

5 Profits Tax Rate and Aggregate Profits

The impact of a change in the profits tax rate on aggregate profits is given as:

$$dP/dt_p = \{- I(s_w)(1 - t_w)/[(1 - t_p)(1 - \alpha)(1 - c_c) + s_w(1 - t_w)\alpha]^2\}$$
$$\{\alpha(1 - \alpha) + (1 + j)(1 - t_p)\alpha^2 k_{tp}\} > = < 0 \quad (3.8A)$$

6 Derivation of the Investment Equation with a Non-zero Trend

Generally, the investment equation is represented as the sum of the trend and cyclical components of investment. The trend level of investment in time $t + \tau$ is written as:

$$y_{t+\tau} = (q - r)y_t + s\Delta(y_t) + B(t) \quad (3.9A)$$

By adding and subtracting y_t on the right-hand side of equation (3.9A), and by multiplying both sides through by y_t and solving for y_t yields:

$$y_t = B(t)/[1 - (q - r) + (y_{t+\tau} - y_t - s\Delta(y_t))/y_t] \quad (3.10A)$$

Kalecki assumes:

$$g \geq |(y_{t+\tau} - y_t - s(1 - a)(\Delta y_t))/y_t| \quad (3.11A)$$

where g is expected to have a small absolute value. Given this expression, the trend value of investment can be written as:

$$y_t = B(t)/[1 - (q - r) \pm g] \quad (3.12A)$$

By multiplying and dividing equation (3.12A) by $[1 - (q - r)]$, the trend value of investment is rewritten as:

$$y_t = B(t)[d_t]/[1 - (q - r)] \qquad (3.13A)$$

where:

$$1/[1 + g/(1 - (q - r))] = d_t = 1/[1 - g/(1 - (q - r))] \qquad (3.14A)$$

Assuming d_t is fairly stable within the range specified, then the maximum growth rate in y_t will closely follow that of $B(t)$, (Kalecki, 1968/1971, p. 177), and a change in taxation will have a negligible impact on d_r.

By combining equations (3.13A) and (3.12), the investment equation is given as:

$$I_{t+\tau} = B(t + \tau)[d_{t+\tau}]/[1 - (q - r)] + (q - r)(I_t - y_t) + s[\Delta(I_t - y_t) \qquad (3.15A)$$

7   The Impact of Taxation on Investment

The impact of taxation of investment over the business cycle is found by differentiating equation (3.15A) with respect to the wage and profits tax rates as described in equation (3.15) and the partial derivatives of equations (3.16) and (3.17) are given as:

$$\partial(I_{t+\tau})/\partial q = B(t + \alpha)[d_{t+\tau}]/[1 - (q - r)]^2 + (I_t - y_t) \qquad (3.16A)$$

$$\partial(I_{t+\tau})/\partial s = \Delta(I_t - y_t) \qquad (3.17A)$$

$$dq/dt_w = \{[\lambda + (r/P)\delta]s_w(1 - t_p)/[(1 - t_p)(1 - \alpha)(1 - c_c) + s_w(1 - t_w)\alpha]^2\}$$
$$\{\alpha(1 - \alpha) + (1 - t_w)(1 + j)\alpha^2 k_{t_w}\} > = < 0 \qquad (3.18A)$$

$$ds/dt_w = \{(s_w)(r/P)n(1 - t_p)/[(1 - t_p)(1 - \alpha)(1 - c_c) + s_w(1 - t_w)\alpha]^2\}$$
$$\{\alpha(1 - \alpha) + (1 - t_w)(1 + j)\alpha^2 k_{t_w}\} > = < 0 \qquad (3.19A)$$

$$dq/dt_p = \{-[I + (r/P)d]s_w(1 - t_w)/[(1 - t_p)(1 - \alpha)(1 - c_c) + s_w(1 - t_w)\alpha]^2\}$$
$$\{\alpha(1 - \alpha) + (1 - t_p)(1 + j)\alpha^2 k_{t_p}\} > = < 0 \qquad (3.20A)$$

$$ds/dt = \{-(s_w)(r/P)n(1 - t_w)/[(1 - t_p)(1 - \alpha)(1 - c_c) + s_w(1 - t_w)\alpha]^2\}$$
$$\{\alpha(1 - \alpha) + (1 - t_p)(1 + j)\alpha^2 k_{t_p}\} > = < 0 \qquad (3.21A)$$

Equations (3.16A) to (3.21A) can be used to analyse the impact of a change in the wage and profits tax rates on investment during the eight different stages of the business cycle for varying trends, $B(t + \tau) > = < 0$, and for varying shifting assumptions, $k_{t_w} > = < 0$, and $k_{t_p} > = < 0$. As a consequence, for the balanced budget stance, the impact of taxation on investment could be examined for 96 different cases: eight business cycle stages times three trends times two types of tax changes times two shifting assumptions.

REFERENCES

Atkinson, A. and Stiglitz, J.E. (1980), *Lectures on Public Economics*, New York, McGraw-Hill.

Asimakopulos, A. and Burbidge, J.B. (1979), 'Harberger and Kalecki on the incidence of taxation: a critical comparison', *Greek Economic Review*, 70–81.

Courvisanos, J. (1996), *Investment Cycles in Capitalist Economies*, Cheltenham, Edward Elgar.

Coutts, K., Godley, W. and Nordhaus, W. (1978), *Industrial Pricing in the United Kingdom*, Cambridge, Cambridge University Press.

Kalecki, M. (1937), 'A theory of commodity, income and capital taxation, *Economic Journal*, **47**, 444–50.

Kalecki, M. (1968/1971), 'Trend and the business cycles reconsidered', *Economic Journal*, **78**. Reprinted in *Selected Essays on the Dynamics of the Capitalist Economy*, 1933–1970, Cambridge, Cambridge University Press.

Laramie, A.J. (1991) 'Taxation and Kalecki's distribution factors', *Journal of Post Keynesian Economics*, **4**, 583–94.

Laramie, A.J. and Mair, D. (1991) 'Taxation's Impact on the Trade Cycle: A Kaleckian Perspective,' Department of Economics, Heriot-Watt University, Discussion Paper No. 6.

Laramie, A.J. and Mair, D. (1992) 'Taxation and Economic Growth: A Post-Keynesian Perspective,' Department of Economics, Heriot-Watt University, Discussion Paper, No. 7.

Laramie, A.J. and Mair, D. (1996), 'Taxation and Kalecki's theory of the business cycle', *Cambridge Journal of Economics*, **20** (4), 451–64.

Laramie, A.J., Mair, D., Miller, A.G. and Stratopoulos, T. (1996), 'The impact of taxation on gross private nonresidential fixed investment in a Kaleckian model: some empirical evidence', *Journal of Post Keynesian Economics*, **19**, 243–56.

Musgrave, R.A. and Musgrave, P. (1989), *Public Finance in Theory and Practice*, New York, McGraw-Hill.

Paladini, R. (1989), 'Kalecki and fiscal policy', in Sebastiani, M. (ed.), *Kalecki's Relevance Today*, London, Macmillan.

Sylos-Labini, P. (1979/1988), 'Industrial pricing in the United Kingdom, *Cambridge Journal of Economics*, **3**, 153–63. Reprinted in Sawyer, M.C. (ed.), *Post Keynesian Economics*, Aldershot, Edward Elgar.

Weintraub, S. (1979), 'Generalizing Kalecki and simplifying macroeconomics', *Journal of Post Keynesian Economics*, **1** (3), 101–106.

Weintraub, S. (1981), 'An eclectic theory of income shares', *Journal of Post Keynesian Economics*, **4** (1), 10–24.

4. The long-run effects of taxation in a Kaleckian model

1 INTRODUCTION

In this chapter we present a Kaleckian approach to the long-run effects of taxation stability, growth and unemployment. By presenting a model in which the micro and macroeconomic elements are fully integrated and theoretically compatible, we can demonstrate the long-term impact of taxation on economic stability, growth and unemployment. To do so requires us to abandon the standard approach in which pre-Keynesian microeconomics is harnessed to Keynesian macroeconomics (or some variant thereof).

As we have seen in Chapter 1, Kalecki (1937) had demonstrated that the publication of Keynes's *General Theory* required a new approach to the effects of taxation on the level of effective demand. He showed that, under conditions of less than full employment, the legal and economic incidence of taxes on commodities, incomes and capital can vary even in the short period and that the economic incidence of taxation has an impact on the aggregate levels of income and employment. This early profound insight of Kalecki's has been largely ignored in the literature on public finance. Kalecki himself did not pursue the implications of his 1937 paper into his later work on business cycles and growth in which he generally assumed a minimal role for taxation and government spending. We have shown in the previous chapter how taxation can be integrated into Kalecki's business cycle theory. In this chapter we now extend the analysis to consider the effects of taxation on stability, the rate of growth and unemployment.

There are, in our opinion, three principal grounds for preferring Kalecki to Keynes as the starting point from which to study the macroeconomic effects of taxation as they affect the long-term behaviour of the economy. First, although Keynes and Kalecki may be regarded as the co-founders of modern macroeconomics, Kalecki was always concerned to try to understand the dynamics of capitalist economies in a way that Keynes never was. Second, income distribution, and its effects on aggregate economic behaviour, plays a central role in Kalecki, whereas Keynes never appreciated that a consequence of the *General Theory* had to be the abandonment of the marginal productivity theory of income distribution (Rothschild, 1961). But the third, and most important, reason is the one which addresses directly the concern expressed in Chapter 1 regarding the dichotomy between micro and macroeconomics.

In order to address the issue of how taxation may affect the long-term behaviour of the economy, we now integrate taxation into Kalecki's theory of growth. Unfortunately, we are unable to proceed directly to utilize Kalecki's growth theory because of the unsatisfactory state to which he had developed it by the time of his death. This, however, has been rectified by Gomulka, Ostaszewski and Davies (hereafter G.O.D.) (1990) who correct the mistake in Kalecki's (1962) version of his theory and explore the mathematical properties of Kalecki's theory of the business cycle and trend.[1]

In this chapter, we further extend Kalecki's analysis of the dynamic effects of taxation by introducing the effects of wage and profit taxes into his growth theory as amended by G.O.D. In so doing, we consider we have produced a theory which addresses the long-term effects of taxation on stability, growth and unemployment by integrating the micro and macroeconomic elements in a consistent manner, not hitherto achieved.

In simple terms, the micro–macro relationships in Kaleckian tax theory are as follows. At the macroeconomic level, aggregate spending flows determine the level of profits. At the microeconomic level, the degree of monopoly determines the distribution of income. Tax policy can affect the aggregate flow of spending and profits, but pricing decisions, as reflected in firms' price/cost markups, determine the intra/inter-industry and class distributions of income. Ultimately, the confluence of these factors determines the short-period incidence of taxes and this incidence, insofar as it has an impact on firms' investment decisions, generates a long-period effect. These relationships are developed formally in the model below.

The structure of the chapter is as follows. First, we rewrite Kalecki's (1962) growth equation, as corrected by G.O.D., to account for the effects of wage and profit taxes; next, we consider the effects of wage and profit taxes on economic stability, the balanced rate of growth, the nature of capitalism, and the trend rate of unemployment under non-shifting and shifting assumptions of each tax; we conclude the chapter by summarizing our findings.

---

1. Kalecki (1962) examined the determinants of the trend rate of growth by expressing the investment-to-capital ratio as a lagged function of the savings-to-capital ratio, (workers' savings assumed to be zero), the change in the profitability of investment, and innovations-induced investment. In integrating the profit equation into the investment equation, Kalecki failed to account for innovations-induced investment's impact on the trend rate of profits (which impacts on future investment).

2   KALECKI'S CORRECTED GROWTH EQUATION

Kalecki, like Keynes, focused on the private sector, particularly investment as a source of cyclical fluctuations and economic growth. Kalecki believed that changes in the economic environment of the firm guide investment decisions, and that these changes were reflected in firms' savings out of profits and in changes in the level of profitability of firms. Following Kalecki, we ignore the effect of changes in the rate of interest. Thus, investment decisions, in the absence of innovations, can be written as:

$$D_t = aSp_t + b(K_t\Delta\ (P/K))/\Delta\ t \qquad (4.1)$$

where D_t = investment decisions, Sp = savings out of profits, P = profits, K = the capital stock, $K_t[\Delta\ (P/K)]$ = change in the level of profits, Δt = the time period in which changes in profitability are monitored for the purpose of making investment decisions (G.O.D., 1990, p. 528) and where a, $b > 0$. These investment decisions are then translated into actual investment expenditures, I, via a lag; i.e.: $I_{t+1} = D_t$. Thus actual investment expenditures are written as:

$$I_{t+1} = aSp_t + b(K_t\Delta\ (P/K))/\Delta t \qquad (4.1')$$

Net investment is rewritten by approximating the change in profitability as the difference between the change in total profitability, ΔP, and the change in the trend profitability, $(P^*/K^*)\Delta K$; i.e.: $(K_t\Delta\ (P/K) = \Delta P - (P^*/K^*)\Delta K^*$, where '*' denotes a trend value and by adding innovations-induced investment, εK^*, as a determinant (see G.O.D. 1990, p. 528); i.e.:

$$I_{t+1} = aSp_t + b[\Delta P_t - (P^*_t/K^*_t)\Delta K_t]/\Delta\ t + \Delta K^*_{t+1} \qquad (4.2)$$

The net investment equation is transformed into a difference equation by finding expressions for savings, Sp, and the change in the level of profits, ΔP_t. This difference equation is then used to illustrate the impact of taxation on the trend rate of growth, economic stability and unemployment.

To achieve this, we derive expressions for national income, Y, and profits. We define national income so as to include government purchases. We write national income as:

$$Y = I + C_1 + C_2 + G \qquad (4.3)$$

where C_1 = consumption out of profits, C_2 = consumption out of wages and G = government purchases. Following Kalecki (1968), we write profits, ignoring the foreign sector, as:

$$P = I + C_1 + G - T - Vs \qquad (4.4)$$

where T = taxes (and $T = T_p + T_v$; where T_p = profit taxes; and T_v = wage taxes); and Vs = worker savings.

Assuming that:

$$C_1 = c_1(P) + A_1 \qquad (4.5)$$

$$V_g = \alpha(Y) \qquad (4.6)$$

where Vg = pre-tax wage income, and α = the wage share;[2] and where:

$$T_v = t_v(V_g) \qquad (4.7)$$

where Tv = wage tax receipts and t_v = wage tax rate; and where:

$$C_2 = c_2(V_g - T_v) \qquad (4.8)$$

where C_2 = consumption derived from wage income, and c_2 is the marginal propensity to consume out of wage income.

Thus, worker savings can be written as:

$$V_s = (1 - t_v)(1 - c_2)\alpha\,(Y) \qquad (4.9)$$

and profits and national income can be rewritten as:

$$P = [I + A_1 + G - T]m_1 \qquad (4.10)$$

and

$$Y = [I + A_1 + G - T]m_2 \qquad (4.11)$$

where:

$$m_1 = [(1 - \alpha)(1 - t_p)]/[(1 - \alpha)(1 - t_p)(1 - c_1) + \alpha(1 - t_v)(1 - c_2)];$$

and:

$$m_2 = 1/[(1 - \alpha)(1 - t_p)(1 - c_1) + \alpha(1 - t_v)(1 - c_2)];$$

2. Kalecki (1968/1971) originally expressed the wage share as: $V/Y = \beta/y + \alpha$; where β = the fixed portion of the wage bill.

where $m_1 > 1$, $m_2 > 1$, and $m_2 > m_1$, where $m_1/m_2 = (1 - \alpha)(1 - t_p)$.

To simplify, we suppose that $G = T$ and, like Kalecki, assume that the ratio of non-investment determinants of profits to the trend capital stock, K^* is constant. Equations (4.10) and (4.11) are rewritten as:

$$P = m_1(I) + n_1(K^*) \qquad\qquad (4.10')$$

$$Y = m_2(I) + n_2(K^*) \qquad\qquad (4.11')$$

where:

$$n_1(K^*) = [A_1]m_1 \qquad\qquad (4.12)$$

$$n_2(K^*) = [A_1]m_2 \qquad\qquad (4.13)$$

Given equations (4.10') and (4.11') and by noting that savings out of profits is equal to total savings less worker savings, $Sp = S - Vs$, and that total savings equals investment ($S = I$), by incorporating the G.O.D. correction to Kalecki's original equation that $P^*/K^* = m_1(I^*/K^*) + n_1,$[3] and assuming $\Delta t = h$, equation (4.2) can be rewritten as:

$$I_{t+1} = \{a' - b[m_1(I^*_t/K^*_t) + n_1][I_t] + (bm_1/h)[\Delta I_t] + bn_1(I^*_t) + \varepsilon'K^*_{t+1}\} \qquad (4.2')$$

where $a' = a[1 - (1 - t_v)(1 - c_2)\alpha m_2]$; and $\varepsilon' = \varepsilon - a(1 - t_v)(1 - c_2)\alpha n_2$.

Now we can consider briefly the impact of taxation on investment. The wage tax rate and the profits tax rate affect investment through; 1) the level of savings out of profits; and 2) changes in profitability. These effects are reflected in equation (4.2') in the parameters a', m_1 and ε'.

The impact of taxes on profits is reflected in equation (4.10'). Assuming a balanced budget constraint, a constant and positive propensity to save out of wages ($0 < c_2 < 1$), a constant propensity to save of profits ($0 < c_1 < 1$), an increase in the wage tax rate reduces worker savings and increases profits and savings out of profits through a balanced budget multiplier effect and, therefore, increases net investment (if $I_t > 0$ and $\Delta I_t > 0$). The increases in profits, savings out of profits and net investment are dampened, if the wage tax is shifted. The

3. As mentioned in note 1, Kalecki mistakenly ignored the impact of innovations investment on the trend rate of profits, and, therefore, simply treated the trend rate of profits as a parameter in the model.

shifting of the wage tax is reflected in a reduction in the markup over prime costs which increases the wage share, increasing the distribution of income in favour of pre-tax wages. This pushes up worker savings which dampens the effects of the wage tax on profits, savings out of profits, and net investment.

An increase in the profit tax rate, assuming a balanced budget constraint, reduces the level of profits. An increase in the profit tax causes national income to increase, given the wage share. The increase in national income pushes up the wage bill and worker savings. The rise in worker savings reduces the level of profits and savings out of profits. However, the shifting of the profits tax, as reflected in an increase in the markup of price over prime costs, reduces the wage share and worker savings and heightens the effects of the profits tax on profits, savings out of profits and net investment.[4]

As G.O.D. (1990, p. 529) note, Kalecki developed a third version of the investment equation to comply with the Harrod requirement that investment which justifies itself results in a constant investment to trend capital stock ratio. The investment equation is adjusted accordingly and is written as:

$$I_{t+1}/K^*_{t+1} = \{a' - b[m_1(I^*_t/K^*_t) + n_1][I_t/K^*_t]\}$$
$$+ (bm_1/h)[\Delta I_t/K^*_t] + bn_1(I^*_t/K^*) + \varepsilon' \qquad (4.14)$$

By defining $I_t/K^*_t = g_t$ and $\Delta I_t = \Delta(g_t K^*_t) = \Delta g_t K^*_t + g_{t-h}\Delta K^*_t = \Delta g_t K^*_t + g_{t-h}hI^*_t$, we derive the G.O.D. corrected version of Kalecki's growth equation:

$$g_{t+1} = a'g_t + [bm_1/h](g_t - g_{t-h}) + bm_1 g_t(g_{t-h} - g_t) + \varepsilon' \qquad (4.15)$$

This expression is used to consider the impact of taxation on stability, economic growth, the nature of capitalism and unemployment.

3 TAXATION AND ECONOMIC STABILITY

Following G.O.D. (1990, pp. 531–2), a sufficient condition for an asymptotically stable growth rate can be found. In terms of equation (4.15), a sufficient

---

4. We ignore the impact of taxation on the marginal propensities to save out of profits and wages, but such effects are easy to consider. If, for example, the marginal propensities to consume vary positively with the profits and wage tax rates, then the effects of taxation as described above are to some degree modified. An increase in the marginal propensity to consume out of wages, reduces workers' savings and increases profits, savings out of profits and investment, and, therefore heightens the effect of a wage tax increase. Likewise, an increase in the marginal propensity to consume out of profits, increases capitalists' consumption, profits, savings out of profits and investment.

condition for stability, using the corrected version of Kalecki's growth equation, can be written as:

$$h > h^* = 2bm_1/(1-a')^5 \qquad (4.16)$$

The wage and profits tax rates affect the conditions for stability through the terms m_1 and a'. Recall that m_1 is the investment coefficient in the profit equation and that a' is the savings coefficient in the investment equation. By differentiating h^* with respect to the wage and profits tax rates, we consider the impact of changes in the tax rates on economic stability. A change in any parameter that increases h^* relative to h and makes h^* greater than h causes the growth rate to be unstable. In addition, if h^* initially is greater than h, a change in any parameter that increases h^* increases the instability of the growth rate; and if h^* is initially less than h, a change in any parameter that reduces h^* increases the stability of the growth rate. For example, as mentioned above, with a balanced budget constraint an increase in the wage tax rate, t_v, increases profits and savings out of profits and net investment. Therefore, an increase in the wage tax rate would tend to increase the likelihood that the growth rate is unstable, and this effect would be dampened if the wage tax rate is shifted. If the profits tax rate, t_p increases, profits and savings out of profits decline assuming the tax change is unshifted; and, the increase in the profits tax rate would reduce h^* relative to h, and increase the likelihood that the growth rate is stable. If the profits tax is shifted, profits and savings out of profits both increase and, thus, increase the likelihood that the growth rate is unstable. These results are formally presented in the Appendix.

4   THE IMPACT OF TAXATION ON THE BALANCED RATE OF GROWTH

For balanced growth to occur: $g_t = g_{t-h} = g_{t+1}$. Thus, from equation (4.15), the balanced growth rate, g^*, can be written as:

$$g^* = \varepsilon'/(1-a') \qquad (4.17)$$

As implied, the balanced growth rate is positive when both ε' and $(1-a')$ are positive or both are negative. If we suppose that ε' is positive, then for the

---

5. G.O.D (1990, p. 532) state that the zero solution is unstable when $h^* > h$ and 'either h is irrational, or h is rational and is of the form p/q, with p odd and q even'. These conditions suggest that growth rate is 'virtually only stable,' if equation (4.16) is satisfied, since most numbers are irrational.

balanced growth rate to be positive, $(1 - a')$ must also be positive. For $(1 - a')$ to be positive, a' must be between zero and one $(1 > a' > 0)$.[6]

We now consider the impact of taxation on the balanced growth rate. These results are formally presented in the appendix. Taxation affects the balanced rate of growth through changes in ε', the constant in the investment function, and a', the savings coefficient in the investment function. An increase in the wage tax rate that is not shifted reduces workers' savings, which increases profits and savings out of profits. The increase in the wage tax rate simultaneously causes both ε' and a' to increase $((1 - a')$ to decrease), which increases the balanced rate of growth. If the wage tax is shifted, $k_{tv} < 0$, then these effects are diminished, because the shifting of the wage tax results in an increase in worker savings, a reduction in savings out of profits.

The change in the balanced growth rate with respect to a change in the profits tax rate is negative, if the markup is constant with respect to a change in the profits tax. An increase in the profits tax reduces the level of profits and savings out of profits. If the markup is positively related to the profits tax, then the shifting of the profits tax dampens the negative effect that the profits tax has on the balanced rate of growth.

From the discussion above, two implications arise. First, taxation and fiscal policy modify the 'nature' of capitalism. Second, the incidence and effects of taxation have an impact on the long-run unemployment rate when 1) the growth rate is stable; and 2) when the growth rate is unstable. We consider each briefly.

5   TAXATION AND THE NATURE OF CAPITALISM

In describing the stability characteristics of Kalecki's growth theory, G.O.D. distinguish two types of capitalism – 'rash' and 'cautious' – and show that 'cautious' capitalism arises when 1) investors react slowly to changes in profitability (b is relatively small or h is relatively large in equation (4.16)); and 2) either the rate of innovation is low or the response of innovators to innovations is weak. The results presented above imply that fiscal policy can counter or reinforce the nature of capitalism. For example, an increase in the wage tax that is not shifted, coupled with a balanced budget constraint, heightens instability (or reduces the degree of stability). In other words, 'rash' capitalism is being accommodated. The opposite is true with respect to increases in the profits tax, if the profits tax is unshifted and a balanced budget constraint is maintained. Furthermore, these results suggest that budget deficits (surpluses)

6. Generally, since $a > 0$, $1 > a'$, if $1/a' > [(1 - \alpha)(1 - c_1)(1 - t_p)]/[(1 - \alpha)(1 - c_1)(1 - t_p) + \alpha(1 - c_2)(1 - t_v)]$.

heighten (dampen) economic stability, but that the ultimate effect of fiscal policy, in particular tax changes, on stability depends upon the reaction of the markup and the marginal propensity to save out of wage income.

6   TAXATION AND TREND UNEMPLOYMENT

We can now consider the implications for unemployment when the growth rate is stable and unstable. We begin by examining the impact of taxation on the trend growth rate in employment when the growth rate is stable.

As implied above, assuming no government sector, the growth rate of output, g^*, is positively related to the rate of innovation-induced investment, ε. Kalecki (1962) assumed that innovations-induced investment is positively related to the rate of innovation, λ. Thus, growth in employment can be written as:

$$g_L = g^*(\varepsilon(\lambda)) - \lambda \qquad (4.18)$$

where g_L = the trend employment growth rate.

Assuming that g^* is less than the 'natural' growth rate (the growth rate in the labour force plus the rate of innovations), the employment growth rate is demand-determined, determined by ε, and is less than the 'natural' employment growth rate. When the government sector is absent and when $\lambda = 0$, then ε and g are zero, and $g_L = 0$. Under this condition, assuming the labour force is growing, the trend level of unemployment is increasing and the trend level of employment is constant. For the trend unemployment rate to remain constant, the rate of innovation-induced investment, ε would have to be of a magnitude ε^* such that $g(\varepsilon^*) - \lambda = g_L$. Kalecki did not develop his theory sufficiently to say anything specific about the properties of ε. But his theory implies that if $g_L > 0$, then either the rate of innovation or the investment-inducing power of innovations would have to be sufficiently high to prevent the unemployment rate from increasing. G.O.D. (p. 526) call this proposition that technological innovation is good for employment 'Kalecki's Growth Proposition' and it is this they argue that brings Kalecki close to Schumpeter and away from Marx.

With our modifications, we now rewrite the trend employment growth rate. In the discussion above, the national income multiplier, m_2, was implicitly held constant. Thus, the trend rate of growth in output was identical to the trend rate of growth in investment, g^*. Since we are allowing for changes in tax rates, and, therefore, changes in the income multiplier, the rate of growth in output can be approximated as the sum of the rate of growth in investment and the rate of growth in the income multiplier. The rate of growth in investment, g^*, depends on the tax rates, t_v and t_p, the wage share, α, and the rate of innovations induced investment $\varepsilon(\lambda)$. The growth rate in the income multiplier, g_{m2}, depends upon the tax rates, t_v and t_p, the wage share, α. Thus the trend growth rate in output is given as:

$$g^*_y = g^*(t_v, \alpha, t_p, \varepsilon(\lambda)) + g_{m_2}(t_v, t_p, \alpha) \qquad (4.19)$$

Since $g^*_Y = g_L + \lambda$, the growth rate of employment is now written as:

$$g_L = g^*(t_v, \alpha\ t_p, \varepsilon(\lambda)) - \lambda + g_{m_2}(t_v, t_p, \alpha) \qquad (4.19')$$

As suggested by equation (4.19'), tax policy impacts on the trend employment rate through two channels: 1) g^*, the trend rate of capital accumulation; and 2) g_{m_2}, the rate of growth in the multiplier effect. We now consider both of these channels.

The impact of taxation on g^* is described above. Given the rate of innovations and the rate at which these innovations are absorbed into new investment, increases in the wage tax rate increase the trend rate of employment when a balanced budget constraint is imposed and when the tax is not shifted. Likewise, an increase in the profits tax rate decreases the trend rate of employment only when the tax is unshifted (again, assuming a balanced budget constraint).

Assuming the tax rates, the marginal propensities to consume and the wage share have no trends, the trend rate of growth in the income multiplier is zero. Thus, the introduction of a tax change temporarily shocks the multiplier and alters the rate of growth in output. For example, the income multiplier is positively related to changes in the wage tax rate and the profits tax rate (where the taxes are not shifted). Thus, following an increase in either tax, the trend rate of growth in employment may increase, via the shock to the multiplier, but then be restored to the rate of growth that is determined by the trend rate of capital accumulation.

When the rate of growth is unstable, we are able to obtain some quite different results. Following G.O.D. (p. 534), the average of the floor and ceiling levels of investment is used to approximate the trend growth rate. Whenever investment is below the ceiling, unemployment arises. Thus, the greater the gap between the ceiling and the floor levels of investment, the greater will be the average (trend) unemployment rate (relative to any measure of full employment unemployment). To consider how taxation impacts on the trend unemployment rate, we therefore determine how taxation impacts on the ceiling and floor levels of investment. Any change in taxation that widens the gap between the floor and the ceiling increases the trend rate of unemployment.

The floor level of net investment is defined as the difference between the innovations-induced gross investment, εK^*_t, and the depreciated capital stock, δK^*_t; i. e.:

$$I_t > = \varepsilon K^*_t - \delta K^*_t = I^f_t \qquad (4.20)$$

where I^f_t = the floor level of net investment.

The ceiling level of net investment, as determined by available resources, is derived from equation (4.11') where 'labour is the only binding input' (G.O.D., p. 535), and is given as:

$$I_t < = [1/m_2](y_t(L_t) - n_2 K^*_t) = I^c_t \qquad (4.21)$$

where y = labour productivity; L = the supply of labour; I^c_t = the labour-constrained ceiling level of investment. By defining the gap as the difference between the ceiling and the floor, we have:

$$GAP = I^c_t - I^f_t \qquad (4.22)$$

Now we consider the impact of changes in the wage and profits tax rates on the *GAP*. (The mathematical results are presented in the Appendix.) Again, the results depend on whether or not the taxes are shifted. Assuming no tax shifting, an increase in the wage tax rate reduces the ceiling level of investment and raises the floor level of investment, and, therefore reduces the trend unemployment rate. If the wage tax is shifted, the shifting increases the negative effect of the tax on the ceiling and heightens the positive effect of the tax on the floor causing a further decline in the gap between the ceiling and floor levels of investment, further reducing trend unemployment.

With no tax shifting, an increase in the profits tax reduces the ceiling level of investment and increases the floor level of investment, and, therefore, reduces trend unemployment. However, if the profits tax is shifted, the shifting of the tax heightens the negative effect of the tax on the ceiling (makes the effect more negative) and dampens the positive effect of the tax on the floor. Thus under a tax shifting scenario, the impact of the profits tax on the gap between the ceiling and floor levels of investment is indeterminate.

7   CONCLUSION

The Kaleckian approach set out in this paper avoids the micro–macro tensions that bedevil the orthodox approach. The microeconomic elements are captured in the pricing decisions of firms in response to changes in wage or profits taxation. The ability of firms or workers to shift increased tax burdens depends on the 'degree of monopoly' which is reflected in the markup of price over prime cost (Reynolds, 1996). Increases in markups have an inverse effect both on real wages and on the income share of wages, thereby affecting the level of aggregate consumption. Thus, tax-induced changes in income distribution have an important role to play in a Kaleckian model. The level of consumption and the distribution of income as between wages and profits have a critical role in the determination of profits and investment. And what happens to investment critically affects the long-run performance of the economy.

We have used the corrected version of Kalecki's theory of the business cycle to assess the effects of tax policy on stability, the balanced rate of growth, the nature of capitalism, and unemployment. With a balanced government budget constraint, increases in the wage tax rate, when the wage tax is unshifted, increase the degree of instability, and, therefore, accommodate rash capitalism. The shifting of the wage tax diminishes this effect. An increase in the profits tax rate, when the profits tax is unshifted, promotes stability. However, an increase in the profits tax, when unshifted, increases the degree of instability. The shifting of increases in profits taxes dampens the negative effect that the tax has on instability.

Unshifted increases in the wage tax increase the balanced rate of growth, while unshifted increases in the profits tax reduce the balanced rate of growth. The shifting of taxes dampens their respective effects.

These results have implications for the trend unemployment rate. If the growth rate is stable, the trend (un)employment rate is tied to the rate of capital accumulation (the balanced rate of growth). If the growth rate is unstable, the average of the ceiling and the floor is positively related to the trend (long-period) unemployment rate. With a balanced budget constraint, an increase in the wage tax or profit tax rates results in lower long-period unemployment. The shifting of the wage tax further reduces long-period unemployment, but the shifting of the profit tax has an indeterminate effect.

APPENDIX

1   The Impact of Taxation on Stability

To consider formally the impact of changes in the wage and profits tax rates on economic stability, we allow for tax shifting through the change in the impact of the markup on the wage share, α, as in Chapter 3. The wage share is simply written as:

$$\alpha = (1/k) \qquad (4.1A)$$

where k is the markup of price over prime costs.

From equation (4.16) the change in h^* with respect to the tax rate i, where $i = v, p$, is found by substituting the expressions for m_1 and a' into equation (4.16) and is written as:

$$dh^*/dt_i = (\partial h^*/\partial m_1)(\partial m_1/\partial t_i) + (\partial h^*/\partial a')[\partial a'/\partial t_i$$
$$+ (\partial a'/\partial m_2)(\partial m_2/\partial t_i) + (\partial a'/\partial \alpha)(\partial \alpha/\partial t_i)] \qquad (4.2A)$$

where:

$$(\partial h^*/\partial m_1) = 2b/(1 - a') > 0, \text{ if } 0 < a' < 1 \qquad (4.3A)$$

$$(\partial m_1/\partial t_v) = \{\alpha(1 - c_2)(1 - \alpha)(1 - t_p) + (1 - t_p)(1 - c_2)(1 - t_p)\alpha^2 k_{tv}\}/$$
$$[(1 - \alpha)(1 - t_p)(1 - c_1) + \alpha(1 - t_v)(1 - c_2)]^2 > = < 0, \text{ but}$$
$$> 0, \text{ if } k_{tv} = 0 \qquad (4.4A)$$

$$(\partial m_1/\partial t_p) = \{-\alpha(1 - c_2)(1 - a)(1 - t_v) + (1 - t_p)(1 - c_2)(1 - t_p)\alpha^2 k_{tp}\}/$$
$$[(1 - \alpha)(1 - t_p)(1 - c_1) + \alpha(1 - t_v)(1 - c_2)]^2 > = < 0, \text{ but } < 0, \text{ if } k_{tp} = 0 \quad (4.5A)$$

$$\partial h^*/\partial a' = 2bm_1/(1 - a')^2 > 0 \qquad (4.6A)$$

$$\partial a'/\partial t_v = a\alpha m_2(1 - c_2) > 0 \qquad (4.7A)$$

$$(\partial a'/\partial m_2) = -a\alpha (1 - t_v)(1 - c_2) < 0 \qquad (4.8A)$$

$$(\partial m_2/\partial t_v) = [\alpha(1 - c_2) - [(1 - t_p)(1 - c_1) - (1 - t_v)(1 - c_2)]\alpha^2 k_{tv}]$$
$$/[(1 - \alpha)(1 - t_p)(1 - c_1) + \alpha(1 - t_v)(1 - c_2)]^2 > 0 \qquad (4.9A)$$

$$(\partial m_2/\partial t_p) = [(1 - \alpha)(1 - c_1) - [(1 - t_p)(1 - c_1) - (1 - t_v)(1 - c_2)]\alpha^2 k_{tp}]$$
$$/[(1 - \alpha)(1 - t_p)(1 - c_1) + \alpha(1 - t_v)(1 - c_2)]^2 > = < 0, \text{ but } > 0, \text{ if } k_{tv} = 0$$
$$(4.10A)$$

$$(\partial a'/\partial \alpha)(\partial \alpha/\partial t_v) = am_2(1 - t_v)(1 - c_2)\alpha^2 k_{tv} < 0, \text{but} = 0, \text{ if } k_{tv} = 0 \qquad (4.11A)$$

$$(\partial a'/\partial \alpha)(\partial \alpha/\partial t_p) = am_2(1 - t_v)(1 - c_2)\alpha^2 k_{tv} > 0, \text{ but} = 0, \text{ if } k_{tp} = 0 \qquad (4.12A)$$

where:

$$\partial \alpha/\partial t_v = k_{tv} < 0.$$

To consider the effect of the wage tax on h^*, we first assume that the wage tax is not shifted. Under this assumption, we can show that h^* is positively related to the wage tax. First assume that $(\partial h^*/\partial m_1) > 0$, thus $(\partial h^*/\partial m_1)(\partial m_1/\partial t_v) > 0$. Since $\partial h^*/\partial a' > 0$, $\partial a'/\partial t_v > 0$, and $(\partial a'/\partial m_2) < 0$, and since $(\partial m_2/\partial t_v) > 0$ and $(\partial a'/\partial \alpha)(\partial \alpha / \partial t_v) = 0$ (when no shifting is present), then the sign of the derivative of h^* with respect to t_v can be written as:

$$
\begin{array}{cccccc}
(+) & (+) & (+) & (+) & (-) & (+) \\
\end{array}
$$
$$
dh^*/dt_v = (\partial h^*/\partial m_1)(\partial m_1/\partial t_v) + \partial h^*/\partial a'[\partial a'/\partial t_v + (\partial a'/\partial m_2)(\partial m_2/\partial t_v) +
$$

$$
(0)
$$
$$
(\partial a'/\partial \alpha)(\partial \alpha - \partial t_v)] > 0, \text{ if } k_{tv} = 0 \qquad (4.13A)
$$

The term in brackets is strictly positive. To prove this, assuming no shifting, the term in brackets is given as: $a\alpha m_2(1 - c_2) - a\alpha(1 - t_v)(1 - c_2) [\alpha (1 - c_2)]/ [(1 - \alpha)(1 - t_p)(1 - c_1) + \alpha(1 - t_v)(1 - c_2)]^2$. This term is greater than zero, since $(1 - \alpha)(1 - t_p)(1 - c_1) > 0$.

If the wage tax is shifted, the shifting reduces the positive effect of a change in the wage tax on h^*. As reflected above, the shifting of the wage tax increases the wage share, α. The increase in the wage share directly reduces a', and indirectly reduces a' through an increase in m_2 while the decline in a' reduces h^*. In addition, the shifting of the wage tax reduces m_1, which reduces h^*. One further note, if the marginal propensity to consume out of disposable wage income is assumed to equal one (worker savings is equal to zero), then the wage tax, whether shifted or not, has no impact on h^* or economic stability.

To consider the effect of the profits tax on h^*, we first assume that the profits tax is not shifted. Under this assumption, we can show that h^* is negatively related to the profits tax. This conclusion holds under the following conditions: $(\partial h^*/\partial m_1) > 0$, thus $(\partial h^*/\partial m_1)(\partial m_1/\partial t_p) < 0$. Since $\partial h^*/\partial a' > 0$, $\partial a'/\partial t_p = 0$, and $(\partial a'/\partial m_2) < 0$, and since $(\partial m_2/\partial t_p) > 0$ and $(\partial a'/\partial \alpha)(\partial \alpha/\partial t_v) = 0$

$$
\begin{array}{cccccc}
(+) & (-) & (+) & (0) & (-) & (+) \\
\end{array}
$$
$$
dh^*/dt_p = (\partial h^*/\partial m_1)(\partial m_1/\partial t_p) + \partial h^*/\partial a'[\partial a'/\partial t_p + (\partial a'/\partial m_2)(\partial m_2/\partial t_p) +
$$

$$
(0)
$$
$$
(\partial a'/\partial \alpha)(\partial \alpha/\partial t_p)] < 0, \text{ if } k_{tv} = 0 \qquad (4.14A)
$$

If the profits tax is shifted, the shifting reduces the negative effect of a change in the profits tax on h^*. The shifting of the profits tax reduces the wage share, α. The reduction in the wage share directly increases a', and indirectly increases a' through a decrease in m_2 while the increase in a' increases h^*. In addition, the shifting of the profit tax increases m_1, which increases h^*. Again, if the marginal propensity to consume out of disposable wage income is assumed to equal one (worker savings is equal to zero), then the profits tax, whether shifted or not, has no impact on $h*$ or economic stability.

2   The Impact of Taxation on the Balanced Rate of Growth

By differentiating equation (4.17) with respect to the wage and profits tax rates; i.e.:

$$dg*/dt_i=(\partial g*/\partial \varepsilon')[(\partial \varepsilon'/\partial t_i) + (\partial \varepsilon'/\partial \alpha)(\partial \alpha/\partial t_i)] + (\partial g*/\partial a')[(\partial a'/\partial t_i)$$
$$+ (\partial a\alpha/\partial \alpha)(\partial \alpha/\partial t_i) + (\partial a'/\partial m_2)(\partial m_2/\partial t_i)] \qquad (4.15A)$$

where $i = v$ and p, and where:

$$\partial g*/\partial \varepsilon' = 1/(1 - a') > 0; \text{ if } 0 < a' < 1 \qquad (4.16A)$$

$$(\partial \varepsilon/\partial t_v) + (\partial \varepsilon'/\partial \alpha)(\partial \alpha/\partial t_v) = an_2(1 - c_2)(\alpha + (1 - t_v)\alpha^2 k_{tv}) >= < 0,$$
$$\text{but} > 0 \text{ if } k_{tv} = 0 \qquad (4.17A)$$

$$(\partial \varepsilon'/\partial t_p) + (\partial \varepsilon'/\partial \alpha)(\partial \alpha/\partial t_p) = an_2(1 - c_2)(1 - t_v)\alpha^2 k_{tp} > 0,$$
$$\text{but} = 0 \text{ if } = k_{tp} = 0 \qquad (4.18A)$$

$$\partial g*/\partial a' = \varepsilon/(1 - a')^2 > 0 \qquad (4.19A)$$

$$(\partial a'/\partial t_v) + (\partial a'/\partial \alpha)(\partial \alpha/\partial t_v) = a\alpha m_2(1 - c_2)[1 + (1 - tv)\alpha k_{tv}] > = < 0,$$
$$\text{but} > 0, \text{ if } k_{tv} = 0 \qquad (4.20A)$$

$$(\partial a'/\partial t_p) + (\partial a'/\partial \alpha)(\partial \alpha/\partial tp) = am_2(1 - t_v)(1 - c_2)\alpha^2 k_{tp} > 0, \text{ if } k_{tp} > 0; \qquad (4.21A)$$

$$(\partial a'/\partial m_2) = -a\alpha(1 - c_2)(1 - t_v) < 0 \qquad (4.22A)$$

$$(\partial m_2/\partial t_v) = [\alpha (1 - c_2) - [(1 - t_p)(1 - c_1) - (1 - t_v)(1 - c_2)]\alpha^2 k_{tv}]/$$
$$[(1 - \alpha)(1 - t_p)(1 - c_1) + \alpha(1 - t_v)(1 - c_2)]^2 > 0 \qquad (4.23A)$$

$$(\partial m_2/t_p) = [(1 - \alpha)(1 - c_1) - [(1 - t_p)(1 - c_1) - (1 - t_v)(1 - c_2)]\alpha^2 k_{tp}]/$$
$$[(1 - \alpha)(1 - t_p)(1 - c_1) + \alpha(1 - t_v)(1 - c_2)]^2 >= < 0, \text{ but} > 0, \text{ if } k_{tv} = 0 \qquad (4.24A)$$

To consider the effects of taxation on the balanced rate of growth, first assume the shifting effect is zero. Thus the derivatives of the balanced rate of growth with respect to a change in the wage and profit tax rates are given as:

$$\overset{(+)}{dg^*/dt_v} = (\partial g^*/\partial \varepsilon')[\overset{(+)}{(\partial \varepsilon'/\partial t_v)} + (\partial \varepsilon'/\partial \alpha)(\partial \alpha/\partial t_v)]$$

$$\overset{(+)}{+ (\partial g^*/\partial a')}\{[\overset{(+)}{(\partial a'/\partial t_v)} + \overset{(-)}{(\partial a'/\partial \alpha)(\partial \alpha/\partial t_v)}] + \overset{(+)}{(\partial a'/\partial m_2)(\partial m_2/\partial t_v)}\} > 0, \text{ if } k_{tv} = 0$$
$$\text{(4.25A)}$$

and:

$$\overset{(+)}{dg^*/dt_p} = (\partial g^*/\partial \varepsilon')[\overset{(+)}{(\partial \varepsilon'/\partial t_p)} + \overset{(0)}{(\partial \varepsilon'/\partial \alpha)(\partial \alpha/\partial t_p)}]$$

$$\overset{(+)}{+ (\partial g^*/\partial a')}\{[\overset{(+)}{(\partial a'/\partial t_p)} + \overset{(0)}{(\partial a'/\partial \alpha)(\partial \alpha/\partial t_p)}] + \overset{(-)}{(\partial a'/\partial m_2)(\partial m_2/\partial t_p)}\} < 0, \text{ if } k_{tp} = 0$$
$$\text{(4.26A)}$$

The derivative of the balanced rate of growth with respect to wage tax rate is strictly positive, assuming no tax shifting, because the term in brackets, {.}, is strictly positive as shown for equation (4.14A). The shifting of the wage tax dampens this positive effect. The shifting of the wage tax increases the wage share and directly reduces a' and indirectly reduces a' through an increase in m_2 (assuming $c2 > c1$). The reduction in a' reduces the balanced rate of growth.

The derivative of the balanced rate of growth with respect to the profit tax rate is strictly negative, assuming no tax shifting. The shifting of the profits tax dampens this negative effect. The shifting of the tax reduces the wage share. The reduction in the wage share directly increases a', and indirectly increases a' through a reduction in m_2. The increase in a' increases the balanced rate of growth.

3 The Impact of Taxation on Trend Unemployment when the Growth Rate is Unstable

To illustrate the impact of a change in the wage or profit tax rates on the gap between the ceiling and floor levels of investment consider the following:

$$dGap/dt_i = dI^C_t/dt_i - dI^f_t/dt_i \tag{4.27A}$$

where $i = v, p$ and where:

$$dI^C_t/dt_i = [(\partial I^C_t/\partial m_2) + (\partial I^C_t/\partial K^*)(\partial K^*/\partial m_2)](\partial m_2/\partial t_i) \tag{4.28A}$$

and

$$dI^f/dt_i = (\partial I^f/\partial K^*)(\partial K^*/\partial m_2)(\partial m_2/\partial t_i) \qquad (4.29A)$$

By finding expressions for equations (4.15A) and (4.16A), we can consider the effects of a change in the wage and profits tax rates on gap and the trend unemployment rate. The derivatives of equation (4.29A) are given as:

$$(\partial I^c_t/\partial m_2) = [-1/m_2^2](y_t(L_t) - n_2K^*_t) > 0 \qquad (4.30A)$$

$$(\partial I^c_t/\partial K^*) = -n_2/m_2 < 0 \qquad (4.31A)[7]$$

$$(\partial K^*/\partial m_2) = [1/n_2] > 0 \qquad (4.32A)$$

$$(\partial m_2/\partial t_v) = [\alpha(1 - c_2) - [(1 - t_p)(1 - c_1) - (1 - t_v)(1 - c_2)]\alpha^2 k_{tv}]$$
$$/[(1 - \alpha)(1 - t_p)(1 - c_1) + \alpha(1 - t_v)(1 - c_2)]^2 > 0 \qquad (4.33A)$$

$$(\partial m_2/\partial t_p) = [(1 - \alpha)(1 - c_1) - [(1 - t_p)(1 - c_1) - (1 - t_v)(1 - c_2)]\alpha^2 k_{tp}]$$
$$/[(1 - \alpha)(1 - t_p)(1 - c_1) + \alpha(1 - t_v)(1 - c_2)]^2 >=< 0, \text{ but}$$
$$> 0, \text{ if } k_{tv} = 0 \qquad (4.34A)$$

Thus:

$$\overset{(-)}{} \qquad \overset{(-)}{} \qquad \overset{(+)}{} \qquad \overset{(+)}{}$$
$$dI^c_t/dt_v = [(\partial I^c_t/\partial m_2) + (\partial I^c_t/\partial K^*)(\partial K^*/\partial m_2)](\partial m_2/\partial t_v) < 0 \qquad (4.35A)$$

and assuming the profits tax is not shifted:

$$\overset{(-)}{} \qquad \overset{(-)}{} \qquad \overset{(+)}{} \qquad \overset{(+)}{}$$
$$dI^c_t/dt_p = [(\partial I^c_t/\partial m_2) + (\partial I^c_t/\partial K^*)(\partial K^*/\partial m_2)](\partial m_2/\partial t_p) < 0 \qquad (4.36A)$$

Since $(\partial I^f_t/\partial K^*) = \varepsilon - \delta$, and assuming that this term is greater than zero, the change in the floor level of investment with respect to a change in the tax rates can be written as:

$$\overset{(+)}{} \qquad \overset{(+)}{} \qquad \overset{(+)}{}$$
$$dI^f_t/dt_v = (\partial I^f_t/\partial K^*)(\partial K^*/\partial m_2)(\partial m_2/\partial t_v) > 0 \qquad (4.37A)$$

and, assuming the profits tax is not shifted:

7. Recall $n_2(K^*_t) = m_2(A_1)$, thus, $(K^*_t) = [m_2/n_2](A_1)$.

$$dI^f_t/dt_i = \overset{(+)}{(\partial I^f_t/\partial K^*)}\overset{(+)}{(\partial K^*/\partial m_2)}\overset{(+)}{(\partial m_2/\partial t_p)} > 0 \qquad (4.38A)$$

The shifting of the profits tax reduces the positive effect that an increase in the profits tax has on the income multiplier, m_2.

REFERENCES

Gomulka, S., Ostaszewski, A. and Davies, R.O. (1990), 'The innovation rate and Kalecki's theory of the trend, unemployment and the business cycle', *Economica*, **57**, 525–40.

Kalecki, M. (1937), 'A theory of commodity, income and capital taxation', *Economic Journal*. **47**, 444–50.

Kalecki, M. (1962), 'Observations on the theory of growth', *Economic Journal*, **72**, 134–53.

Kalecki, M. (1968/1971), *Selected Essays on the Dynamics of the Capitalist Economy*, Cambridge University Press, Cambridge.

Kriesler, P. (1996), 'Microfoundations: a Kaleckian perspective' in *An Alternative Macroeconomic Theory: The Kaleckian Model and Post-Keynesian Economics*, King, J.E. (ed.), Boston, Kluwer.

Rothschild, K.W. (1961), 'Some recent contributions to a macroeconomic theory of income distribution', *Scottish Journal of Political Economy*, 173–99.

5. The incidence of the corporate profits tax[1]

1 INTRODUCTION

In this chapter we extend our analysis of the incidence and effects of taxation into an area that has been and continues to be dominated by the mainstream neo-classical literature, the incidence and effects of the corporate profits tax. As we show below, if aggregate demand matters in affecting income, production and employment, the incidence of the corporation income tax must be understood in the context of a macroeconomic model. We outline such a model below.

There are a great variety of views regarding the incidence of the corporate profits tax, and the economics profession has not yet reached a definite conclusion as to who bears the burden of the tax. Pechman (1980) cites a number of studies and describes the various short- and long-run shifting mechanisms that have been adopted in assessing the incidence of the corporate profits tax. However, Pechman does not consider the post Keynesian or Kaleckian contributions. In this chapter, we consider the incidence of the corporate profits tax explicitly within the Kaleckian tradition.[2] In this tradition, the economy is assumed to operate with excess supplies of labour and capacity. As a consequence, changes in broad-based taxes, such as the corporate profits tax, have an impact on aggregate demand, employment and real output, and these macroeconomic effects come to bear on the incidence of corporate profits tax.

The standard mainstream approaches derive from Harberger (1962). In this chapter, we consider the Harberger-type approach in light of the potential of our Kaleckian model. We discuss the short- and long-period incidence of the corporate profits tax and set up an analytical framework for analysing its incidence. We conclude by presenting some empirical results for the US. We

---

1. This chapter is revised from Laramie (1994).
2. Taxes derived from other sources of capital income will be ignored as the incidence of these taxes, as shown by Asimakopulos and Burbidge (1974), is determined by the operation of different influences in the economy. In the neoclassical approach, taxes on income from capital (taxes on profits, dividends and interest) affect the user costs of capital and, therefore, the demand for capital. It is this theory that allows for the lumping of taxes on income from capital into the analysis of corporate tax incidence.

show that the incidence of the corporate profits tax is largely dependent on: 1) the government's budget stance; 2) corporate pricing decisions; 3) corporate investment decisions; and 4) household savings decisions. We consider these latter private-sector effects, insofar as they mitigate the impact of the government's budget stance on the incidence of the tax, to be indirect and relatively weak. As a consequence, we conclude that the government's budget stance is the primary factor determining the incidence of the corporate profits tax. In light of these findings, we reconsider the arguments concerning the desirability of the corporate profits tax and we explore some policy implications.

2   HARBERGER-TYPE MODELS

According to Gravelle and Kotlikoff (1989, p. 750), the corporate profits tax model as developed by Harberger (1962) has become 'remarkably influential, [has] vanquished earlier analyses, and has shifted the debate from one of theory to [one of] proper measurement of the model's parameters'. The Harberger model assesses the incidence of the corporate profits tax using a two-sector (corporate and non-corporate) pre-Keynesian model. The basic assumptions of the Harberger model are perfect competition and profit maximization, with full utilization of capital and labour. In the model, the impact of saving, if it takes place at all, is on the level of investment. In the short run, the imposition of the corporate profits tax reduces the after-tax rate of profits causing corporate capital to bear the full incidence of the tax. In the long run, the extent to which the corporate profits tax is shifted depends on the relative shifts in the demand for and supply of corporate capital. The corporate profits tax reduces the demand for capital through two channels: 1) a reduction in the after-tax rate of return; and 2) an increase in the relative price of goods produced in the corporate sector.[3] The decline in the supply of corporate capital is caused by a capital flight into the non-corporate sector. If the decline in the demand for capital is greater than the reduction in the supply of corporate capital, then corporations, in the long run, bear some, all, or more than all of the increase in the corporate profits tax.

Gravelle and Kotlikoff (1989) modify the standard Harberger model by allowing for corporate and non-corporate production in the same sector,[4] and

3. The corporation income tax increases the price of capital relative to labour. The increase in the relative price of capital induces a greater use of labour. The increased use of labour results in an increase in marginal cost and in the corporate price level (see Stiglitz (1988) pp. 567–71).
4. According to Gravelle and Kotlikoff (1989, p. 750), the standard Harberger model allows for differential tax analysis of capital producing different products but not for the analysis of corporate taxation *per se*.

by allowing for intra-sector substitution of products and factors while maintaining the basic pre-Keynesian assumptions. As a consequence, the thrust of their conclusions is the same as Harberger's, namely that corporate capital bears the full burden of the corporate profits tax in the short run. The long-run incidence depends, among other things, on the elasticities of substitution of factors and products and on the relative elasticities of product demand. Gravelle and Kotlikoff (1989, p. 779) end their discussion by hoping for a 'rebirth of analytical attention to the [question of] . . . what the corporate profits tax precisely does'.

Harberger-type models have enjoyed great popularity in the mainstream literature and have served as the basis for a number of empirical studies. However, these models have been shown by post Keynesians to be irrelevant for two reasons. First, they ignore the central features of a capitalist economy and, second, they are empirically inconsistent, incorporating *ad hoc* Keynesian cyclical variables into pre-Keynesian models (Burbidge, 1976). In assessing the impact and incidence of taxation, Asimakopulos and Burbidge (1974) have shown that aggregate demand effects must be considered following a change in any broad-based tax. These aggregate demand effects are related to the government's budget stance, and to the response of business pricing decisions. Thus, government may increase its spending or reduce other taxes in response to an increase in the corporate profits tax, and/or corporations may increase their markups and prices in response to increases in the corporate profits tax.

As we mention at the beginning of Chapter 3, post Keynesians have found it convenient to decompose the study the study of taxation into two parts: 1) a study of short-period tax incidence; and 2) a study of long-period tax incidence. In the Harberger-type approaches, the short run is defined as the time period during which the capital stock of the corporate sector remains unchanged following a change in the corporate profits tax. With an unchanged capital stock, no change in demand conditions and with no substitution of labour for capital, marginal cost, and, thus, price remain unchanged following a change in the corporate profits tax rate.

In contrast, post Keynesians, like Asimakopulos and Burbidge (1979), define the short period as the time during which investment is fixed, having been determined by past decisions, and capacity utilization varies with respect to changes in aggregate demand. They argue that the short period, so defined, can be measured in 'calendar time, for example a quarter of a year, a half of a year or even a year' (Asimakopulos and Burbidge, 1979, p. 71). The long period is that period of time during which capacity varies, that is, when past investment decisions have an impact on the present.

3 A FRAMEWORK FOR ASSESSING TAX INCIDENCE

In order to analyse the incidence of the corporate profits tax, we derive an accounting identity for corporate profits from the US *National Income and Product Accounts* (NIPA). This identity is similar to Kalecki's (1968) famous profit identity, discussed in previous chapters, which shows the various sources of aggregate profits. The corporate profits identity utilized here was pioneered by Levy and Levy (1983). In aggregate, profits are shown to be related, amongst other things, to investment, the government budget surplus and personal savings. Aggregate profits are caused by investment, for example, because businesses cannot decide to earn profits but businesses can make decisions that have an impact on profits (Kalecki, 1968, p. 55). As Levy and Levy (1983) show, manipulation of the savings and investment identity in the NIPA yields the following expression for corporate profits (see the Appendix for the complete derivation):

Post-tax corporate profits (with adjustments for inventory valuation and capital consumption) =

Gross investment
+
Government budget deficit
+
Dividends
−
Personal savings
−
Consumption of fixed capital
−
Wage accruals (less disbursements)
−
Capital grants received by the US (net)
−
Statistical discrepancy

To yield a measure of corporate profits that better approximates the corporate net cash flow we modify the Levy identity. We do so by recognizing that the consumption of fixed capital can be broken down into corporate and non-corporate components; by adding the corporate component to both sides; by subtracting the capital consumption and inventory valuation adjustments from both sides; and by adding corporate net interest to both sides, i.e. (see the Appendix):

Gross post-tax corporate profits (undistributed corporate profits + dividends + corporate net interest + corporate consumption of fixed capital) =

Gross investment

−

Corporate inventory valuation adjustment

−

Corporate capital consumption adjustment

+

Government budget deficit

+

Dividends

+

Corporate net interest

−

Personal savings

−

Non-corporate capital consumption allowance (with inventory valuation and capital consumption adjustments)

−

Wage accruals (less disbursements)

−

Capital grants received by the US (net)

−

Statistical discrepancy

This latter expression serves as the basis for analysing the incidence of the US corporate profits tax.

Determining what post-tax corporate profits would be in the US in the absence of a change in the corporate profits tax is more complicated than is implied by the truism that a $1 increase in the corporate profits tax reduces post-tax corporate profits by $1. The complication arises because other things may not be constant with respect to the change in the corporate profits tax. Following a change in the corporate profits tax, other tax receipts and/or government purchases may change, and these changes can generate aggregate demand effects (see Burbidge, 1976, p. 229). As a consequence, we analyse the incidence of the corporate profits tax by considering the macroeconomic adjustments that result from a change in the tax and how these adjustment come to bear on corporate profits. As Asimakopulos and Burbidge (1979, p. 79) stress, a 'causal story' is needed to explain the incidence of the corporate profits tax. And, as Burbidge (1976, p. 233) stresses, 'macro models *with micro foundations* [Burbidge's emphasis] which link short-period stories will provide a consistent and useful approach' for analysing the incidence of taxation. Unfortunately, post-Keynesian macroeconomic models have not explicitly considered the incidence question, for example, Arestis and Driver (1988) and Eichner (1979). To address this problem, we construct in the next section a causal story of a small macro model to illustrate the short-period and long-period incidence of the corporate profits tax.

4   A CAUSAL STORY

To illustrate the incidence of the corporate profits tax, suppose that the latter four categories of the post-tax corporate profits identity are zero, i.e. non-corporate capital consumption allowance, wage accruals, capital grants and statistical discrepancy. As a result, the analysis of the incidence of the corporation profits tax can be limited to the impact of the tax on gross investment, the government budget deficit and the difference between the sum of corporate net interest and dividends and personal savings. In the short period, assuming gross investment is fixed by past decisions, the incidence of the corporate profits tax is limited to the impact of the tax on the government budget deficit, and the difference between the sum of corporate net interest and dividends and personal savings. As Asimakopolus and Burbidge (1974) show, under a balanced budget constraint (with compensating changes in other taxes and government spending), a tax change, such as an increase in the corporate profits tax, that leads to an increase in aggregate demand, say, through a balanced budget multiplier effect, will, under competitive conditions,[5] cause an increase in business markups and prices which will, in turn, reduce reduce real wages and personal savings, and increase post-tax corporate profits.[6] Under non-competitive conditions, with personal savings insensitive to changes in current income, aggregate post-tax profits will be unaffected by a change in the tax. In the long period, assuming competitive conditions, the short-period increase in profits leads to additional profits to finance investment, and, as a consequence, current investment decisions and future investment expenditures and profits increase.[7] In contrast to the Harberger-type models, the post Keynesian approach allows for partial, full or more than full shifting of the corporate profits tax in the short run, even under competitive conditions; and the impact of the corporate profits tax in the long period is tied to, not

5. Competitive conditions refer to a situation where the price of wage goods rises in response to a change in aggregate demand (see Asimakopulos and Burbidge (1979) p. 76), and non-competitive conditions refer to a situation where the price of wage goods remains constant with respect to a change in aggregate demand.
6. On the basis of this conclusion, Burbidge (1976) considered the Harberger-type models to be irrelevant and inconsistent when such models include *ad hoc* Keynesian cyclical variables.
7. This line of reasoning ignores the depreciation effect outlined in Chapter 3.

independent of, the tax incidence in the short period. We express these results more formally below in a simple macro model.

5   A CORPORATE PROFITS TAX INCIDENCE MODEL

We begin by rewriting the profits identity as:

$$P = I + Xf - (Tn - G) + D - Sp - Z \qquad (5.1)$$

where P = post-tax gross corporate profits; I = gross private domestic investment (less the inventory valuation adjustment); Xf = net foreign investment; Tn = government receipts (net of transfer payments); G = government purchases; D = the sum of corporate net interest and dividends; Sp = personal savings; and Z = the sum of non-corporate consumption of fixed capital, wage accruals less disbursements, capital grants received by the US and the statistical discrepancy.

In order to determine the incidence of the corporate profits tax, we consider the structural determinants of the variables on the right-hand side of the identity. For the sake of simplicity, net foreign investment and the sum of wage accruals less disbursements, capital grants to the US and the statistical discrepancy are treated as exogenous variables.

1   Gross Private Investment

Gross private investment, by definition, is the sum of gross fixed investment, residential construction and changes in business inventories. To simplify the analysis, we consider only the determinants of business fixed investment and ignore the other categories. Following Kalecki (1968 and 1968/1971), we express fixed investment as a function of the past level of entrepreneurial savings and changes in the past level of profits; i.e.:

$$I_t = I(E_{t-t}, \Delta P_{t-t}) \qquad (5.2)$$

where E = entrepreneurial savings (the internal savings of the corporation plus the personal savings of controlling group (Kalecki, 1968, p. 97)); and t = the time lag necessary for investment decisions to be translated into investment expenditures.

According to Kalecki (1968), firms will be induced to undertake new investment following a change in the economic environment. A change in the economic environment occurs when businesses accumulate savings out of profits and when the rate of profit changes. The latter term in equation (5.2) largely determines the change in the rate of profit. Since no precise measure of the personal savings (E) of the controlling group exists, we assume it to be a function of corporate profits and we write it as:

$$E = E(P) \tag{5.3}$$

Thus, we rewrite equation (5.2) as:

$$I_t = I(P_{t-t}, \Delta P_{t-t}) \tag{5.2'}$$

2 Government Purchases

We assume that government purchases are dependent on net tax receipts and the purchases of the previous period; i.e.:

$$G_t = G(Tn_t, G_{t-1}) \tag{5.4}$$

We use this equation to judge the short-period government budget stance, and we ignore any long-period dynamic relationship between government purchases and net tax receipts.[8]

3 Net Government Receipts

Net government receipts by definition equal gross government receipts less transfer payments. Here, we define transfer payments broadly as government expenditures less government purchases of final goods and services. Thus, we write net tax receipts as:

$$Tn = Tp + Tc + Ti + Tcsi - GTP \tag{5.5}$$

where Tn = net tax receipts, Tp = personal tax receipts; Tc = corporate profit tax receipts (accruals); Ti = indirect business tax receipts; $Tcsi$ = contributions to social insurance; and GTP = government transfer payments.

As a first approximation, we find expressions for the right-hand side of equation (5.5). Total personal taxes are written as a function of personal income, i.e.:

$$Tp = Tp(Yp) \tag{5.6}$$

where Yp = personal income.

---

8. The presence of a long-period (dynamic) relationship between government spending and taxation has been described by Peacock and Wiseman (1961). Although this has not yet been considered, their theory of public sector growth has relevance for the analysis of tax incidence.

In a similar manner, we write the corporate profits tax as a function of pre-tax corporate profits and the corporate profits tax rate, i.e.:

$$Tc = Tc(t_c, Pg) \qquad (5.7)$$

where t_c = corporate profits tax rate; and Pg = pre-tax net corporate profits.

We combine the remaining variables in net tax receipts and simply express them as a function of aggregate income, i.e.:

$$T' = T'(Y) \qquad (5.8)$$

where T' = the sum of indirect business taxes, contributions for social insurance less government transfer payments; and Y = aggregate income.

4   Corporate Net Interest and Dividends

As a first approximation, we express the sum of corporate net interest and dividends simply as a function of gross post tax profits, i.e.:

$$D = D(P) \qquad (5.9)$$

5   Personal Savings

We represent personal savings simply as a function of disposable personal income and a past level of personal savings. Thus, personal savings are expressed as:

$$Sp_t = Sp(Yd_t, Sp_{t-1}) \qquad (5.10)$$

where Yd = disposable personal income.

6   Aggregate Income

As in Kalecki's 1968 model, we express aggregate income as a function of a distribution parameter, the wage share,[9] which may vary with respect to the

---

9. Kalecki (1968) illustrated this relationship by writing the wage and salary share as: $V/Y = \beta/Y + \alpha$, where Y = value added; V = the pre-tax wage and salary bill; β = pre-tax salaries; and $\hat{a}$ = share of wages in value added. By defining $V = Y = Pg$ and collecting terms $Y = [\beta + Pg]/(1 - \alpha)$. According to Kalecki, (1968, p. 61), 'national income ... is pushed up to a point at which profits out of it are determined by the distribution factors'.

change in corporate profits tax (see Laramie and Mair 1993), and in the
aggregate level of pre-tax corporate profits, i.e.:

$$Y = Y(\alpha, Pg) \qquad (5.11)$$

where a = the wage share; and the wage share, a, can be written as:

$$\alpha = \alpha(t_c) \qquad (5.12)$$

To complete the model, we define in turn disposable personal income, pre-tax
net profits and disposable personal income. To simplify the analysis we assume
that disposable income can be written as:

$$Yd_t = Y_t - NCCAo - T' - Tp - (Pg' - D)^{10} \qquad (5.13)$$

where $NCCAo$ = the non-corporate consumption of fixed capital (assumed to
be exogenous); $Pg' = P + Tc + CCCo$, where $CCCo$ = the corporate consumption
of fixed capital (assumed to be exogenous).

Pre-tax corporate profits are defined as:

$$Pg = P + Tc \qquad (5.14)$$

and personal income is defined as:

$$Yp = Yd + Tp \qquad (5.15)$$

We now discuss both the short-period and long-period tax incidence within
this framework. In particular we consider two cases: 1) fixed government
purchases, i.e. $dG/dT = 0$; and 2) a balanced budget constraint, i.e $G = T$.

6 FIXED GOVERNMENT PURCHASES

In this case, assuming that the increase in the corporate profits tax rate results
in an increase in government tax revenues, corporate post-tax profits fall. To
illustrate this conclusion, let us consider the case where all profits are retained

10. *The NIPA definition of disposable personal income is:* $Y + (RFI - PFI) - NCCAo - T' - SD - (Pg' - D) + IPCB - BTPF - WAD - Tp$; *where RFI receipts of factor income from rest of world; PFI* = *payments of factor income to rest of world; SD* = *statistical discrepancy; IPCB* = *interest paid by consumers to businesses; BTFP* = *business transfer payments to foreigners; WAD* = *wage accruals less disbursements.*

by businesses and the only tax is the corporate profits tax. Given that investment is exogenous in the short period, an increase in the corporate profits tax has no impact on aggregate demand, aggregate income, disposable personal income and personal savings.[11] The decline in corporate profits is attributable to the decline in the government budget deficit. This decline in corporate profits is dampened if corporations increase their markups with respect to the increase in corporate profits tax rate and if the increase in markups reduces personal savings. The increase in the corporate profits tax rate, via a change in corporate markups, reduces the distribution parameter, α, and aggregate demand, which, in turn, reduces the levels of income and personal savings. It is through the decline in personal savings that the corporation income tax is shifted in this contractionary budget stance.[12]

In the long period, investment may respond to these changes. Insofar as the increase in the profits tax rate has reduced the level of profits, future investment will decline. This decline in investment will increase the burden of the corporation tax burden over the long period, as investment is a source of profits. If businesses increase their markups and, hence, personal savings decline, the level of profits may be restored to its pre-tax level, but the resulting fall in the aggregate levels of demand and income may discourage future investment and, thus, increase the long-period tax burden.

7   A BALANCED BUDGET CONSTRAINT

In the short period, with constant markups, the change in the corporate profits tax still has a negative impact on the level of profits, but this negative impact is less than in the previous case. The increase in the corporate profits tax, insofar as it results in additional profit tax revenues, will increase the level of gross profits, via the balanced budget multiplier effect, and, given the distribution parameter, will increase the levels of aggregate and disposable income. The rise in disposable personal income increases personal savings and reduces after-tax profits. In this case, a sufficient, but not necessary, condition for post-tax profits to remain constant is for personal savings to remain unchanged with respect to the increase in disposable income.[13] Again, if corporations

---

11. The increase in the corporate tax has no impact on disposable personal income because pre-tax profits, which are removed from aggregate income in deriving disposable personal income, are unaffected by the increase in the corporate profits tax.
12. In an open economy, assuming import substitution, the ability of domestic corporations to raise markups with respect to an increase in the corporate profits tax is limited by the degree of international competition. An increase in imports diminishes the degree to which the corporate profits tax is shifted.

alter their markups in response to the change in the corporate profits tax rate, then the effect described in the previous case applies.[14] Corporations regain some of their profits but at the expense of the aggregate level of income. Again, we present these results formally in the Appendix for the model outlined above.

The extent to which the long-period tax burden changes depends on the effects mentioned above. The rise in the corporate profits tax may inhibit further investment and increase the long-period burden of the tax. Again, if corporations alter their markups in response to the tax change, the results of the previous case hold.

8   CORPORATE TAX CHANGES AND PROFIT CHANGES: EVIDENCE FROM US DATA

As we hypothesize above, the short-period incidence of the corporation profits tax is substantially influenced by two factors: 1) the government budget stance; and 2) the reaction of personal savings to a change in the corporate profits tax. An examination of annual corporate profits data, published in the US NIPA, suggests that conditions have been such as to ameliorate some of the effects the corporate profits tax has had on post-tax profits, following changes in the corporate tax code (the data are presented in Table 5.1A in the Appendix). These offsetting effects are not only reflected in changes in the government budget deficit and personal savings but also in changes in gross investment, which, in the short period, may represent a hangover effect.

In assessing the impact of the corporate profits tax on corporate profits, we examine the overall trend in gross pre-tax profits, gross after-tax profits and the corporate profit tax shares of GDP. We consider four changes in the corporate profits in the USA: 1) the increase in the corporate profits tax during the Korean war; 2) the imposition of a surtax on corporate profits during the Viet Nam War (1968 and 1969); 3) the increase in corporate profits tax following the 1986 Tax Reform Act; and 4) the reduction in the corporate profits tax following

---

13. An implication derived from this result is that government would have to increase its deficit with respect to the increase in the corporate profits tax in order for post-tax corporate profits to remain constant. Also, it might be appropriate to consider the special case where the marginal propensity to save is approximately one (as in Friedman's permanent income hypothesis). The incidence of the tax lies somewhere between the constant government purchase and the balanced budget case where $0 < MPS < 1$.

14. Damania and Mair (1992), in the Kaleckian tradition, have argued that under conditions of oligopoly, the markup may actually fall during an increase in aggregate demand. Conceivably, this kind of aggregate demand pressure may swamp any pressure to increase markups following an increase in the corporate profits tax.

the Economic Recovery Act of 1981. We have deflated each of the sources of profits using the GDP deflator instead of its own particular deflator. We adopt this convention to ensure that the right-hand side of the profits identity adds up to profits on the left-hand side.[15]

Overall, during the period 1947 to 1991, the share of gross post-tax corporate profits in GDP appears to move inversely with the corporate tax share of GDP. The gross post-tax corporate profit share of GDP appears to increase on a long-run trend, and the corporate profits tax share of GDP appears to decrease on a long-run trend. If the two series are combined, then gross pre-tax profits' share of GDP appears to exhibit a zero trend. This evidence suggests that US corporations have been able to increase their share of GDP primarily through reductions in their corporate tax liability and that the incidence of the corporate profits tax, over the long period, has fallen by and large on corporations, in the sense that corporations have been able to capture the reduction in the corporate tax share of GDP. The evidence also suggests that changes in the corporate tax code have altered the economic incidence of the profits tax.

Following the outbreak of the Korean war in 1950, an excess profits tax was placed on corporate profits in the US and the corporate profits tax rate was increased from 42 per cent in 1950 to 50.75 per cent in 1951 (Pechman, 1987). In 1950, the real corporate profit tax liability jumped by about 73 per cent, and real profits increased by about 20.2 per cent. Moreover, in 1950, the corporate profit tax and profit shares of GDP increased respectively by 2.3 and 1.2 percentage points. In 1951, some of these effects were offset. The real corporate tax liability increased by about 20 per cent while corporate profits fell by 9 per cent; the corporate profit tax share increased by 0.6 of a percentage point and the profit share fell by 2.2 percentage points. If 1950 and 1951 are combined, then the 2.9 percentage point increase in the corporate profit tax share can be compared to a 1 percentage point decrease in the corporate profit share. These relative movements in the respective tax shares suggest some shifting of the corporate profits tax.

It is interesting to consider the sources of changes in corporate profits during these years. In 1950, the increase in corporate profits occurred during an investment rebound, with gross fixed investment increasing by 53.8 per cent over the previous year. Fixed, inventory and residential construction all jumped significantly during 1950. However both public and private savings also rose significantly. The real government deficit in 1949 of $16.6 billion was

15. Kalecki (1968, p. 119) assumed that the price index to deflate investment goods was identical to the gross domestic product deflator. Ideally, profits should be deflated according to some weighted index of consumer goods and capital goods that are purchased out of profits. However, no such index exists. Moreover, if each of the variables were deflated according to its own price index, there is no guarantee that the deflated sum of sources on the right-hand side of the identity would add up to the deflated value of profits.

transformed into a real government budget surplus of $35.1 billion in 1950, while real personal savings rose by $25.7 billion or by 73 per cent. Moreover, personal savings minus the sum of corporate net interest and dividends increased by about $19.3 billion or by 1830 per cent.[16] In 1951, real gross investment continued to grow and the government budget surplus declined, but real personal savings increased relative to the sum of net interest and dividends. The $21 billion increase in personal savings relative to the sum of net interest and dividends accounts for much of the decline in profits.

The effects of the surtax on corporate profits during the Viet Nam War are somewhat similar. A surtax during the years 1968 and 1969 increased the corporate tax rate from 48 per cent to 52.8 per cent and the investment tax credit was suspended during the latter part of 1969 (Pechman, 1987). The surtax was reduced to 49.2 per cent in 1970 and eliminated in 1971. In 1968, the real corporate profits tax liability jumped by about 15 per cent as real corporate profits increased by 1.5 per cent. The real corporate profit tax share of real GDP increased by 0.4 of a percentage point, while the corporate profits share fell by 0.3 of a percentage point. As in 1950, the increase in profits can be attributed, in part, to an increase in investment, as the government deficit fell. Gross investment increased by about 4.5 per cent. Moreover, real personal savings declined by about 8.7 per cent, and the difference between personal savings and the sum of corporate net interest and dividends decreased by about $17.6 billion, or by about 30 per cent. In 1969, real corporate profit taxes decreased by 4.1 per cent and corporate profits declined by 1.2 per cent as real gross investment rose by 6.6 per cent. The decline in corporate profits can be attributed to the increase in the real government budget surplus offsetting the combined effects of the fall in the difference between real personal savings and the sum of corporate net interest and dividends and the rise in gross investment. In this year, the shares of GDP of both real profits and the taxes fell. Overall, during the period, the corporate profits tax share increased by 0.1 of a percentage point, while the profit share declined by 0.7 of a percentage point.

In 1986, following the Tax Reform Act, depreciation rates were reduced and the investment tax credit was eliminated, the definition of taxable income was broadened and the corporate tax rate was reduced from 46 per cent to 32 per cent. The real corporate profits tax liability increased respectively by 7.5 per cent and by 15.6 per cent in 1986 and 1987. In 1986, real corporate profits fell by 1 per cent, while real gross investment declined by 5.9 per cent. This fall in investment accounts for a large part of the decline in profits as the real

16. The difference between the sum of net interest and dividends and personal savings is akin to Kalecki's (1968) measures of the difference between capitalists' consumption and workers' savings. A rise in workers' savings relative to capitalists' consumption reduces the level of profits.

government deficit increased and the difference between real personal savings and the sum of corporate net interest and dividends declined. In 1987, real profits recovered as investment increased and the deficit contracted. The increase in profits in this year can, by and large, be attributed to a 26.6 per cent reduction in personal savings (as the sum of corporate net interest and dividends remained roughly constant) and to the 4.4 per cent increase in gross investment. In 1986, the corporate profits tax share remained roughly constant while the profit share declined by about 0.5 of a percentage point. In 1987, both shares increased. If both 1986 and 1987 are combined, the profit and tax shares both increased by 0.4 of a percentage point.

Following the Economic Recovery Act of 1981, which accelerated the depreciation rates and liberalized the investment tax credit, the real corporate tax liability fell by about 26.7 per cent in 1982 and then increased by 17.9 per cent in 1983. In 1982, corporate profits fell by about 6.2 per cent as real gross investment decreased by about 19.4 per cent. The 238 per cent increase in the government budget deficit reduced the fall in profits. In this year, both the profit tax and profit shares decreased respectively by 0.7 and 0.6 of a percentage point. In 1983, profits increased by 3 per cent as gross investment declined by 6.7 per cent, because the government budget deficit increased by 23.9 per cent and personal savings relative to the sum of corporate net interest and dividends fell by 23.6 per cent. For 1982 and 1983 combined, the corporate tax and profit shares declined respectively by 0.4 and 0.7 of a percentage point.

Table 5.1 below summarizes the movements in the real corporate profits tax, real post-tax corporate profits, profits share of GDP and the tax share of GDP for the above mentioned years. The less than or equal sign between the last two columns indicates whether the change in the profit share was less than, greater than or equal to the change in the tax share.

Table 5.1   The movement in post-tax profits immediately following major corporate tax changes in US 1950–87

Years	Corporate Profits Tax	Post-Tax Corporate Profits	Profits Share of GDP		Tax Share of GDP
1950–51	+	–	–	<	+
1968–69	+	–	–	>	+
1982–83	–	+	–	>	–
1986–87	+	+	+	=	+

The evidence suggests that the impact of changes in the corporation profits tax on corporate post-tax profits has been mitigated by changes in other factors despite the contractionary government budget stances in some years. In particular, when corporate tax rates have been increased, and the government surplus increased, either increases in gross investment, perhaps due to a hangover effect, or a reduction in personal savings relative to the sum of net corporate interest and dividends have offset, to some extent, the decline in profits. The important question, as we indicate above, is how are the factors on the right-hand side of the profits identity related to each other and to the corporate profits tax? In order to determine this, the structural parameters of the model have to be estimated, and these parameters can only be estimated in a properly formulated macroeconomic model.

9   CONCLUSIONS

Our purpose in this chapter has been to consider the factors that have an impact on the economic incidence of the corporate profits tax. If we drop the assumptions that all markets clear and that the economy is at continuous full employment, then the incidence of the corporate profits tax can be analysed using a Kaleckian macroeconomic model. Within such a model the incidence of the corporate profits tax is determined by two sets of effects: 1) a public sector effect which depends on the government's budget stance; and 2) a private sector effect which depends on: a) the reaction of personal savings to the tax; b) the reaction of investment to the tax in the long period; and c) the change in corporate markups with respect to the tax. As we have shown, a $1 increase in the corporate profits tax, holding other things constant, results in a $1 reduction in post-tax corporate profits, but this effect is mitigated depending upon the public and the private sector effects. If the government spends the corporate profit tax receipts on final goods and services, the incidence on corporations of the profits tax is reduced depending on the reaction of personal savings to the resultant change in aggregate income. Moreover, if corporations respond to the tax by altering markups, then the economic incidence of the tax may vary further from the legal incidence. These various effects have their impact on future investment, through profits, which may lead to cumulative incidence effects.

In determining the economic incidence of the corporate profits tax, the relative strengths of these various effects must be considered. The government's budget stance is a policy decision and little can be said *a priori* about that. However, we can indulge in some speculation about the relative strengths of the private sector effects. The private sector effects are likely to be relatively weak. First, consider the behaviour of savings. If the marginal propensity to save is low, then any change in personal disposable income, given a change in the corporate profits tax, is likely to have a small impact on post-tax corporate profits. Second, the degree to which corporations are able to shift the corporate profits tax through changes in corporate markups and the extent to which changes in profit margins have an impact on aggregate post tax profits is diluted by a number of factors. As stressed by Pechman (1987), businesses only know their tax liability *ex post*, and, therefore, immediate shifting of the profits tax through changes in markups is unlikely. Inter-firm rivalry may also inhibit the degree to which the tax is shifted forwards or backwards. These sentiments are also expressed by Sylos-Labini (1979) in that non-direct costs may not be passed along due to 'interfirm' differences.[17] However, with UK data, Coutts, Godley and Nordhaus (1978), in analysing the relationship between profit margins and corporate taxes, have found that little shifting occurs in the short period (a year or less), but that there is full or more than full shifting in the medium and long runs respectively.

Even if full shifting or more than full shifting is the result, then the extent to which such shifting has an impact on the level of aggregate post-tax corporate profits depends on: 1) the change in aggregate income with respect to the change in profit margins; and 2) the extent to which personal savings change with respect to the change in aggregate income. Again, if the marginal propensity to save is relatively low, the change in corporate profits with respect to a change in corporate markups is expected to be relatively small. Moreover, if the marginal propensity to save is negative, the change in corporate post-tax profits with respect to the change in corporate markups is negative when shifting through changes in the markup is present. With the relatively small private sector effects, the incidence of the corporation income tax depends largely on the government budget stance. This means that the economic incidence of the corporation profits tax is determined politically, as reflected in the government's budget stance!

The major economic policy issue associated with the corporation profits tax is whether such a tax should exist at all. One of the arguments against the corporate profits tax is that it results in the double taxation of income which distorts the resource allocation of capital. Clearly, if the government takes an appropriate budget stance with respect to the corporate profits tax, then such double taxation of income for the corporate sector as a whole, need not arise.

Another important issue is whether the corporate profits tax should be reduced while government is downsized as a means of ending an era of stagnation (for example, see Norton, *Fortune*, 9/16/93, pp. 34–48). As implied by the discussion above, such a policy is not likely to have much impact on corporate profits, and it may actually reduce them if the government reduces

17. Ed Slattery has pointed out to Laramie that the corporate profits tax is neither a direct cost nor an overhead cost. It is not a direct cost because it is not known at the time of production. It is not an overhead cost because, in all likelihood, it varies with production.

the size of its deficit as a result. Furthermore, the process of downsizing is likely to reduce aggregate income through a balanced budget multiplier effect.

In the same context, there have been calls to reduce or replace the corporate profits tax with some other type of tax, such as a value-added tax. The discussion above indicates that there may be only small benefits from doing so. Taxes, in most forms, if not accompanied by government spending, have a depressing effect on corporate profits. This depressing effect may be increased if the imposition of the value-added tax results in an increase in the marginal propensity to save. However, some gains could be derived from replacing the corporate profits tax with a value-added tax. First, the introduction of the value-added tax is more likely to generate a certain private sector shifting effect, as value-added tax is more like a direct cost than is the profits tax.[18] As a consequence, the incidence of the tax will be better understood than the incidence of the corporate profits tax. Second, the value-added tax may result in a more efficient allocation of resources within the corporate sector. This can come about as relatively small corporations and large corporations have the same shifting basis, and investment and financial decisions are no longer based upon tax considerations but upon economic considerations. However, whether these changes would result in additional future investment and higher corporate profits remains an unresolved issue. Moreover, the impact on aggregate income of replacing the corporate profits tax with the value-added tax is unknown.

Whatever the possibilities for the future, if we accept the old adage that 'the best tax is an old tax', then the corporation profits tax is here to stay in some form. The question then is what can be done with the corporation income tax, or for that matter tax revenue in general, to ensure economic growth. The realization that the economic incidence of corporation profits tax, or any tax, is determined politically leads to some policy questions. For example:

1. Should the government make use of the corporate profits tax to finance public projects to build and rebuild infrastructure? If so, given a positive marginal propensity to save, how much of a deficit should the government run to ensure that the economic incidence of the corporate profits tax is zero?
2. Should the government use the corporate profits tax as a means of reducing poverty? If the recipients of government transfer payments have a marginal propensity to save equal to zero, then the tax incidence issues will be the same as in the previous case.
3. Should the corporate profits tax be hypothecated for specific purposes, for example projects that provide joint benefits to the corporate sector like

18. Laramie is grateful to Tom Karier for pointing this out to him.

research and development, job training and education? The private costs of these goods may be too high for individual corporations to bear. If the government makes provisions for these goods, by spending the corporate profits tax, then the economic incidence of the tax will be slight in the short run and negative in the long run as corporations benefit from the resulting productivity gains.

Finally, in this chapter, we have considered the determinants of the economic incidence of corporate sector as a whole and we have ignored the economic incidence of the corporate profits tax for an individual corporation. When government plays a large role in determining the economic incidence, it is the distribution by government of spending and taxation across corporations that determines by and large individual corporations' tax incidence. The winners are those corporations that receive the benefits of government spending (directly or indirectly) in excess of their tax payments. The losers (and even some winners) may attempt to shift the tax through altering markups. Insofar as these individual corporations are able to adjust their markups, the corporate incidence of the profits tax may be negative. In contrast, if government plays a passive role, where the budget process is totally *ad hoc*, where corporate profit taxes are unrelated to the rest of the budget, then the economic incidence of the corporate profits tax on individual corporations rests with the ability of individual corporations to shift the tax through altering markups.

APPENDIX

Deriving the Corporate Profits Identity from the US National Income and Product Accounts (*NIPA*)

In the US *NIPA* the following relationships are defined:

GDP (expenditures)   = Personal Consumption Expenditures (*C*)
                       + Gross Private Investment (*I*)
                       + Net Exports (*XNET*)
                       + Government Purchases (*G*)

GNP   = *GDP*
                       + Receipts of factor income from the rest of the world (*XSF*)
                       – Payments of factor income to the rest of the world (*MSF*)

GDP = GNP
- Receipts of factor income from the rest of the world (*XSF*)
+ Payments of factor income to the rest of the world (*MSF*)

National Income (*NI*) = GNP
- Consumption of Fixed Capital (*NCCAJ*)
- Indirect Business Taxes (*NBTAX*)
- Business Transfer Payments (*NBTRAN*)
- Statistical Discrepancy (*NBSTAT*)
+ Subsidies less current surplus of government enterprises (*NGSUB*)

or:

National Income (*NI*) = Compensation to Employees (*YLE*)
+ Proprietors' Income (with capital consumption and inventory valuation adjustments) (*YOP*)
+ Rental Income (with capital consumption adjustment) (*YRI*)
+ Corporate Profits (with inventory valuation and capital consumption adjustments) (*YCP*)

Corporate Profits with *IVA* (*YCVA*)
Profits before tax (*YCBT*)
Profits tax liability (*YCTL*)
Profits after tax (*YCAT*)
Dividends (*YCAD*)
Undistributed Corporate Profit (*YCAU*)
Inventory Valuation Adjustment (*YCIVA*)
Capital Consumption Adjustment (*YCCA*)
Net interest (*YNI*)

Given these definitions, *GDP* is rewritten as:

$$GDP = YLE + YOP + YRI + YCP + YNI + NCCAJ + NBTAX$$
$$+ NBTRAN + NBSTAT - NGSUB - XSF + MSF \qquad (5.1A)$$

or as:

$$GDP = C + I + XNET + G \qquad (5.2A)$$

Setting equation (5.1A) equal to equation (5.2A) and by defining consumption of fixed capital as:

$$NCCAJ = BALO + SANCALO \qquad (5.3A)$$

where $BALO$ = corporate consumption of fixed capital; and $SANCALO$ = non-corporate consumption of fixed capital, and by solving for the sum of after tax corporate profits with inventory valuation and capital consumption adjustments, yields:

$$YCAT + YCIVA + YCCA + BALO = C + I + XNET + G + NGSUB$$
$$- YCTL - NBTAX - SANCALO - YLE - YOP - YRI$$
$$- YNI - NBTRAN - XSF + MSF - NBSTAT \qquad (5.4A)$$

In order to derive the profit identity in the text, the following are added to and subtracted from the right-hand side of the equal sign in equation (5.4A): dividends $(YCAD)$; personal tax receipts $(GRPTX)$; government transfer payments $(GEXTR)$; net interest paid by government $(GNETI)$; dividends received by government $(GDIVC)$; government wage accruals less disbursements $(GWAGE)$; contributions for social insurance $(GRCSI)$; wage accruals less disbursements $(WAGE)$; personal transfer payments to foreigners $(PTPF)$; capital grants received by the US (net) (XG); and net corporate interest $(YCNINT)$.

This process yields:

$$YCAT + YCIVA + YCCA + BALO = C + I + XNET - GBAL$$
$$+ NGSUB - YCBT - NBTAX - SANCALO - YLE - YOP$$
$$- YRI - YNI - NBTRAN - XSF + MSF - NBSTAT + YCAD$$
$$- YCAD + YPX + GRCSI - GEXTR - GNETI + GDIVC$$
$$+ GWAGE + SAWA - WAGE + PTPF - PTPF + XG$$
$$- XG + YCNINT - YCNINT \qquad (5.5A)$$

where $GBAL$ = the government budget surplus, and is defined as:

$$GBAL = (YPX + YCTL + NBTAX + GRCSI) - (G + GEXTR$$
$$+ GNETI + GDIVC - GSUB + GWAGE) \qquad (5.6A)$$

Given the following *NIPA* definitions, the following expression for corporate profits can be derived.

$$YCAD = YCDV + GDIVC \qquad (5.7A)$$

where $YCDV$ = personal dividend income; and $GDIVC$ = dividend payments to government;

$$SAWA = GWAGE + WAGE \qquad (5.8A)$$

where $SAWA$ = total wage accruals less disbursements;

$$NBTRAN = NBTRNP + NBTRNF \qquad (5.9A)$$

where $NBTRNP$ = business transfer payments to persons; and $NBTRNF$ = business transfer payments to foreigners;

$$GEXTR = GEXTRP + GEXTRF \qquad (5.10A)$$

where $GEXTRP$ = government transfer payments to persons; and GEXTRF = government transfer payments to foreigners;

$$GNETI = (GIPD - GIREC) + GIPDF \qquad (5.11A)$$

where $GIPD$ = interest paid by government to persons and business; $GIREC$ = interest received by government; and $GIPFD$ = net interest paid by government to the rest of the world;

$$YNI = YPIN - (GIPD - GIREC) - YNICB \qquad (5.12A)$$

where $YPIN$ = personal net interest; and $YNICB$ = interest paid by consumers to businesses;

$$YP = NI - YCP - YNI - GRCSI - SAWA + YPIN + YPDV + GEXTRP + NBTRNP \qquad (5.13A)$$

where YP = personal income;

$$YPD = YP - YPX \qquad (5.14A)$$

where YPD = disposable personal income;

$$YPSV = YPD - C - YNICB - PTPF \qquad (5.15A)$$

where $YPSV$ = personal savings;

$$MINET = XNET + XG + XSF - MSF - GEXTRF - PTPF - GIPDF - NBTRNF \qquad (5.16A)$$

Combining expressions (5.5A) to (5.16A) yields:

$$YCAT + YCIVA + YCCA + BALO = (I + MINET) - GBAL + YCAD + YCNINT$$
$$- YPSV - SANCALO - SAWA - XG - RBS - YCNINT \quad (5.17A)$$

To derive the expression for gross post-tax profits, the inventory valuation adjustment and the capital consumption adjustment are subtracted from both sides of equation (5.17A) and corporate net interest is added to both sides of equation (5.17A), i. e.:

$$YCAT + BALO + YCNINT = (I + MINET - YCIVA - YCCA) + YCAD$$
$$+ YCNINT - YPSV - SANCALO - SAWA - XG - RBS - YCNINT$$
$$(5.18A)$$

Table 5.1A(a)   Real corporate profits and sources (constant dollars, 1987 = 100) (US NIPA)

Year	Real Corporate Profits (1)	Percentage Real Change	Real Gross Investment (2)	Percentage Real Change
1947	112.299	–	236.898	–
1948	143.500	2.8	252.500	6.6
1949	149.246	4.0	188.945	−25.2
1950	146.535	−1.8	159.406	37.3
1951	148.357	1.2	287.324	10.8
1952	157.674	6.3	254.419	−11.5
1953	155.000	−1.7	250.000	−1.7
1954	166.216	7.2	243.694	−2.5
1955	191.703	15.3	303.057	244
1956	190.678	−0.5	317.797	4.9
1957	193.443	1.4	309.016	−2.8
1958	184.337	−4.7	262.651	−1.5
1959	208.984	13.4	303.125	15.4
1960	207.308	−0.8	315.385	4.0
1961	211.027	1.8	312.548	−0.9
1962	235.316	11.5	341.264	9.2
1963	248.897	5.8	361.765	6.0
1964	269.314	8.2	394.585	9.1
1965	297.183	10.3	437.324	10.8
1966	306.803	3.2	456.803	4.5
1967	304.620	−0.7	434.323	−4.9
1968	301.572	−1.0	445.597	2.6
1969	290.120	−3.8	470.060	5.5
1970	269.034	−7.3	440.909	−6.2
1971	294.609	9.5	476.550	8.1
1971	294.609	9.5	476.550	8.1
1972	320.051	8.6	521.080	9.3
1973	329.298	2.9	609.927	17.1
1974	296.239	−10.0	555.088	−9.0
1975	342.683	15.7	502.846	−9.4
1976	367.304	7.2	564.436	12.2
1977	402.683	9.6	624.508	10.6
1978	424.046	5.3	701.990	12.4
1979	421.189	−0.7	735.061	4.7
1980	387.448	−8.0	668.201	−9.1
1981	405.830	4.7	719.265	7.6
1982	396.181	−2.4	597.733	−16.9
1983	451.206	13.9	587.486	−1.7
1984	478.705	6.1	685.950	16.8
1985	489.513	2.3	631.886	−7.9
1986	474.097	−3.1	594.324	−5.9
1987	500.400	5.5	594.200	−0.0
1988	535.260	7.0	650.867	9.5
1989	528.361	−1.3	684.070	5.1
1990	538.482	1.9	644.660	−5.8
1991	529.312	−1.7	631.521	−2.0

(1) Defined as real corporate profits after taxes and before the corporate capital consumption allowance (with the capital consumption and inventory valuation adjustments).
(2) Defined as the sum of gross private domestic investment and net foreign investment.

A dynamic theory of taxation

Table 5.1A(b)

Real Gov't Budget Surplus	Percentage Real Change	Dividends	Percentage Real Change	Personal Savings	Percentage Real Change
77.005	–	33.690	–	26.738	–
47.000	–39.0	35.000	3.9	54.500	103.8
–16.583	–135.3	36.181	3.4	35.176	–35.5
35.149	312.0	44.059	21.8	60.891	73.1
26.291	–25.2	40.376	–8.4	77.934	28.0
–16.279	–161.9	40.000	–0.9	80.000	2.7
–25.909	–59.2	40.455	1.1	82.273	2.8
–32.883	–26.9	41.892	3.6	72.973	–11.3
12.664	138.5	46.288	10.5	69.432	–4.9
22.881	80.7	48.305	4.4	90.254	30.0
3.279	–85.7	48.361	0.1	93.033	3.1
–43.775	–143.5	46.586	–3.7	96.787	4.0
–12.109	72.3	49.609	6.5	85.938	11.2
13.846	214.3	51.538	3.9	79.231	–7.8
–11.407	–182.4	53.232	3.3	94.677	19.5
–10.781	–5.5	56.134	5.5	96.283	1.7
5.882	–154.6	59.191	5.4	90.809	–5.7
–5.776	–198.2	64.982	9.8	113.718	25.2
4.577	–179.2	71.127	9.5	121.831	7.1
–3.061	–166.9	71.088	–0.1	123.810	1.6
–45.545	–1388.7	72.937	2.6	151.155	22.1
–14.465	68.2	77.358	6.1	138.050	–8.7
29.940	307.0	75.449	–2.5	129.641	–6.1
–32.670	–209.1	67.330	–10.8	163.352	26.0
–51.752	–58.4	64.151	–4.7	176.280	7.9
–10.026	80.6	66.324	3.4	153.728	–12.8
16.707	266.6	68.039	2.6	208.475	35.6
–9.956	–159.6	67.257	–1.1	206.637	–0.9
–131.707	1222.9	61.179	–9.0	203.862	–1.3
–73.231	44.4	68.069	11.3	177.820	–12.8
–30.054	59.0	72.987	7.2	157.245	–11.9
4.975	116.6	76.119	4.3	178.773	13.7
14.482	191.1	79.878	4.9	187.957	5.1
–49.233	–440.0	82.287	3.0	214.644	14.2
–38.403	22.0	87.706	6.6	243.093	13.3
–129.594	–237.5	83.532	–4.8	238.067	–2.1
–160.505	–23.9	93.226	11.6	193.685	–18.6
–119.429	25.6	90.779	–2.6	243.688	25.8
–132.733	–11.1	97.881	7.8	200.530	–17.7
–151.496	–14.1	113.313	15.8	193.498	–3.5
–111.700	26.3	106.200	–6.3	142.000	–26.6
–94.701	15.2	111.175	4.7	150.000	5.6
–71.363	24.6	123.941	11.5	140.055	–6.6
–122.242	–71.3	135.481	9.3	150.044	7.1
–166.695	–36.4	116.737	–13.8	171.198	41.1

Table 5.1A(c)

Real Noncorporate Capital Consumption Allowance	Percentage Real Change	Corporate Tax Receipts	Percentage Real Change
44.920	–	60.428	–
48.500	8.0	62.500	3.4
52.764	8.8	51.256	−18.0
55.941	6.0	88.614	72.9
61.033	9.1	106.103	19.7
64.651	5.9	90.233	−15.0
66.364	2.6	92.273	2.3
68.468	3.2	79.279	−14.1
70.306	2.7	96.070	21.2
74.153	5.5	93.220	−3.0
75.410	1.7	87.705	−5.9
76.305	1.2	76.305	−13.0
76.953	0.8	92.578	21.3
78.846	2.5	87.308	−5.7
79.848	1.3	86.692	−0.7
80.669	1.0	89.219	2.9
82.721	2.5	96.324	8.0
84.838	2.6	101.083	4.9
87.676	3.3	108.803	7.6
90.816	3.6	114.626	5.4
94.389	3.9	107.921	−5.8
97.799	3.6	123.899	14.8
103.593	5.9	118.862	−4.1
105.966	2.3	97.443	−18.0
110.243	4.0	101.887	4.6
119.794	8.7	107.455	5.5
124.697	4.1	119.370	11.1
130.752	4.9	114.602	−4.0
136.992	4.8	103.455	−9.7
140.727	2.7	122.753	18.7
148.122	5.3	130.590	6.4
157.711	6.5	138.474	6.0
168.598	6.9	134.146	−3.1
176.848	4.9	118.271	−11.8
181.242	2.5	102.788	−13.1
185.442	2.3	75.298	−26.7
184.615	−0.4	88.749	17.9
183.754	−0.5	103.293	16.4
187.182	1.9	102.225	−1.0
190.299	1.7	109.907	7.5
194.500	2.2	127.100	15.6
198.844	2.2	131.985	3.8
209.945	5.6	130.110	−1.4
206.973	−1.4	122.330	−6.0
206.287	−0.3	110.365	−9.8

A dynamic theory of taxation

Table 5.1A(d)

Real Profits Share of Real GDP	Percentage Real Change	Corporate Profits Tax Share of Real GDP	Percentage Real Change
9.0	–	4.8	–
11.0	23.0	4.8	−0.4
11.5	3.9	3.9	−18.1
10.3	−10.0	6.2	58.5
9.5	−7.6	6.8	9.3
9.7	1.7	5.5	−18.6
9.2	−4.9	5.5	−1.1
9.9	7.9	4.7	−13.5
10.9	9.1	5.4	14.7
10.6	−2.8	5.2	−5.2
10.5	−0.3	4.8	−7.6
10.1	−4.1	4.2	−12.4
10.8	7.2	4.8	14.8
10.5	−3.0	4.4	−7.8
10.4	−0.6	4.3	−3.0
11.1	6.1	4.2	−2.1
11.2	1.4	4.3	3.5
11.5	2.5	4.3	−0.6
12.0	4.3	4.4	1.8
11.7	−2.4	4.4	−0.4
11.3	−3.3	4.0	−8.3
10.8	−4.9	4.4	10.3
10.1	−6.3	4.1	−6.6
9.4	−7.2	3.4	−18.0
10.0	6.3	3.4	1.5
10.3	3.5	3.5	0.5
10.1	−2.3	3.7	5.5
9.2	−8.9	3.6	−2.8
10.6	15.8	3.2	−9.6
10.9	2.2	3.6	13.1
11.4	5.0	3.7	1.9
11.5	0.4	3.7	1.1
11.1	−3.1	3.5	−5.5
10.6	3.0	2.7	−14.5
10.5	−0.2	2.0	−25.1
11.5	9.5	2.3	13.3
11.5	0.0	2.5	9.7
11.4	−0.9	2.4	−4.1
10.8	−5.9	2.5	4.4
11.0	2.4	2.8	12.2
11.3	2.9	2.8	−0.1
10.9	−3.6	2.7	−3.7
11.0	0.7	2.5	−7.1
10.9	−1.0	2.3	−9.2

REFERENCES

Arestis, P. and Driver, C. (1988), 'The macrodynamics of the US and UK economies through two post Keynesian models', in Arestis P. (ed.), *Post Keynesian Monetary Economics*, Aldershot, Edward Elgar.

Asimakopulos, A. and Burbidge, J.B. (1974), 'The short-period incidence of taxation', *Economic Journal*, **84**, 267–88.

Asimakopulos, A. and Burbidge, J.B. (1979), 'Harberger and Kalecki on the incidence of taxation: a critical comparison', *Greek Economic Review*, 70–81.

Burbidge, J. (1976), 'Internally inconsistent mixtures of micro- and macro-theory in empirical studies of profits tax incidence' *Finanzarchiv*, **35**, 218–34.

Coutts, K., Godley, W. and Nordhaus, W. (1978), *Industrial Pricing in the United Kingdom*, Cambridge, Cambridge University Press.

Damania, D. and Mair, D. (1992), 'The short-period incidence of taxation revisited', *Cambridge Journal of Economics*, **16**, 195–206.

Eichner, A.S. (1979), 'A post Keynesian short-period model', *Journal of Post Keynesian Economics*, **1**, 38–63. Reprinted in Sawyer, M.C (ed.), *Post Keynesian Economics*, Aldershot, Edward Elgar.

Gravelle, J. and Kotlikoff, L. (1989), 'The incidence and efficiency costs of corporate taxes when corporate and non-corporate firms produce the same good', *Journal of Political Economy*, **97** (4), 749–80.

Harberger, A.C. (1962), 'The incidence of the corporation income tax', *Journal of Political Economy*, **70**, 215–240.

Kalecki, M. (1968), *Theory of Economic Dynamics*, New York, Monthly Review Press.

Kalecki, M. (1968/1971), *Selected Essays on the Dynamics of the Capitalist Economy*, Cambridge, Cambridge University Press.

Laramie, A.J. (1994), 'Taxation and business fixed investment', mimeo, Jerome Levy Economics Institute, Bard College, NY.

Levy, S.J. and Levy, D.A. (1983), *Profits and the Future of American Society*, New York, Harper and Row.

Peacock, A. and Wiseman, J. (1961), *The Growth of Public Expenditure in the United Kingdom*, Princeton, Princeton University Press.

Pechman, J.A. (1980), *Federal Tax Policy*, Washington, D.C., The Brookings Institution.

Stiglitz, J.E. (1988), *Economics of the Public Sector*, New York, W.W. Norton and Company.

Sylos-Labini, P. (1979), 'Industrial pricing in the United Kingdom', *Cambridge Journal of Economics*, **3**, 153–63. Reprinted in Sawyer, M.C. (ed.), *Post Keynesian Economics*, Aldershot, Edward Elgar.

6. The impact of taxation on gross private non-residential fixed investment[1]

1 INTRODUCTION

In this chapter we compare the neoclassical and Kaleckian approaches to identifying the effects of taxation on fixed investment. In support of our Kaleckian approach we provide a statistical illustration from the United States. We follow Kalecki's methodology in attempting 'to show the plausibility of the relations between economic variables arrived at theoretically rather than to obtain the most likely coefficients of these relations' (Kalecki, 1954, p. 5, cited from Courvisanos, 1996, p. 11).

The 1980s brought major changes in the tax treatment of business fixed investment in the United States which raised the level of debate over the effects of tax incentives on business fixed investment. A sample of the neoclassical literature suggests that investment tax incentives had little impact on investment or investment's share of GDP.[2] None of this literature, however, considered the incidence effects of taxation on investment.

2 PROBLEMS OF NEOCLASSICAL MODELS

One of the purposes of economic theory is to generate questions and to sort out explanations for economic phenomena. The structural models used by economists are typically designed to sort out the confluence of factors impacting on a particular economic variable, like business fixed investment. These structural models are supported by a set of assumptions which form a theory. As Robinson (1980) states, if the theory is logical, then debate over the appro-

---

1. This chapter is a revision of Laramie, Mair, Miller and Stratopoulos (1996).
2. See Auerbach (1983), Auerbach and Hassett (1990), Auerbach and Hines (1988), Auerbach, Hines and Oliner (1992), Bosworth (1985), Chirinko (1988), Clark (1993), DeLong and Summers (1992), Fazzari, Hubbard and Petersen (1988a and 1988b), Hall and Jorgensen (1976), Summers (1981a and 1981b). Ironically, the need to improve economic efficiency is the result of the tax wedge between corporate and non-corporate capital (see Summers, 1981b). For criticisms of this approach see Crotty (1992), Gordon (1992) and Vickers (1992).

priateness of the theoretical model hinges upon the relevance of the assumptions. These assumptions condition the types of questions asked and the subsequent interpretation of empirical results. For example, the neoclassical theory of investment tax incentives is based upon the notion that individuals maximize utility, that the production and demand for investment goods is the consequence of that process, and, therefore, the neoclassics examine how marginal tax changes affect investment. Moreover, the theories of aggregate production, factor demand and income distribution are subordinated to the theory of utility maximization. The debate over these theories occupied economics for the better part of two decades, and, yet, it appears that the sides have 'declared victory and gone home'.[3] The purpose of this section is to examine a critique of the neoclassical theory of investment so that an alternative theory of investment tax incentives might be considered.

1 The Relevance of the Standard Assumptions

The neoclassical approach to investment is typically governed by the following assumptions: 1) utility maximization and its derivatives govern economic decisions; 2) product, factor and financial markets, with some exceptions, are efficient; and 3) an analysis of representative firm(s) (financially unconstrained or constrained) can be generalized to an understanding of the aggregate level of investment; 4) the firm (or firms) operates in equilibrium in the long-run, and this equilibrium level is consistent with long-run equilibrium for the economy as a whole; 5) the short-run position of the firm and of the economy is independent of the firm's and the economy's long-run equilibrium; 6) savings cause investment; and 7) true uncertainty does not exist. All of these assumptions at one time or another have been dismissed as irrelevant to the understanding of the 'laws' and motions of capitalism. Rather than covering this burgeoning literature, we present a brief review of some criticisms of the neoclassical theory of investment. We then consider some applications to the theory of investment tax incentives.

2 Static Equilibrium and the Incidence of Taxation

Following the publication of the *General Theory*, Kalecki (1937a and 1971/1937) made two important and separate contributions. The first contribution was a criticism of Keynes's Marginal Efficiency of Capital and the second was on the incidence and effects of taxation (which we discuss in

3. For examples of critiques of the neoclassical approach, see Harcourt, (1972), Robinson, (1980) and Schwartz (1977).

Chapter 1). Both of these criticisms are relevant to the neoclassical theory of investment tax incentives.

The first criticism is that investment decisions do not generate an equilibrium path. In a given neoclassical disequilibrium situation, for example, where the marginal product of capital exceeds the user cost of capital, the adjustment requires additional investment. This additional investment generates additional incomes (profits). The additional incomes alter the state of expectations. The change in the expectations generates a new disequilibrium and a new set of investment decisions. This process continues through calendar time. A static capital stock or a steady state growth rate is unlikely to be obtained.

The second criticism is that the businesses sector, as shown in previous chapters, does not necessarily bear the burden of business taxes. Following an increase in business taxes, assuming those business taxes are spent by government on goods or services or on doles to the unemployed, where workers spend all they receive, and investment is fixed in the short period and, thus, insensitive to the change in business taxes, the level of national income will rise to maintain the aggregate level of after-tax profits. In short, when considering the effects of taxation on investment, the incidence of tax must also be considered. As described in the previous chapters, to understand fully the incidence of the tax, the impact of a change in the business tax on various categories of government expenditures and receipts, and the impacts of the changing composition of the government budget on aggregate income and profits must be understood. The neoclassical theory of investment, with its rigorous adherence to market clearing at full employment prohibits consideration of these incidence effects.

3   The Fallacy of the Core Assumptions of the Neoclassical Theory of Investment: the Gordon Critique

Gordon (1992) argues that the neoclassical theory of finance, which supports the neoclassical theory of investment, is based on a number of false assumptions:

- real persons are portfolio investors who hold only financial assets; while corporate persons hold and invest in real productive assets
- each corporation serves its stockholders
- the value of the corporation is independent of:
- its capital structure; and
- its dividend policy
- current investment opportunities are independent of the past.

Gordon rejects the first assumption because of the presence of uncertainty and risk aversion. A risk-averse individual may maximize utility at some level of wealth below the maximum amount (Gordon, 1992, p. 428). The investment decisions of corporations to maximize wealth are thus inconsistent with a financial asset holder's objective of maximizing utility. He rejects the second assumption because of the principal–agent problem. Corporate managers and stockholders are in conflict over the objectives of the firm. Gordon (1992, p. 429) cites Crotty (1990):

> Stockholder interests constrain the pursuit of management objectives. The neoclassical treatment of management as inside stockholders and, then posing the problem as a conflict between inside and outside stockholders is inappropriate, because: a) management may not be stockholders; and b) management holdings are not diversified; so management maximizes utility not net worth.

Gordon rejects the third assumption on the grounds that capital markets are not perfectly competitive. When capital markets are perfectly competitive, one form of finance is a perfect substitute for another form of finance, debt, equity or retained earnings, and the firm's financial policy is independent of its equilibrium value. However, studies have shown that the value of the firms is related to financial policy and, therefore, market imperfections are present. The tax deductibility of interest payments (where the personal tax rate is less than the corporate tax rate), the desire to hold corporate leverage over personal leverage, expected bankruptcy costs, unequal information, etc., all generate imperfections. In light of these imperfections, the neoclassical literature has been unable to explain why the optimal corporate leverage rates exceed actual leverage rates. Moreover, in light of market imperfections, firms should not pay dividends, and firms that pay dividends should have lower values. However, the evidence indicates that dividends have a positive impact on the value of the firm. In the neoclassical literature, imperfect capital markets are viewed not as a problem with the model, but as a problem with the real world.

The final assumption is the most questionable and it cuts right to the first-order condition in setting an optimal stock of capital. Implicit in this condition is that the required rate of return is independent of investment in all other periods. According to Gordon (1992, p. 436), this means that investment opportunities arise independently of the corporation's history! A corporation with no history has the same investment opportunities as if it had a history.

4 Uncertainty and Institutions: Vickers' and Crotty's Criticisms

Vickers (1992) spelled out five propositions in order clarify the issues involved in understanding investment behaviour. First, a macrofoundation is required to support a microeconomic argument (Vickers, 1992, p. 447). A macrofoundation is required when Say's law is non-operable and unemployment is present, and where uncertainty abounds and incoherence is present. Moreover, the rejection of Say's law raises the question: 'Where does the money come from' to finance investment, and at what cost? The answer to this question requires a knowledge of the financial structure and the determinants of money flows. The aggregate flows of money and the institutional structure contribute to the macro-foundations which have an impact on individual investment decisions. Second, investment decisions are made in the context of uncertainty subject to conjectures and ignorance, and, thus, neoclassical investment demand curves are unlikely to exist. Third, the short run takes precedence over the long run in the analysis of the investment decision. The presence of uncertainty and lack of coherence suggest that economic decisions are conditioned within the current institutional setting. Within this context the long-run history is made up of the consequences of short-run decisions, and the existence of a centre of gravity, like a steady-state capital stock, is denied. Fourth, the marginal efficiency of investment or capital, properly understood within this framework, remains a useful tool for understanding investment. The marginal efficiency of investment, defined as the discount rate that equates the demand price to the supply price of capital, can be 'rehabilitated' by removing from it any neoclassical notions about steadiness or smoothness. Fifth, 'investment expenditures are not subject to a savings constraint but to a finance constraint' (Vickers, 1992, p. 459), and credit expansions, increases in the money supply or increases in the velocity of money, lead to increased savings. The institutional structure and the resulting full marginal cost of relaxing the financing constraints to undertake new investment must be understood.

Crotty (1992) takes further issue with three core assumptions. First, the principal–agent problem has not been resolved. The notion that corporations operate to maximize the utility of owners is not empirically supported. With the rejection of this assumption, a single neoclassical theory of the firm does not exist, and the financial and real sectors operate semi-autonomously. The semi-autonomous operation of these sectors is inconsistent with the neoclassical vision of the economy. Second, the existence of neoclassical risk is unfounded. Known probability distributions of future outcomes do not exist, and, therefore, agents cannot have knowledge of them. Rather, economic decisions are made by social conventions, for example, as described by Keynes (1936). These conventions are 'fragile' and subject to change. Third, physical capital is illiquid and, thus, many investments are irreversible. In the neoclassical theory, the secondary markets are so well developed that a firm's only cost of capital is its rental value. If adjustment costs are included, these adjustment costs do not account for the irreversibility of investment decisions. The existence of irre-versibility, combined with uncertainty, destroys the vision of a well-functioning neoclassical economy.

5 Summary

The criticisms of Kalecki, Gordon, Vickers and Crotty raise the important question of how relevant the neoclassical theory is to its empirical conclusions. A sampling of the neoclassical literature indicates that the lack of convergence on specific issues, like the empirical definition of user costs, the impact of inflation, and a definitive conclusion as to the impact of taxation on investment is the result of a theoretically weak research programme. Perhaps this weakness can be best illustrated by considering the definition of user cost. User cost represents the expected present value of the stream of costs generated by an additional investment during its life. The fact that this *ex ante* value of user costs is not known is problematic in empirically testing for the determinants of investment. One solution to this problem is to assume that the *ex post* value is somehow related to the *ex ante* value. For example, Auerbach (1991, p. 193) states:

In principle, a solution is to follow the now common approach of specifying that, under a rational expectations hypothesis, the ex post value of a future value of [user cost] ... is distributed with an error around its true expected value.

Another solution is to use a variant of Tobin's *q*, (Tobin, 1978), where *q* captures expectations. To Vickers (1992) and Crotty (1992) these solutions are untenable. For them, the sort of behaviour that underlies these approaches is beyond the realm of the real world. For example, Crotty (1992, p. 486) states:

Where the information required to connect decision to outcome is incomplete and undependable, neoclassical theories have nothing – literally – to say.

These criticisms represent an indictment of the neoclassical approach. They suggest that many wrong questions are being asked, wrong hypotheses tested, dubious explanatory variables are being employed, and that the interpretations of the theoretical results are questionable. In attempting to consider the effects of taxation an alternative theory of investment is required.

3 THE IMPACT OF TAXATION ON INVESTMENT IN A KALECKIAN MODEL

As we have already explained in previous chapters, in a Kaleckian approach, the economy is assumed to operate at below full employment. Investment determines savings. Both microeconomic and macroeconomic foundations are present. The microeconomic foundations are present in the pricing behaviour of the firm that comes to bear on the distribution of income and the incidence of taxation. The macroeconomic foundations determine aggregate profit/cash flow and the financial structure. This Kaleckian approach has certain desirable features described by Crotty (1992, pp. 494–5). Firms are risk averse, the capital structure and degree of competition (monopoly) both matter and the theory is historically contingent. The approach is highly aggregative. With these features, Kalecki's core investment theory provides a useful point for extensions and refinements (see Courvisanos (1996)).

We now consider a statistical illustration as to how we have introduced taxation into Kalecki's theory of investment. From Chapter 3, Kalecki's investment equation can be written as:

$$I_{t+\tau} = \lambda P_t + r(\{[nDP + \delta P]/\pi\} - I_t) + B(t) \qquad (6.1)$$

where P = the level of profits, $\lambda = E/P$, n = the portion of new profits captured by new investment, π = the standard rate of profits, and δ = the rate of depreciation in the sense that it represents the rate at which profits are lost to existing capital, gained by new capital, as the result of technical progress.

As we show in Chapter 3, the impact of the tax system on investment is through the level of profits and the rate of depreciation. With no tax shifting, a change in the wage tax has no impact on rate of depreciation, and when the wage is shifted an increase in the wage tax rate increases the rate of depreciation. In contrast, an increase in the tax rate on profits, t_p, increases the rate of depreciation, and, if the profits tax is shifted, the shifting dampens the increase in the rate of depreciation.

To review our previous findings, the impact of taxation on the level of profits and, therefore, investment, depends on the type of tax change, the government budget stance and the nature of tax shifting. Assuming that government purchases and tax receipts are unrelated, an increase in the wage tax, if the wage tax is unshifted, reduces the level of profits. If the government has a balanced budget stance, an increase in the wage tax, through a reduction in workers' savings, increases the level of profits. If the wage tax is shifted, then this positive impact is reduced depending on the degree of shifting. In contrast, an unshifted increase in the profits tax reduces profits through a balanced budget multiplier effect, if workers' savings is non-zero. However, if the profits tax is shifted, this negative effect is reduced.

In summary, an increase (decrease) in the profits tax rate has two opposing impacts on investment. An increase in the profits tax tends to reduce profits while increasing the rate of depreciation. An increase in the wage tax rate has a negative impact on profits only if government expenditures are independent of the level of wage taxes.

4 SOME POLICY IMPLICATIONS

Our analysis suggests a number of policy implications. First, as shown in Chapter 3, changes in all taxes have an impact on the level of profits, depending upon mitigating effects, and, therefore, the definition of tax incentives should be broadened to include the impact of non-business taxes. For example, an increase in the regressiveness of the tax system, such as an increase in social security taxation will, holding other things constant, reduce the government budget deficit and profits and act as a disincentive to investment. If this additional tax is paid for by a reduction in personal (or worker) savings, the investment disincentive is reduced. Moreover, increases in taxes on dividends or increases in taxes on capital gains, if paid for by reductions in personal savings, will have no impact on profits (see Chapter 5). Increases in the business profits tax, if accompanied by increases in government purchases of infrastructure or by transfers to the unemployed, may have only a small impact on post-tax profits.

Second, the existence of these incidence effects has implications for the design of tax policy. It may be possible to stimulate investment with a minimal impact on the government budget deficit while, at the same time, fulfilling equity objectives. An increase in taxes on dividends or on capital gains, if largely paid for out of reduced personal savings, will have little impact on post-tax profits. If these additional tax revenues are used to finance transfers to the unemployed, post-tax corporate profits may actually increase resulting in new investment. The state, by redistributing income from the wealthy to the poor, may actually stimulate investment without any additional public debt burden.

5 EVIDENCE FROM THE US

We estimate a variant of equation (6.1) for the United States for the period beginning in the first quarter of 1980 and ending in the first quarter of 1993. We transform equation (6.1) by adding the capital consumption allowance, Co, to both sides, and by adding and subtracting the capital consumption allowance to the net investment term on the right-hand side. Thus, gross private nonresidential fixed investment, I', is written as:

$$I'_{rtt} = Co(1 + r) + \lambda P_t + r(\{[nDP_t + \delta P_t]/\pi\} - I'_t) + B(t) \qquad (6.2)$$

Equation (6.4) is rewritten as:

$$I'_{t+\tau} = Co(1 + r) + (\lambda + rn/\pi + (r/\pi)[\delta])P_t - rn/\pi(P_{t-1}) - rI'_t + B(t) \quad (6.2')$$

1   The Impact of Tax Rates on Investment

Now we can consider the impact of tax rates on investment. Given that both
wage (private sector compensation to employees) and profits taxes result in
changes in the flow of profits and the rate of depreciation, both taxes have an
impact on investment. By controlling for changes in one tax rate, the effect of
a change in the other tax rate on the investment can be measured. To consider
the effects of tax rates on investment, we derive a reduced form equation from
equation (6.2') i.e.:

$$I'_{t+\tau} = F(t, t_w, t_p, I'_t, I'_{t-1}) \tag{6.3}$$

where $F_{t_w} > = < 0$ and $F_{t_p} > = < 0$, depending on the relative impacts of a change
in the respective tax rates on the rate of depreciation and the level of profits;[4]
$F(I'_t) > 0$, because investment in time t generates profits and new investment
decisions in time t; and $F(I'_{t-1}) < 0$, because past investment depresses the
current rate of profits.

We estimate investment using a third degree polynomial, lagged twelve
quarters, with a far end point constraint, in order to capture the effects of
adjustment costs on investment. In the presence of adjustment costs, investment
decisions do not instantaneously change in response to changes in the profitability of investment. The empirical definitions of the average profits and
wage tax rates are given in the Appendix. We include a time variable as an
independent variable in order to capture Kalecki's 'innovations' factor. To
satisfy the stationarity condition, we estimate equation (6.3) in first difference
form. By first differencing, the constant in the investment function drops out
and the constant in the estimated equation is interpreted as the time trend
coefficient. All the results reported below are for first differences in the
variables. The tests for stationarity are summarized in the Appendix.

Table 6.1 below summarizes six sets of regression results for different com-
binations of independent variables. The first equation (see Table 6.1) is
investment regressed on lagged average profits and wage tax rates and itself.
The constant or trend coefficient is positive and statistically different from
zero. The cumulative effect of the average profits tax rate on investment is

---

4. In neoclassical economics, an increase in wage tax raises the real pre-tax wage, this higher
    wage could encourage investment as business seek to replace labor with capital. This neoclas-
    sical incidence effect is ignored in their investment tax incentive approaches, because the wage
    tax is seen as a disincentive to supply labour reducing the natural growth rate. In our Kaleckian
    approach, the effect of wage taxation on investment is through the profit and depreciation
    effects, and since less than full employment growth is allowed, we recognize that aggregate
    demand effects through changes in investment come to play in determining the volume of
    employment.

Table 6.1 *Gross private nonresidential fixed investment regressed on lagged average wage and profits tax rates and lagged investment. (All estimates were derived by using the maximum likelihood iterative technique, provided by TSP, or the Cochrane–Orcutt iterative technique.) Third Degree Polynomial Distributed Lag (12 quarters, far end constraint)*

Sample Period	Constant (t)	Σtp_{t-1}	Σtw_{t-1}	$\Sigma I'_{t-1}$	$\rho*$
1983:Q2 to	14.72	1072.5	– 20421	– 2.93	0.578
1993:Q1	(2.30)	[1746.5][†]	[7680.9][†]	[0.095][†]	(4.03)
SER = 8.37	Adj R^2 = 0.294	DW = 1.98	F 9,30 = 2.80		

Coefficients on lagged average profits tax rate

Lag	t – 1	t – 2	t – 3	t – 4	t – 5	t – 6
	– 58.92	– 11.09	33.69	73.99	108.38	135.40
	(– 0.349)	(– 0.068)	(0.181)	(0.367)	(0.524)	(0.648)
Lag	t – 7	t – 8	t – 9	t – 10	t – 11	t – 12
	153.74	161.87	158.39	141.90	110.95	64.12
	(0.716)	(0.722)	(0.688)	(0.639)	(0.589)	(0.544)

Coefficients on lagged average wage tax rate

Lag	t – 1	t – 2	t – 3	t – 4	t – 5	t – 6
	17.85	– 693.17	– 1304.4	– 1807.1	– 2192.4	– 2451.7
	(0.042)	(– 1.047)	(– 1.52)	(– 1.87)	(– 2.20)	(– 2.60)
Lag	t – 7	t – 8	t – 9	t – 10	t – 11	t – 12
	– 2576.1	– 2556.1	– 2385.3	– 2052.6	– 1550.0	– 868.7
	(– 2.88)	(– 3.18)	(– 3.38)	(– 3.46)	(– 3.39)	(– 3.22)

Coefficients on lagged investment

Lag	t – 1	t – 2	t – 3	t – 4	t – 5	t – 6
	– 0.490	– 0.394	– 0.324	– 0.276	– 0.245	– 0.225
	(– 2.96)	(– 3.45)	(– 3.39)	(– 2.97)	(– 2.67)	(– 2.50)
Lag	t – 7	t – 8	t – 9	t – 10	t – 11	t – 12
	– 0.213	– 0.202	– 0.188	– 0.166	– 0.130	– 0.077
	(– 2.33)	(– 2.09)	(– 1.84)	(– 1.62)	(– 1.45)	(– 1.33)

Notes:
*ρ = the serial correlation coefficient.
† The terms in square brackets represent the standard errors of the sum of the lagged coefficients.

A dynamic theory of taxation

Table 6.2   Gross private nonresidential fixed investment regressed on lagged average profits tax rate and lagged investment. (All estimates were derived by using the maximum likelihood iterative technique, provided by TSP, or the Cochrane–Orcutt iterative technique.) Third Degree Polynomial Distributed Lag (12 quarters, far end constraint)

Sample Period	Constant (t)	Σtp_{t-1}	Σtw_{t-1}	$\Sigma I'_{t-1}$	$\rho*$
1983:Q2 to	5.22	− 236.95	[−]	− 0.768	− 0.051
1993:Q1	(2.63)	[857.06]	[−]	[0.630]	(− 0.294)
SER = 9.02	Adj R^2 = 0.33	DW = 1.99		F 6,33 = 4.27	

Coefficients on lagged average profits tax rate

Lag	$t-1$	$t-2$	$t-3$	$t-4$	$t-5$	$t-6$
	11.92	48.16	59.69	51.89	30.16	− 0.138
	(0.071)	(.370)	(0.487)	(0.436)	(2.74)	(− 0.0014)
Lag	$t-7$	$t-8$	$t-9$	$t-10$	$t-11$	$t-12$
	− 33.62	− 64.90	− 88.61	− 99.35	− 91.75	− 60.40
	(− 0.037)	(− 0.685)	(− 0.865)	(− 0.940)	(− 0.965)	(− 0.970)

Coefficients on lagged investment

Lag	$t-1$	$t-2$	$t-3$	$t-4$	$t-5$	$t-6$
	0.114	0.0296	− 0.035	− 0.0815	− 0.112	− 0.129
	(0.759)	(0.346)	(− 0.652)	(− 1.78)	(− 2.46)	(− 2.83)
Lag	$t-7$	$t-8$	$t-9$	$t-10$	$t-11$	$t-12$
	− 0.133	− 0.127	− 0.112	− 0.090	− 0.062	− 0.032
	(− 2.78)	(− 2.32)	(− 1.78)	(− 1.34)	(− 1.01)	(− 0.079)

Notes:
*ρ = the serial correlation coefficient.
† The terms in square brackets represent the standard errors of the sum of the lagged coefficients.

positive, but none of the average profits tax rate coefficients is statistically different from zero. The cumulative effect of the average wage tax rate is negative. The coefficient indicates that a one percentage point increase in the first difference in the average wage tax rate over twelve quarters reduces the first difference in investment by about $204 billion. The coefficients on the lagged average wage tax rate are statistically different from zero at the 95 per cent confidence level for lags five through twelve quarters. The coefficient on the fourth quarter lagged average wage tax rate is statistically significant at the 90 per cent level. The coefficients on lagged investment are negative at the 95 per cent confidence level for lags one through eight.

Table 6.3 Gross private nonresidential fixed capital formation regressed on average wage tax rate and lagged investment. (All estimates were derived by using the maximum likelihood iterative technique provided by TSP or the Cochrane–Orcutt iterative technique.) Third Degree Polynomial Distributed Lag (12 quarters, far end constraint)

Sample Period	Constant (t)	Σtp_{t-1}	Σtw_{t-1}	$\Sigma I'_{t-1}$	$\rho*$
1983: Q2 to	14.88		– 18029	– 3.06	– 0.632
1993: Q1	(3.76)		[6220.9]	[0.875]	(– 4.89)
SER = 8.04	Adj R^2 = 0.36		DW = 1.97 F 6,33 = 4.69		

Coefficients on lagged average wage tax rate:

Lag	t – 1	t – 2	t – 3	t – 4	t – 5	t – 6
	194.4	– 384.5	– 926.4	– 1411.5	– 1820.4	– 2133.5
	(0.593)	(– 0.751)	(– 1.38)	(– 1.85)	(– 2.30)	(– 2.76)
Lag	t – 7	t – 8	t – 9	t – 10	t – 11	t – 12
	– 2331.2	– 2394.0	– 2302.3	– 2036.6	– 1577.4	– 905.0
	(– 3.18)	(– 3.54)	(– 3.76)	(– 3.83)	(– 3.77)	(– 3.62)

Coefficients on lagged investment

Lag	t – 1	t – 2	t – 3	t – 4	t – 5	t – 6
	– 0.556	– 0.420	– 0.325	– 0.264	– 0.230	– 0.213
	(– 3.78)	(– 4.09)	(– 3.73)	(– 3.13)	(– 2.73)	(– 2.52)
Lag	t – 7	t – 8	t – 9	t – 10	t – 11	t – 12
	– 0.209	– 0.208	– 0.203	– 0.188	– 0.157	– 0.094
	(– 2.39)	(– 2.25)	(– 2.10)	(– 1.98)	(– 1.86)	(– 1.80)

Notes:
*ρ = the serial correlation coefficient.
† The terms in square brackets represent the standard errors of the sum of the lagged coefficients.

Similar results are obtained for different sets of independent variables. In Table 6.2, for the first equation, investment is regressed on the lagged values of average profits tax rate and on lagged values of itself. The cumulative effect of the average profits tax rate on investment is now negative, but the lagged coefficients are not statistically different from zero. For the second equation, investment is regressed on lagged values of the average wage tax rate and on lagged values of itself. The results are qualitatively the same as those reported in Table 6.1. In Table 6.4, for the equation, investment is regressed on the lagged values of the average profits and wage tax rates (the lagged dependent variable is dropped). The coefficients on the lagged average profits tax rate are

A dynamic theory of taxation

Table 6.4   Gross private nonresidential fixed investment regressed on average wage and profits tax rates. (All estimates were derived by using the maximum likelihood iterative technique, provided by TSP, or the Cochrane–Orcutt iterative technique.) Third Degree Polynomial Distributed Lag (12 quarters, far end constraint)

Sample Period	Constant (t)	Σtp_{t-1}	Σtw_{t-1}	$\Sigma I'_{t-1}$	ρ^*
1983: Q2 to	6.185	− 522.02	− 12984.0	–	− 0.313
1993: Q1	(2.62)	[1259.5]	[5966.5]	–	(− 1.92)
SER = 9.27	Adj R^2 = 0.13		DW = 2.05	F 6,33 = 1.94	

Coefficients on lagged average profits tax rate

Lag	$t-1$	$t-2$	$t-3$	$t-4$	$t-5$	$t-6$
	− 161.7	− 128.7	− 98.9	− 72.5	− 49.5	30.1
	(− 0.968)	(− 0.896)	(− 0.629)	(− 0.440)	(− 0308)	(− 0.195)
Lag	$t-7$	$t-8$	$t-9$	$t-10$	$t-11$	$t-12$
	− 14.24	− 2.10	− 6.24	− 10.72	− 11.23	− 7.68
	(− 0.091)	(− 0.013)	(− 0.034)	(− 0.058)	(− 0.069)	(− 0.074)

Coefficients on lagged average wage tax rate

Lag	$t-1$	$t-2$	$t-3$	$t-4$	$t-5$	$t-5$
	− 176.4	− 821.3	− 1272.1	− 1550.8	− 1680.0	− 1681.0
	(− 0.397)	(− 1.49)	(− 1.86)	(− 2.04)	(− 2.15)	(− 2.23)
Lag	$t-7$	$t-8$	$t-9$	$t-10$	$t-11$	$t-12$
	− 1578.2	− 1392.1	− 1145.4	− 860.6	− 559.9	− 265.6
	(− 2.26)	(− 2.21)	(− 2.05)	(− 1.80)	(− 1.50)	(− 1.19)

Notes:
*ρ = the serial correlation coefficient.
† The terms in square brackets represent the standard errors of the sum of the lagged coefficients.

negative, but, again, the coefficients are not statistically different from zero. The coefficients on the lagged average wage tax rate are, again, all negative. In this case, the pattern of the statistical coefficients changes and the size of the cumulative effect decreases. In equation 6.3, investment is regressed on lagged values of the average profits tax rate (the average wage tax rate and the lagged dependent variables are dropped). The coefficients on the lagged average profits tax rate are negative, the coefficients for lags eight through twelve quarters are statistically different from zero. In Table 6.3, investment is regressed on the average wage tax rate (the average profits tax rate and the lagged dependent

Table 6.5   Gross private nonresidential fixed investment regressed on lagged average profits tax rate. (All estimates were derived using the maximum likelihood iterative technique provided by TSP or the Cochrane–Orcutt iterative technique.) Third Degree Polynomial Lag (12 quarters, far end constraint)

Sample Period	Constant (t)	Σtp_{t-1}	Σtw_{t-1}	$\Sigma I'_{t-1}$	ρ^*
1983: Q2 to 1993: Q1	4.02 (1.91)	– 1597.7 [957.65]			– 0.289 (– 1.81)
SER = 9.54	Adj R² = 0.08		DW = 2.06 F 3,36 = 2.11		

Coefficients on lagged average profits tax rate

Lag	t – 1	t – 2	t – 3	t – 4	t – 5	t – 6
	– 99.20	– 2.20	33.08	20.30	– 26.85	– 94.69
	(– 0.656)	(– 0.018)	(– 0.262)	(– 0.156)	(– 0.214)	(– 0.814)
Lag	t – 7	t – 8	t – 9	t – 10	t – 11	t – 12
	– 169.6	– 237.8	– 285.6	– 299.4	– 265.6	– 170.3
	(– 1.54)	(– 2.11)	(– 2.39)	(– 2.47)	(– 2.46)	(– 2.42)

Notes:
*ρ = the serial correlation coefficient.
† The terms in square brackets represent the standard errors of the sum of the lagged coefficients.

Table 6.6   Gross private nonresidential fixed investment regressed on average wage tax rate (All estimates were derived by using the maximum likelihood iterative technique, provided by TSP, or the Cochrane–Orcutt iterative technique.) Third Degree Polynomial Distributed Lag (12 quarters, far end constraint)

Sample Period	Constant (t)	Σtp_{t-1}	Σtw_{t-1}	$\Sigma I'_{t-1}$	ρ^*
1983: Q2 to 1993: Q1	5.65 (2.82)		– 11295 [3603.1]		0.262 (– 1.63)
SER – 9.00	Adj R² = 0.19 DW = 2.01 F 3,36 = 1.94				

Coefficients on lagged average wage tax rate

Lag	t – 1	t – 2	t – 3	t – 4	t – 5	t – 6
	– 56.4	– 716.7	– 1167.1	– 1434.4	– 1545.1	– 1525.8
	(– 0.161)	(– 2.04)	(– 2.84)	(– 3.18)	(– 3.36)	(– 3.42)
Lag	t – 7	t – 8	t – 9	t – 10	t – 11	t – 12
	– 1403.8	– 1205.1	– 956.79	– 685.4	– 417.68	– 180.3
	(– 3.33)	(– 3.10)	(– 2.61)	(– 2.07)	(– 1.55)	(– 1.09)

Notes:
*ρ = the serial correlation coefficient.
† The terms in square brackets represent the standard errors of the sum of the lagged coefficients.

variables are dropped). The results are similar to those presented above. The cumulative effect of changes in the average wage tax rate remains quite large, and the coefficients are statistically different from zero for lags two to ten quarters.

In summary, the evidence indicates that average tax rates on profits and wages have an impact on the aggregate level of investment. Moreover, the results show that the average wage tax rate has a negative and relatively large effect on investment for different sets of independent variables.[5] In contrast, the results show that the average profits tax rate has a relatively small effect on investment. The evidence of this effect is only apparent when the other independent variables are dropped from the variable list. This conclusion requires the definition of tax incentives to be modified to account for the incidence effects of wage taxes on profits and, perhaps, the depreciation effect of wages and profits taxes on investment. Moreover, given that changes in the average wage tax rate have a relatively larger impact on investment than do changes in the average profits tax rate, this result suggests that changes in the average wage tax rate might be preferable in order to effect changes in investment.

This conclusion is useful for understanding how traditional tax stimulus policies, policies designed to reduce the corporate tax rate on new or existing investment goods, might be swamped by other factors. A relatively large reduction in the average profits tax rate, given a relatively small tax base, may only generate a small increase in profits and investment, whereas a relatively small increase in the average wage tax rate, given a relatively large tax base, may result in a relatively large reduction in profits and investment. This latter effect may be useful in explaining the failure of 'traditional' investment tax incentives to alter significantly the investment share of GDP in the United States during the 1980s. As US data show (available on request from the authors), the average tax rate on wages has been drifting up while the share of investment share in GDP has been declining.

6   CONCLUSION

In this chapter, Kalecki's theories of investment and tax incidence have been combined to illustrate the effects of taxation on investment. We have tested the theories using recent US data and we have derived some 'surprising results' of 'practical importance'. In particular, we provide evidence that changes in average wage tax rates swamp the effects of changes in average profits tax

5. This relatively larger effect is to be expected given that the wage tax base is much greater than the profits tax base.

rates. These results provide evidence that undermines the neoclassical position on three points. First, average tax rates as opposed to marginal tax rates do matter. Second, the economic incidence of taxation must be explicitly considered when considering the effectiveness of tax incidence. Finally, equity considerations need not be subordinated to efficiency objectives. A redistribution of income, through the tax system, from higher to lower income groups, may actually increase the profitability of investment. These conclusions are also relevant to the balanced budget debate in the US. The elimination of the low income tax credit coupled with reductions in the capital gains tax may frustrate supply-siders, and other such 'trickle down' policies will likely reduce investment and its share of GDP, in other words, cause further stagnation.

APPENDIX

1 Deriving the Average Wage Tax Rate

The wage tax rate was calculated by, first, finding private sector compensation to employees and then by estimating the taxes paid on private sector compensation to employees, and by dividing this amount by pre-tax compensation to employees. Private sector compensation to employees is measured as total compensation to employees less compensation to government employees. The taxes paid out of private sector compensation were approximated by multiplying private sector compensation's share of personal income by personal and indirect business taxes and by multiplying private sector compensation's share of total compensation to employees by contributions to social insurance. The sum of these two products is the estimate of taxes paid on private sector compensation. The average tax rate on private sector compensation to employees, t_w, equals the estimate of the tax divided by the private sector pre-tax compensation to employees.

2 Deriving the Average Profits Tax Rate

The average tax rate on profits, t_p, was derived by including an estimate of the taxes paid on personal dividends and net corporate interest. The sum of the shares of personal dividends and net corporate interest in personal income were multiplied by personal and indirect tax receipts. This amount was added to corporate tax receipts to derive total profit taxes. Total profits taxes divided by gross corporate profits yields the average profits tax rate. Gross corporate profits are defined as the sum of undistributed corporate profits, dividends, corporate net interest, corporate consumption of fixed capital and corporate tax receipts.

3   Tests for Stationarity

Tests for stationarity were derived using the Augmented Dickey–Fuller method
as provided by Micro-TSP. For the business fixed investment series, the null
hypothesis that the series was non-stationary was not rejected. The test results
are available upon request. For the first differences in the investment series, the
null hypothesis was rejected using three different regression equations: 1)
without the constant and the trend; 2) with the constant, but without the trend;
and 3) with the constant and the trend. As is shown in Table 6.1A, the
Dickey–Fuller T-statistics are greater than the McKinnon critical values at the
5 per cent and 10 per cent confidence levels.

Table 6.1A Tests for stationarity of the first differences in business fixed investment

(a)	Eq 6.1		Eq. 6 2		Eq.6. 3	
Variable:	$\Delta I(-1)$	Constant $\Delta I(-1)$		Constant $\Delta I(-1)$		Trend
Sample period 1981:Q1 to 1993:Q1						
Coefficient	−0.476	1.438	−0.503	0.660	−0.501	0.027
t-stats.	(−3.73)	(1.00)	(−3.86)	(0.202)	(−3.80)	(0.266)
McKinnon Critical Value						
5%	−1.94		−2.92		−3.50	
10%	1.62		−2.90		−3.18	
SER	9.79		9.79		9.88	
Adjusted R^2	0.22		0.22		0.21	
DW	2.15		2.13		2.13	
F	−		14.92		7.34	

(b)	Eq. 6.4		Eq. 6.5		Eq. 6.6	
Variable:	$\Delta I(-1)$	Constant $\Delta I(-1)$		Constant $\Delta I(-1)$		Trend
Sample Period 1983:Q2 to 1993:Q1						
Coefficient	−0.533	2.73	−0.602	7.46	−0.633	−0.138
t-stats.	(−3.69)	(1.65)	(−4.08)	(1.46)	(−4.20)	(−0.98)
McKinnon Critical Value						
5%	−1.95		−2.94		−3.52	
10%	−1.62		−2.61		−3.19	
SER	10.26		10.05		10.05	
Adjusted R^2	0.26		0.29		0.29	
DW	2.03		2.02		2.00	
F	−		16.68		8.81	

REFERENCES

Auerbach, A.J. (1983), 'Corporate taxation in the United States', *Brookings Papers on Economic Activity*, **2**, 451–505.

Auerbach, A.J. and Hassett, K. (1990), 'Investment, tax policy and the Tax Reform Act of 1986', in Slemrod, J. (ed.), *Do Taxes Matter? The Impact of the Tax Reform Act of 1986*, Cambridge, MA, MIT Press.

Auerbach, A.J. and Hines, J.R. (1988), 'Investment tax incentives and frequent tax reforms', *American Economic Review*, **78**, 2, 211–6.

Auerbach, A.J., Hines, J.R. and Oliner, S.D. (1992), 'Reassessing the social returns to equipment investment', *Economic Activity Section Paper* 129, Washington, D.C., Federal Reserve Board of Governors.

Blundell, R., Bond, S., Devereux, M. and Schianterelli, F. (1992), 'Investment and Tobin's *q*', *Journal of Econometrics*, **51**, 233–57.

Bosworth, B.P. (1985), 'Taxes and the investment recovery', *Brookings Papers on Economic Activity*, **1**, 1–38.

Brainard, W.C. and Tobin, J. (1968), 'Pitfalls in financial model building', *American Economic Review*, **58** (2), 99–122.

Chirinko, R.S. (1988), 'Business tax policy, the Lucas Critique lessons from the 1980s', *American Economic Review*, **78** (2), 206–10.

Chirinko, R.S. (1993), 'Business fixed investment spending: modeling strategies, empirical results and policy implications', *Journal of Economic Literature*, **31**, 1875–911.

Clark, P. (1993), 'Tax incentives and equipment investment', *Brookings Papers on Economic Activity*, **1**, 317–437.

Courvisanos, J. (1996), *Investment Cycles in Capitalist Economies*, Cheltenham, Edward Elgar Publishing Ltd.

Crotty, J.R. (1992), 'Neoclassical and Keynesian approaches to the theory of investment', *Journal of Post Keynesian Economics*, **14** (4), 483–96.

Davidson, P. (1983), 'Rational expectations; a fallacious foundation for studying crucial decision-making processes', *Journal of Post Keynesian Economics*, **5** (2), 182–98.

DeLong, J.B. and Summers, L.H. (1992), 'Equipment investment and economic growth: how strong is the nexus?', *Brookings Papers on Economic Activity*, **2**, 157–99.

Fazzari, S., Hubbard, G. and Petersen, B. (1988a), 'Financing constraints and corporate investment, *Brookings Papers on Economic Activity*, **1**, 141–206.

Fazzari, S., Hubbard, G. and Petersen, B. (1988b), 'Investment, financing decisions and tax policy', *American Economic Review*, **78** (2), 200–5.

Feldstein, M.S. (1982), 'Inflation, tax rules and investment: some econometric evidence', *Econometrica*, **50** (4), 825–62.

Feldstein, M.S. (1987), *The Effects of Taxation on Capital Accumulation*, Chicago, University of Chicago Press.

Gordon, M.J. (1992), 'The Neoclassical and a Post Keynesian theory of investment', *Journal of Post Keynesian Economics*, **14** (4), 425–43.

Hall, R.E. and Jorgensen, D.W. (1976), 'Tax policy and investment behaviour', *American Economic Review*, **57**, 391–414.

Harcourt, G.C. (1972), *Some Cambridge Controversies in the Theory of Capital*, Cambridge, Cambridge University Press.

Jorgensen, D.W. (1971), 'Econometric studies of business behavior: a survey', *Journal of Economic Literature*, **9** (4), 1111–47.

Kalecki, M. (1937a), 'Principle of increasing risk', *Economica*, **4** (76), 441–7.

Kalecki, M. (1971/1937), 'A theory of commodity, income and capital taxation', Economic Journal, **47**, 444–50. Reprinted in Kalecki, M. (1971) *Selected Essays on the Dynamics of the Capitalist Economy*, 1933–1970, Cambridge, Cambridge University Press.

Kalecki, M. (1972), *Selected Essays on the Economic Growth of the Socialist and the Mixed Economy*, Cambridge, Cambridge University Press.

Keynes, J.M. (1936), *The General Theory of Employment, Interest and Money*, New York, Harcourt Brace.

Laramie, A.J. Mair, D., Miller, A.G. and Stratopoulos, T. (1996), 'The impact of taxation on gross private nonresidential fixed investment in a Kaleckian model: some empirical evidence', *Journal of Post Keynesian Economics*, **19** (2), 243–56.

Lucas, R.E. (1976), 'Econometric policy evaluation; a critique', *Journal of Monetary Economics*, **1**, 19–46.

Moggridge, D. (1983), *The Collected Writings of John Maynard Keynes: Volume XII Economic Articles and Correspondence*, London, Macmillan.

Robinson, J. (1980), *What are the Questions and Other Essays*, Armonk, NY, M.E. Sharpe, Inc.

Sawyer, M.C. (1985), *The Economics of Michal Kalecki*, London, Macmillan.

Schwarz, J. (1977), *The Subtle Anatomy of Capitalism*, Santa Monica, Goodyear Publishing Co. Ltd.

Summers, L.H. (1981a), 'Taxation and corporate investment: a q-theory approach', *Brookings Papers on Economic Activity*, **1**, 67–127.

Summers, L. H. (1981b), 'Tax policy and corporate investment' in Meyer, L.H. (ed.), *The Supply-Side Effects of Economic Policy*, St. Louis, MO., Center for the Study of American Business.

Tobin, J. (1969), 'A general equilibrium approach to monetary theory', *Journal of Money, Credit and Banking*, **1** (1), 15–29.

Tobin, J. (1978), 'Monetary policies and the economy; the transmission mechanism', *Southern Economic Journal*, **44** (3), 421–31.

Vickers, D. (1992), 'The investment function: five propositions in response to Professor Gordon', *Journal of Post Keynesian Economics*, **14** (4), 445–64.

7. The short-period macroeconomic incidence and effects of state and local taxes[1]

1 INTRODUCTION

Typically, in discussions of fiscal policy, the role of the central or federal government is emphasized and that of states or local governments is ignored. This tendency is not surprising. The fiscal policies of any one state or locality are likely to have only a marginal or minimal impact on the performance of the economy as a whole. However, it would be wrong for a number of reasons to conclude that the fiscal policies of states or localities have no significant impact on the national economy. First, state and local government receipts and expenditures represent a significant share of GDP and, thus, affect aggregate spending and economic growth. Second, the provision of government goods and services is performed primarily at the state or local level and is likely to have both aggregate demand and aggregate supply effects (see the *Economic Report of the President*, February, 1994). Third, the rise in the United States of the 'new fiscal federalism' in the 1980s, the US Federal government budget impasse ('gridlock') and the increased demand for government services have forced states and localities to expand their tax bases and the scope of their activities. Finally, given the existence of national trends in state and local fiscal policies in the US, these factors in concert have come to bear on the aggregate performance of the economy.

In this chapter, we approach the problem of the incidence and macroeconomic effects of state and local taxes in the US from the Kaleckian perspective we have developed in earlier chapters. In particular, we stress that the incidence of state and local taxes on personal income, corporate profits, sales or property depends on institutional factors embodied in the federal system of the US which cause the incidence of these taxes to be different from the incidence of similar taxes levied at the federal level.

Our approach contrasts with the orthodox view as stated for example by Kotlikoff and Summers (1987). The orthodox view on tax incidence is reflected

1. This chapter is a revision of Laramie and Mair (1996) and Laramie and Mair (1997).

in the neoclassical theory of income distribution. Whether taxes are levied on commodities, incomes or wealth (property), they ultimately affect the demand for and supply of factors and, hence, factor returns. Orthodox analysis then compares factor incomes before and after the imposition of a tax to determine its incidence. Within the family of orthodox models, the economic incidence of taxes may be less than, equal to or greater than the legal incidence. This incidence is independent of who pays the tax, whether producer or consumer, or of the level of government, federal, state or local, to which the tax is paid.

Orthodox models of tax incidence range from partial equilibrium to general equilibrium to dynamic and are all supported by the standard set of core assumptions of market clearing and marginal productivity theory of income distribution. Moreover, when considering the effects of taxation in a general equilibrium framework, factors of production are assumed to be in fixed supply and highly mobile. Thus, the aggregate demand effects of tax changes are assumed to be nullified (Mieszkowski, 1972). As we have argued earlier in this book, we consider this to be an inappropriate basis from which to study the macroeconomic effects of taxation.

2 A KALECKIAN FRAMEWORK FOR CONSIDERING THE MACROECONOMIC EFFECTS AND INCIDENCE OF STATE AND LOCAL TAXATION

We develop our Kaleckian analysis along similar lines to earlier chapters. In particular, we combine the theory of national income determination developed in Chapter 2 with the definition of corporate profits presented in Chapter 5. From Chapter 2, the level of national income is written as:

$$Y = \Pi/(1 - \alpha) \tag{7.1}$$

where Y = national income; Π = the level of pre-tax profits; and a = the wage share. If we follow Levy and Levy (1983) and define aggregate profits simply as corporate profits, then:

$$\Pi = P + T_p = I + X + (G - T_v) + D - S_p - Z \tag{7.2}$$

where P = post-tax corporate profits; I = gross private domestic investment minus inventory valuation adjustment; X = net foreign investment; T_p = profit tax receipts; T_v = wage tax receipts; G = government purchases; D = sum of corporate net interest and dividends; S_p = personal savings; and Z = sum of non-corporate consumption of fixed capital, wage accruals less disbursements, capital grants received by the US and the statistical discrepancy (see Chapter 5 for this derivation). National income can be rewritten as a function of expenditures (among other things) assuming:

$$T_v = t_v(V), \quad 0 < t_v < 1 \tag{7.3}$$

$$S_p = s(Y), 0 < s < 1 \tag{7.4}$$

and noting that:

$$V = \alpha(Y) \tag{7.5}$$

that is:

$$Y = [I + X + G + D - Z]/[(1 - \alpha) + (t_v)\alpha + s] \tag{7.6}$$

As a result of defining aggregate profits as corporate profits, our discussion of the effects of taxation on national income, as described in Chapter 2, are modified. As in Chapter 2, national income is pushed up according to the 'distribution factors', in this case the wage share, α, so that profits are realized. However, the channels through which taxation affects the level of profits are modified. Within the context of this definition, our discussion in Chapter 5 on the incidence of taxation on corporate profits is relevant. The incidence of a tax on profits is determined by two sets of effects. The first is a public sector effect that depends on the government's budget stance. The second is a private sector effect that depends on: 1) the reaction of personal savings to the government's tax and budget stance; 2) the reaction of investment to the tax in the long period; and 3) the change in corporate markups with respect to the tax. Holding other things constant, a $1 increase in a profits tax results in a reduction of $1 in post-tax corporate profits, but this effect is mitigated depending on the public and private sector effects. If the government spends the tax receipts on final goods and services, the incidence of the profits tax on corporations is reduced depending on the reaction of personal savings to the resultant change in aggregate income. Moreover, if corporations respond to a tax by altering their markups, then the economic incidence may vary even further from the legal incidence. These various effects will have an impact on future investment, through their effect on profits, which may lead to cumulative incidence effects.

In determining the incidence of a tax, the relative strengths of these various effects must be considered. The budget stance of the Federal or central government is a policy decision and typically, at the national level, little can be said about it *a priori*. However, it is possible to be rather more specific about the relative strengths of the private sector effects. We expect these to be rather weak. First, consider the behaviour of savings. If the marginal propensity to save is low, then a change in income, given a change in taxation, is likely to have a small impact on post-tax corporate profits. Second, the extent to which taxes have an impact on aggregate post-tax profits, via the extent to which taxes are shifted through changes in corporate markups, is diluted by a number of factors. For example, in considering the incidence of the corporate profits tax, Pechman (1987) has stressed that businesses only know their tax liability *ex post*, and, therefore, immediate shifting of a profits tax through changes in markups is unlikely. Also, inter-firm competition may inhibit the extent to which a tax is shifted forwards or backwards.

These views are also expressed by Sylos-Labini (1979) when he argues that non-direct costs may not be passed along because of inter-firm differences. However, Coutts, Godley and Nordhaus (1978), in analysing the relationship between profit margins and corporate taxes with UK data, have suggested that little shifting takes place in the short period (a year or less), but there is some full, or more than full, shifting in the medium and long runs. Even if full, or more than full, shifting is the outcome, the extent to which such shifting has an impact on the level of aggregate post-tax corporate profits depends on: 1) the change in aggregate income with respect to the change in profit margins; and 2) the extent to which personal savings change with respect to the change in aggregate income. Again, if the marginal propensity to save is relatively low, we expect the change in corporate profits with respect to a change in corporate markups to be relatively small.

If the private sector effects are relatively weak, the incidence of the corporation income tax depends largely on the budget stance of the Federal or central government. The economic incidence of the corporate income tax is determined politically or institutionally by the manner in which political and/or institutional factors are reflected in the government's budget stance.

3   A FRAMEWORK FOR CONSIDERING THE SHORT PERIOD EFFECTS AND INCIDENCE OF STATE AND LOCAL TAXES

To consider the effect of state and local taxes on post-tax corporate profits in the US, we rewrite equation (7.2) by separating out the state, local and Federal budget deficits and consider the institutional and political factors that have determined the budget stances of state and local governments,

$$P = I + X + (G - T)_f + (G - T)_{sl} + D - S_p - Z \qquad (7.7)$$

where the subscripts f and sl represent the federal and state and local governments.

We separate out the state and local budgets from the Federal budget for three reasons. First, in the US the state and local governments have an independent authority to raise and spend tax receipts. Second, state and local governments do not have the authority to create money or the economic wherewithal to engage in chronic deficit financing. Finally, state and local governments have various forms of legal limitations on their borrowings (Aaronson and Hilley, 1986).

We argue that the following factors, as mitigated by private sector reactions, have an impact on the incidence of state and local taxes: 1) the structure of state and local government receipts; 2) the expenditure functions of state and local governments; 3) their budget stance as determined by state and local debt and deficit limitations; and 4) inter-governmental relations. Following a brief discussion of these issues, we summarize the factors that have a bearing on the incidence of state and local taxation on corporate profits. We will argue that private sector reactions, because of the budget stances of state and local governments, are unlikely to mitigate the incidence of state and local taxes on corporate profits.

First, we examine the impact of the structure of government receipts by assuming that tax receipts are simply held, but not used, by the state and local governments. By doing so, we consider how the private sector responses to the structure of taxation alone affect corporate profits.

In the US *National Income and Product Accounts* (NIPA), state and local government receipts are divided into personal and non-tax receipts, corporate profits tax accruals, indirect business tax and non-tax accruals, contributions for social insurance and Federal grants-in-aid. During the 1980s and early 1990s, on average the composition of tax receipts was as follows: personal tax and non-tax receipts – 17.8 per cent; corporate profit tax accruals – 3.6 per cent; indirect business tax and non-tax accruals – 50.8 per cent; contributions for social insurance – 8.2 per cent; and Federal grants-in-aid – 19.6 per cent. Holding other things constant (on the right-hand side of equation (8.5)), the change in state and local government tax receipts is inversely related to corporate profits, dollar for dollar. The effect of taxation on corporate profits is mitigated by the extent to which personal savings change, given a change in state and local government tax receipts. To assess the impact of state and local taxes on personal savings, we consider the incidence of these taxes on household incomes.

In the NIPA personal tax and non-tax receipts are divided into personal income taxes, non-taxes and other taxes. During the 1980s and early 1990s, personal income tax was the largest of this category, accounting, on average, for 13.6 per cent of total receipts. On average, non-taxes and other taxes accounted for 1.9 per cent and 2.3 per cent of total receipts respectively. In an attempt to measure the distribution of tax burdens, Pechman (1986) allocated personal income tax to individual taxpayers. We follow the same practice and conclude, therefore, that the impact of this tax on personal savings and, thus, on corporate profits, depends on household marginal propensity to consume.

In the NIPA indirect business tax and non-tax accruals are divided into sales taxes, property taxes and other. Over the period under consideration, indirect business tax and non-tax accruals accounted, on average, for about 51 per cent of state and local government receipts. On average, sales taxes made up 24.4 per cent of total receipts, property taxes 20.5 per cent and other 5.8 per cent. Again following Pechman (1986) we assume that sales taxes are shifted onto consumption. Thus, we assume that consumption expenditures fall by the full amount of the tax and, therefore, that personal savings are unaffected by the tax. We make the same assumption with regard to 'other' indirect business taxes.

Property taxes represent taxes paid on land and improvements and are divided into taxes paid on business property (53 per cent) and taxes paid on homeowners' property (47 per cent). The homeowners' property tax is assumed to fall completely on imputed rental services derived from home ownership (included in personal consumption expenditures). Therefore, like the sales tax, this reduces consumption and the imputed income by the amount of the tax. Corporate profits decline by the amount of the tax if the decline in imputed income causes an equivalent decline in the consumption of goods or services produced in the corporate sector, i.e. there is no impact on personal savings.

The property taxes paid by businesses, both corporate and non-corporate, fall on their respective incomes. These taxes can affect personal savings by altering the distribution of income to households, which is affected in two ways: 1) through an income effect; and 2) through a tax shifting effect via altered business markups. The income effect arises when the tax reduces the income flows to households. For example, corporate businesses may reduce their dividend payments to households or owners of non-corporate businesses may have less personal disposable income following an increase in the business property tax. The markup shifting effect occurs when businesses alter their markups in an attempt to shift the tax. A change in the markup alters the distribution of income and the flow of income to wage earners. Given wage earners' marginal propensity to save, the level of personal savings falls and the level of profits rises, *ceteris paribus*.

Over the period, contributions for social security represented on average 8.2 per cent of state and local government gross receipts. Following Pechman (1986), we treat contributions to social insurance as falling directly on compensation to employees. As a consequence, their impact on corporate profits depends on the marginal propensity to save out of compensation to employees.

As we have indicated above, one of the factors that influences the incidence of state and local government taxes on corporate profits is the reaction of the private sector to the government's budget stance. This reaction depends on what state and local governments do with their tax receipts. If their receipts are saved and paid for via declines in consumption expenditures, corporate profits decline by the full amount of the tax receipts, regardless of the source of these receipts. However, if the tax receipts are used to finance government expenditures, then the impact of taxation depends on how these expenditures flow into the corporate sector. Government purchases of goods and services from the corporate sector, for example, flow directly back into the corporate sector and, therefore, offset the negative impact of the taxes on corporate profits. Government purchases from the non-corporate sector, ignoring the foreign sector, compensation to employees, government transfer payments and government interest payments are payments to households. The flow of these expenditures back to the corporate sector depends on households' marginal propensity to save.

The functions of state and local governments are summarized in their budgets, the bulk of which are devoted to government purchases. Over the 1980s and early 1990s, on average 88.3 per cent of expenditures was devoted to government purchases. Of this amount, 58.7 per cent and 29.7 per cent of total expenditures were devoted to compensation to employees and to other government purchases respectively. Analysis of the various categories of state and local government expenditures suggests that on average over 70 per cent was distributed directly to households.

The data suggest that much of the incidence of state and local taxes on corporate profits in the US over the period depends on the relative impacts of taxes and expenditures on personal savings. The imposition of taxes reduces personal savings, whereas the spending of tax receipts increases personal savings. To determine the relative impacts of these effects, it is necessary to establish the budget stances of state and local governments and the relative marginal propensities to save with respect to changes in various state and local government tax receipts and expenditures.

We now consider the budget stances of state and local governments and the impact of inter-governmental relations. Most states in the US have some form of legal restriction, constitutional or statutory, which limits their budget deficits. According to Fisher (1988), the governor must submit, or the legislature must pass, balanced budgets; another thirty-six states are prohibited from carrying budget deficits into the next fiscal year and many states have debt limitations. The existence of these restrictions has accounted for the surpluses in state and local government budgets. During the 1980s these surpluses ranged between 6 per cent and 12 per cent of the gross receipts of state and local governments. These surpluses have largely disappeared in the 1990s so that by 1992 the budget surplus was only 0.8 per cent of gross receipts. This surplus can be attributed to the surplus in the state and local government insurance fund. The 'other' portion of the state and local government budget surplus has been consistently negative in recent years.

The budget stance of state and local governments implies that the distribution of gross receipts to various uses, as reflected in government expenditures, follows a pattern similar to expenditures. The impact of state and local taxes on corporate profits depends on the redistributive effects of state and local government budgets and the resultant impact on personal savings.

Governmental relations among the Federal, state and local governments in the US encompass many activities, ranging from Federal government mandates, to deductibility of state and local government taxes, to exclusion from Federal taxes of state and municipal bonds, to grants-in-aid. During the 1980s, two of the major changes in fiscal inter-governmental arrangements that occurred were: 1) the elimination of the deduction for sales taxes; and 2) consolidation and reduction in grants-in-aid to state and local governments. The ratio of sales taxes to total receipts or to tax receipts shows no significant trend since its elimination under the Tax Reform Act of 1986. In contrast, the reduction in Federal grants-in-aid has induced state and local governments to reduce their budget surpluses and to increase their reliance on income and property taxes in order to balance rising expenditures. Thus, in determining the incidence of state and local government taxes, we are particularly concerned with the impact of Federal grants-in-aid to state and local governments.

Federal grants-in-aid affect the incidence of state and local government taxes on corporate profits by altering the government budget stance. If the Federal government has a marginal propensity to spend greater than that of state and local governments, then the transfer of tax revenues from the Federal to state and local governments reduces the aggregate propensity to spend out of tax receipts and, thus, alters the impact of taxes on aggregate profits. Moreover, if state and local governments substitute Federal grants-in-aid for other revenue sources, such as personal and property tax receipts, the incidence of these taxes on corporate profits and other forms of income may be altered.

In 1981, President Reagan proposed a 'new' fiscal federalism whose purposes were to make government more responsive and to reduce the Federal government budget deficit (Aaronson and Hilley, 1986). The evidence from the 1980s suggests that the Reagan Administration did have some success as states and local governments became less dependent on Federal grants-in-aid, reduced their surpluses, slowed the rate of increase in their expenditures and increased their reliance on other forms of taxation. However, beginning in 1990, Federal grants-in-aid as a percentage of state and local government receipts have started to increase again. In 1993, grants-in-aid were about 20.5 per cent of state and local government receipts as compared to a low of 17.3 per cent in 1987 and a high of 25 per cent in 1978.

If we assume that Federal tax receipts and expenditures are insensitive to changes in Federal grants-in-aid, then Federal grants-in-aid have reduced the incidence of state and local government taxes on corporate profits. Federal grants-in-aid have allowed the average propensity to spend out of tax receipts of state and local governments to exceed one.

The impact of state and local government taxes on aggregate profits is determined by the difference between state and local government expenditures and tax receipts, mitigated by the net reaction of personal savings to these expenditures and receipts. To identify the incidence of state and local government tax receipts on corporate profits, we must do two things: 1) we must analyse the impact of selected state and local government tax receipts and expenditures on personal savings; and 2) we must estimate the average propensity to consume out of state and local government expenditures directly distributed to households.

To assess the impact of selected state and local tax receipts on personal savings, we estimate a personal savings function. We express personal savings as a function of different definitions of personal disposable income and itself, lagged by one quarter. We express each of the variables in current dollars. The first definition of personal disposable income we use is the standard definition in the NIPA. Our second definition is the first plus net state and local government transfer payments which are defined as the difference between the sum of compensation to employees and transfers to persons and the sum of personal tax receipts and social security contributions. The third definition is the first definition less government transfer payments, defined as compensation to government employees and transfers to persons. Using these various definitions, we derive the regression results presented in Table 7.1.

The results show that all the coefficients, except those on the lagged dependent variable, are not statistically different from zero. These estimates imply that personal savings, at least within one quarter, are insensitive to changes in state and local government net transfer payments, state and local government transfer payments and corporate and indirect business taxes. As a consequence, the incidence of state and local taxes, at least in the short period, is determined by the difference between government expenditures and tax receipts. To test for the robustness of this result, we attempt to estimate the average propensities to consume out of various incomes: private sector compensation to employees; property incomes (the sum of corporate profits, proprietors' income, non-corporate net interest (corporate net interest is already included in corporate profits) and rental income); Federal government expenditures distributed directly to households (government compensation to employees, government transfers to persons and net interest paid by government); and state and local government expenditures distributed directly to households. To estimate these propensities, we use a variant of Weintraub's

Table 7.1   The impact of selected state and local government tax receipts on personal savings in the US 1980:Q2 to 1993:Q1 (ordinary least squares)

Constant	Personal disposable income	Net transfer payments	Transfer payments	Corp. profits tax	Indirect business tax	Personal savings (t − 1)
79.402	0.0129[a]	–	–	–	–	0.545
(3.126)	(0.256)	–	–	–	–	(4.630)

Adjusted R^2 = 0.284 SER = 28.18 F = 1.2 DW = 2.06

| 113.83 | −0.325[b] | 0.263 | – | – | – | 0.476 |
| (3.196) | (−1.288) | (1.370) | – | – | – | (3.740) |

Adjusted R^2 = 0.296 SER = 27.94 F = 8.17 DW = 2.06

| 76.47 | 0.164[c] | 0.408 | – | −2.13 | −1.80 | 0.482 |
| (1.71) | (1.35) | (1.54) | – | (−1.17) | (−1.46) | (3.82) |

Adjusted R^2 = 0.318 SER = 27.5 F = 5.58 DW = 1.96

| 73.06 | 0.163[d] | – | 0.330 | −2.40 | −1.79 | 0.499 |
| (1.60) | (1.33) | – | (1.25) | (−1.31) | (−1.420) | (3.98) |

Adjusted R^2 = 0.310 SER = 27.6 F = 5.76 DW = 1.97

Notes:
a. Defined as the difference between the sum of state and local government compensation to government employees and government transfers to persons minus the sum of personal tax and non-tax receipts and contributions for social insurance.
b. Personal disposable income as defined in the NIPA.
c. Defined as the NIPA definition in b above plus state and local government personal tax and non-tax receipts plus contributions for social insurance less compensation to government employees less transfers to persons.
d. Defined as the NIPA definition in b above less compensation to government employees less transfers to persons.

(1979, 1981) consumption coefficient (Laramie, Mair and Toporowski, 1999). Thus, consumption expenditures are equal to the consumption coefficient times the wage bill.

We alter the consumption equation by including a random shock term. Thus, we write consumption as:

$$C = a(V) + e \qquad (7.8)$$

where C = consumption expenditures; a = the consumption coefficient; V = the wage bill (including salaries) and e = the random shock term.

Since consumption can be defined as the sum of consumption out of private sector compensation to employees, consumption out of property income, consumption out of Federal government distributions to households and consumption out of state and local government distributions to households, equation (7.7) can be written as:

$$c_v(V) + c_p(P') + c_f(FD) + c_{sl}(SD) = a(V) + e \qquad (7.8')$$

where c_i = the average propensity to consume out of pre-tax incomes, where i = v, p, f and sl, and where P' = property income, FD = Federal government direct distributions to households and SD = state and local government direct distributions to households.

By rearranging equation (7.8') and dividing both sides by the wage bill, V, we derive:

$$a = c_y + c_p(P'/V) + c_f(FD/V) + c_{sl}(SD/V) + e/V \qquad (7.9)$$

By estimating equation (7.9), we are able to obtain estimates of the various average propensities to consume (see Table 7.2). As the table shows, during the sample period all the estimates of the average propensities to consume were statistically different from zero, except the average propensity to consume out of property income. The estimates of the average propensities to consume out of pre-tax private sector income, direct Federal government expenditures to households and direct state and local government expenditures to households are 0.837, 0.610 and 1.511 respectively.

Table 7.2 Estimates of the average propensities to consume: private sector compensation to employees (c_y); property income (c_p); Federal government direct distributions to households (c_f); state and local government direct distributions to households (c_{sl}) (maximum likelihood iterative technique)

c_y	c_p	c_f	c_{sl}
0.837	0.688	0.610	1.511
(6.58)	(0.599)	(2.658)	(2.838)
Adjusted R^2 = 0.971 SER = 0.081 F = 568.909 DW = 1.80			

These estimates are remarkable for three reasons. First, the average propensity to consume out of direct state and local government expenditures to households is greater than 1. This suggests that personal savings, at least in the short period, are at best unlikely to change with respect to direct state and local government expenditures to households. Second, the average propensity to spend out of direct Federal government expenditures to households is significantly lower than 1 and is less than the average propensity to spend out of private sector compensation to employees. If the average propensity to spend is inversely related to the level of income over income classes, this result suggests that direct Federal government expenditures to households have provided significant assistance to higher-income households. This result is not surprising in light of the large increases in net interest payments made by the Federal government. Third, these results suggest that the impact of the Federal deficit on corporate profits during the sample period has been mitigated by the relatively low average propensity to consume out of direct Federal government expenditures to households (in addition to the trade deficit).

Now that we have analysed the short-period incidence of state and local government taxation in the US, we can consider some of its effects. As we show in equation (7.6'), the impact of state and local government taxation on national income operates through three variables: the wage tax rate, t_v, the wage share, α; and government purchases, G, *ceteris paribus*. By differentiating equation (7.6') with respect to t_v, α, and G, we derive the following equations:

$$dY/dt_v = -\alpha[I + X + G + D - Z]/[(1 - \alpha) + at_v + s)]^2 \qquad (7.10)$$

$$dY/dG = 1/[(1 - \alpha) + at_v + s)] \qquad (7.11)$$

$$dY/d\alpha = (1 - t_v)[I + X + G + D - Z]/[(1 - \alpha) + at_v + s)]^2 \qquad (7.12)$$

These results indicate that increases in wage tax rate or a decrease in the wage share have a negative impact on national income. In contrast, an increase in a profits tax, assuming that it has no impact on the wage share, will increase national income if the profits tax is used to fund an increase in government purchases.

This result has an interesting implication for the study of state and local government finance in the US. The corporate profits tax represents the weakest revenue source for state and local governments. It has represented only 3.6 per cent of total receipts in recent years. Because of capital mobility, pressure from local businesses and threats of exit, individual states have been constrained in their ability to use the corporate profits tax to fund projects even though such taxes are likely to stimulate growth and have no aggregate incidence impact on corporate profits. Instead, state and local governments have chosen clearly inferior policies that have played income classes off against each other. An increase in indirect business taxes, household property or sales taxes reduces household consumption. But if the tax receipts are spent by state and local governments, there is no impact on corporate profits. The net effect is that some households, particularly middle- or lower-income households who do not receive transfer payments or have major shareholdings in corporations, are made worse off while corporate profits are unaffected. In aggregate corporate profits and household incomes could be unaffected if the corporate profits tax was used to fund state and local government purchases.

The inability of state and local governments to use the corporate profits tax on any significant scale suggests an added rationale for Federal grants-in-aid. The Federal government has much greater latitude and does not face the same constraints as state and local governments in levying corporate profits taxes, even in a global economy. The Federal government could rectify the deficiency in public investment that is a concern of the Clinton Administration by increasing the Federal corporate profits tax and applying the increased revenues to Federal grants-in-aid. The result, in our opinion, would be more balanced economic growth between the public and private sectors of the US economy.

We have shown in this chapter that because of institutional and political factors the macroeconomic effects and incidence of state and local taxes in the US is remarkably different from the incidence of similar Federal taxes on corporate profits. Because of statutory or constitutional requirements, state and local governments have deficit and debt limitations. The US Federal government appears to have an *ad hoc* budget process with little apparent connection between the revenue and expenditure sides of the budget. These state and local government fiscal constraints, coupled with Federal grants-in-aid, cause the propensity to consume of state and local governments out of their tax receipts to exceed unity and, therefore, have a negligible to positive impact on corporate profits.

This conclusion is reinforced by our estimates of the marginal propensities to save out of disposable income and state and local government transfer payments and by the average propensity to consume out of state and local government expenditures distributed directly to households. The marginal propensities to save are not statistically different from zero; households' average propensity to consume out of state and local government compensation to employees, transfer payments and net interest payments is statistically different from zero and greater than one. We have shown that state and local government indirect business and corporate tax receipts have no impact on personal savings in the short period. These estimates suggest that the primary factor determining the short-period incidence of state and local government taxes on corporate profits is the budget stance of state and local governments.

This conclusion poses an interesting public finance problem by suggesting that corporate state and local government profits taxes are preferable to other forms of taxation, such as indirect business taxes, for example, which reduce the incomes of households while having no adverse effects on post-tax corporate profits. In contrast, state and local government corporate profits taxes have no impact on post-tax corporate profits or on household income. Given that the corporate profits tax is the least utilized form of taxation in the US at the state and local government level, a policy conclusion which follows from our analysis is that the Federal government should increase its reliance on the corporate profits tax to fund Federal grants-in-aid and thereby reduce the deficiency in public investment.

4 FISCAL POLICY AND EMU

The analysis we have presented in this chapter also provides a framework within which to consider the macroeconomic effects of fiscal policy in the European Union (Laramie and Mair, 1997). The Treaty of Maastricht has brought back into focus the importance of fiscal policy as a means of achieving the objectives of European economic and monetary union (EMU). An important factor that will help to determine the success or failure of fiscal policy under EMU identified by Roberti and Vissagio (1994) is the robustness of the theoretical model used to analyse the relationships between the targets of economic convergence and the fiscal variables. A number of commentators, such as Eichengreen (1990, 1992a, 1992b, 1993, 1994), Bayoumi and Eichengreen (1994), Buiter, Corsetti and Roubini (1993), Sala-i-Martin and Sachs (1992), have all investigated aspects of fiscal policy in a post-Maastricht Europe. In several cases they have used US experience to illustrate the fiscal issues which arise but within the framework of standard mainstream analysis.

The Treaty of Maastricht established four convergence criteria which countries had to satisfy for the adoption of a single currency, the Euro, and admission to EMU. These were 1) price stability; 2) exchange rate stability; 3) long-term nominal interest rate convergence; and 4) sustainability of public finance situation. In addition, the Treaty imposed two further constraints on member states; 1) prohibition of monetary financing; and 2) indirect tax harmonization.

These conditions were an attempt by the authors of the Treaty of Maastricht to reconcile two conflicting issues. On the one hand, the creation of the European System of Central Banks and the introduction of the Euro will result in a loss of monetary autonomy which needs to be compensated by greater fiscal autonomy (Kenen, 1969; Eichengreen, 1993). With the loss of independent monetary policy, the ability of a member state to take stabilizing fiscal action becomes all the more important. On the other hand, the whole thrust of Community fiscal policy since the earliest days of the EEC has been towards fiscal harmonization and to restrain fiscal policy in order to facilitate attainment of EMU.

The transitional conditions which member states had to satisfy before full operation of EMU reflected the continuing high priority that the Council of Ministers continues to attach to the objective of fiscal harmonization. Eichengreen (1994) has challenged the rationale for this supervision and has asked why the member states cannot be relied upon to manage their fiscal affairs themselves. A concern that has featured prominently in the background papers to the Delors Report and the Treaty itself has been for the international macroeconomic spillovers of national fiscal policies, which may be magnified as a consequence of economic and monetary integration.

Eichengreen (1994) concludes that whether one believes that the closer integration of EMU will create a bias towards excessive deficits, monetization of public debt and inflation depends on the institutional setting and market structure one has in mind. He cites approvingly the model of Canzoneri and Diba (1991) as an approach to the problem. Essentially, this is an application of the Ramsey–Phelps optimal taxation problem to be solved by an optimizing central bank. This model is predicated on increasing international capital mobility and the corresponding adjustments to domestic and foreign interest rates induced by capital mobility. This, in turn, will lead to higher taxes by domestic and foreign governments in order to pay the higher interest charges on outstanding debt.

The framework within which the analysis to date of the role of fiscal policy under EMU has been carried out has been that of mainstream theory where the primary emphasis has been to study the macroeconomic effects of relative price changes. The underlying model has been Harberger's (1962) two-sector general equilibrium tax incidence model in which the emphasis is on the response of factor flows to tax-induced changes in factor incomes.

5   KALECKIAN THEORY AND EMU

The analysis we have presented earlier in this chapter has focused on the incidence and macroeconomic effects of state and local government taxes in the US. The results we have obtained raise interesting questions for the future of corporate profits taxation under EMU. In the US, state governments make only minimal use of the corporate profits tax and it is their weakest revenue source. Due to concerns over capital mobility, the pressures of local business and threats of exit, individual states have been constrained in their ability to use the corporate profits tax even though our analysis suggests that it is likely to stimulate growth and have no aggregate incidence impact on corporate profits. Instead, state governments have chosen inferior fiscal policies. To the extent that the same pressures from the business sector may constrain the use of corporate taxation under EMU, considerations may emerge similar to those that have arisen for the US.

The advent of EMU raises important issues for fiscal policy. There are two levels at which the debate may proceed. The first is the theoretical and we have shown in this chapter how a Kaleckian model may be constructed to examine the macroeconomic effects and incidence of national fiscal policies in an increasingly federal Europe. The second is the policy level. Our analysis suggests that stabilization need no longer depend on the application of orthodox Keynesian policy of running budget deficits during recessions and surpluses during booms. As we have shown in Chapter 4, stabilization objectives can be achieved within given volumes of government revenue and spending by altering the structure of taxation. Recognition of this possibility means that compliance by a member state of EMU to the 3 per cent of GDP budget requirement need not act as a constraint on its ability to use fiscal policy as an instrument of stabilization.

A corollary of this Kaleckian conclusion is that there would have to be a move towards greater heterogeneity in the tax structures of member states. This, of course, would be at variance with the long-standing desire for fiscal harmonization within EMU. This would enable member states to exercise a significant measure of discretion over national macroeconomic priorities while still complying with the budgetary criteria of EMU. For countries whose business cycles are out of phase with those of other members, the ability to pursue independent stabilization policy without violating EMU rules is a considerable advantage.

REFERENCES

Aaronson, J.R. and Hilley, J.L. (1986), *Financing State and Local Governments*, 4th edition, Washington, DC, The Brookings Institution.

Bayoumi, T. and Eichengreen, B. (1994), 'The political economy of fiscal restrictions: implications for Europe from the United States', *European Economic Review*, **38**, 783–91.

Buiter, W., Corsetti, G. and Roubini, N. (1993), 'Excessive deficits: sense and nonsense in the Treaty of Maastricht', *Economic Policy*, **16**, 57–100.

Canzoneri, M. and Diba, B. (1991), 'Fiscal deficits, financial integration and a central bank for Europe', *Journal of the Japanese and International Economies*, **5**, 481–503.

Coutts, K., Godley, W. and Nordhaus, W. (1978), *Industrial Pricing in the United Kingdom*, Cambridge, Cambridge University Press.

Eichengreen, B. (1990), 'One money for Europe? Lessons from the US currency and customs union', *Economic Policy*, **10**, 117–87.

Eichengreen, B. (1992a), 'Is Europe an optimum currency area?', in Borner, S. and Grubel, H. (eds), *European Integration: The View from Outside*, London, Macmillan.

Eichengreen, B. (1992b), 'Should the Maastricht Treaty be saved?' *Princeton Studies in International Finance*, **74**.

Eichengreen, B. (1993), 'European monetary unification', *Journal of Economic Literature*, **31** (3), 1321–57.

Eichengreen, B. (1994), 'Fiscal policy and EMU', in Eichengreen, B. and Frieden, J. (eds), *The Political Economy of European Monetary Unification*, Boulder, Col., Westview Press.

Fisher, R.C. (1988), *State and Local Public Finance*, Glenview, Ill., Scott, Foresman and Co.

Harberger, A.C. (1962), 'The incidence of the corporation income tax', *Journal of Political Economy*, **70**, 215–40.

Kenen, P.B. (1969), 'The optimum currency area: an eclectic view', in Mundell, R. and Swoboda, A. (eds), *Monetary Problems of the International Economy*, Chicago, Chicago University Press.

Kotlikoff, L. and Summers, L. (1987), 'Tax incidence', in Auerbach, A.J. and Feldstein, M.E. (eds), *Handbook of Public Economics, Vol. II*, Amsterdam, North Holland.

Laramie, A.J. (1991), 'Taxation and Kalecki's distribution factors', *Journal of Post Keynesian Economics*, **13** (4), 583–94.

Laramie, A.J. (1994), 'The incidence of the corporate profits tax revisited: a post Keynesian approach', *Working Paper No.* 109, Bard College, NY, Jerome Levy Economics Institute.

Laramie, A.J. and Mair, D. (1996), 'The short-period macroeconomic incidence and effects of state and local taxes', in Pola, G., France, G. and Levaggi, R. (eds) *Developments in Local Government Finance, Theory and Policy*, Aldershot, Edward Elgar.

Laramie, A.J. and Mair, D. (1997), 'The macroeconomic effects of taxation in a federal Europe', in Arestis, P. and Sawyer, M.C. (eds), *The Relevance of Keynesian Economic Policies Today*, London, Macmillan.

Laramie, A.J., Mair, D., and Toporowski, J. (1999), 'Weintraub's consumption coefficient: some economic evidence and implications for the UK', *Cambridge Journal of Economics*, forthcoming.

Levy, S.J. and Levy, D.A. (1983), *Profits and the Future of American Society*, New York, Harper and Row.

Mieszkowski, P.M. (1972), 'The property tax: an excise tax or a profits tax?', *Journal of Public Economics*, **2**, 73–96.

Pechman, J.A. (1987), *Federal Tax Policy*, Washington, DC, The Brookings Institution.

Roberti, P. and Vissagio, M. (1994), 'Fiscal adjustments between fiscal harmonization and the Maastricht convergence criteria', in Baldasarri, M. and Roberti, M. (eds), *Fiscal Problems in the Single-Market Europe*, London, Macmillan.

Sala-i-Martin, X. and Sachs, J. (1992), 'Federal fiscal policy and optimum currency areas' in Canzoneri, M., Grilli, V. and Masson, P. (eds), *Establishing a Central Bank: Issues in Europe and Lessons from the US*, Cambridge, Cambridge University Press.

Sylos-Labini, P. (1979), 'Industrial pricing in the United Kingdom', *Cambridge Journal of Economics*, **3**, 153–63.

Weintraub, S. (1979), 'Generalizing Kalecki and simplifying macroeconomics', *Journal of Post Keynesian Economics*, **3**, 101–6.

Weintraub, S. (1981), 'An eclectic theory of income shares', *Journal of Post Keynesian Economics*, **4**, 10–24.

8. The macroeconomic and regional effects of national and local taxation: a Kaleckian approach

1 INTRODUCTION

In the previous chapter, we demonstrated how our basic Kaleckian model could be adapted to analyse the short-period incidence and macroeconomic effects of state and local taxes. In this chapter, we extend our model of tax incidence and macroeconomic effects model further to examine the local and regional effects of taxation. We first introduce a Kaleckian model of the regional and national effects of taxation. We then consider the aggregate and regional effects of changes in a national wage tax, a national profits tax, a local wage tax and a local profits tax. We illustrate the model by reference to some numerical examples. Finally, we consider some implications of the model. We define these implications according to: 1) those that appear in the short period, such as compensating changes in the budgets of national and local governments, or changes in business markups; and 2) those that appear in the long period, such as changes in the level and patterns of business investment. We then consider some additional implications. We conclude the chapter by summarizing the main results and discussing some of the policy issues.

2 A KALECKIAN MODEL OF THE REGIONAL EFFECTS OF NATIONAL AND LOCAL TAXATION

Tip O'Neil, former Speaker of the US House of Representatives, once said that all politics are local. For this reason, we believe that the Kaleckian approach to taxation that we have presented so far in this book requires further development. In previous chapters, we have focused on the macroeconomic incidence and effects of taxation without considering explicitly how national tax policy may affect the economies of particular jurisdictions or the performance of specific industries in particular jurisdictions. Our purpose in this chapter is: 1) to present an alternative approach to the mainstream economic literature on the question of local taxation; 2) to show how local taxation affects the national economy and how these national effects feed back to the local economy; and 3) to show the local dimensions of national tax policy. In addition, we highlight the various channels through which tax national tax policy works itself out in specific industries and local government jurisdictions, and we highlight the various channels through which local tax policies generate inter-regional effects.

1 Preliminary Assumptions

To begin the analysis, we present the simplest version of the model. In this version, the model is based on the following assumptions:

1. two local jurisdictions with separate fiscal authorities;
2. a single national government with independent fiscal authority;
3. one integrated industry operating over the two jurisdictions;
4. the unit costs of production (prime costs), markups and prices are identical across the two local jurisdictions;
5. trade between the two local jurisdictions is free while foreign trade is nonexistent;
6. trade between the two local jurisdictions is assumed to be initially in balance, i.e. exports from each jurisdiction equal imports into each jurisdiction;
7. to avoid complications, we assume that tax shifting, when allowed, is reflected in changes in the business markup without affecting the market price of output. Increases in wage taxes when shifted result in a lower markup. Increases in profit taxes result in lower wages (and thus a higher markup);
8. we assume the supply of labour is perfectly elastic, and that labour shifts between jurisdictions, in response to real wage differentials, do not take place in the short period.

Given these assumptions, we develop the model following the same approach as we present in Chapter 2.

2 Microeconomic Foundations

We define value added for jurisdiction j as:

$$Y_j = (k_j - 1)(V_j + M_j) + W_j \qquad (8.1)$$

where Y = value added, k = the price/cost mark up, W = the wage bill, and M = the materials bill.

Business profits plus overheads for jurisdiction j are defined as:

$$P_j + O_j = (k_j - 1)(W_j + M_j) \qquad (8.2)$$

where P = profits and O = overhead costs.

The distribution of value added is found by defining the wage share. From equation (8.1) the wage share is given as:

$$W_j/Y_j = 1/[1 + (k_j - 1) + (1 + j_j)] \tag{8.3}$$

where $j_j = M_j/W_j$. The share of profits plus overhead costs of value added is simply $(1 - W_j/Y_j)$.

A question now arises as to what determines the level of wages and material costs in specific industries. Like Keynes, Kalecki considered an economy operating below full employment, with ample unused production possibilities. Similarly, we hypothesize that the rate of innovations and technical progress are such that aggregate demand has difficulty keeping pace with the growth in production possibilities. As with Kalecki, we consider a model where the levels of wages and material costs are constrained by aggregate demand. To consider this further, we must examine the macroeconomic foundations of the model.

3   Macrofoundations

Value added for the economy as a whole is defined as:

$$Y = \Sigma Y_j = Y_1 + Y_2 \tag{8.4}$$

We derive the aggregate markup from equation (8.3) and define aggregate value added in terms of the aggregate markup. For example, by substituting equation (8.1) into equation (8.3), we derive aggregate value added as:

$$Y = (k_1 - 1)(W_1 + M_1) + W_1 + (k_2 - 1)(W_2 + M_2) + W_2 \tag{8.5}$$

Since aggregate value added can also be written as:

$$Y = (k - 1)(W + M) + W \tag{8.5'}$$

where the unsubscripted variables represent aggregates, the aggregate prime cost markup can be written as the weighted average of the industry markups; i.e.:

$$(k - 1) = (k_1 - 1)(W_1 + M_1)/(W + M) + (k_2 - 1)(W_2 + M_2)/(W + M) \tag{8.6}$$

Given equation (8.5), the aggregate wage share can be written as:

$$V/Y = \alpha \tag{8.7}$$

where V = the level of wages (we assume overhead salaries to be zero); and α = the wage share.

Given equation (8.3), the aggregate wage share can be written as:

$$\alpha = 1/[1 + (k - 1) + (1 + j)] \tag{8.8}$$

(see Sawyer 1985).

From equation (8.7), we derive an expression for national income by defining $\Pi = Y - V$, where Π is pre-tax profits, i.e.:

$$Y = (\Pi)/(1 - \alpha) \tag{8.9}$$

Kalecki (1968) states that equation (8.9) shows how the distribution factors, in this case, α, push up the level of income so that profits out of income are realized, where realized profits are determined by aggregate spending flows. Kalecki used the national income accounts, Marx's reproduction scheme, to derive a definition for aggregate profits. He defined aggregate profits (net of taxes), assuming that government transfer payments were completely consumed, as:

$$P = I + Ge - T + Ex - Im + C_c - V_s \tag{8.10}$$

where I = gross private domestic investment, Ge = government expenditures, T = total tax receipts, Ex = exports, Im = imports, C_c = capitalists' consumption and V_s = workers' savings (defined as pre-tax wages and salaries less wage and salary taxes less worker consumption).

For our immediate purposes, we ignore the trade balance and we assume capitalists' consumption, workers' savings and government transfer payments to be zero. Thus, we rewrite equation (8.10) simply as:

$$P + T_p = \Pi = I + G - T_w \tag{8.10'}$$

where P = post-tax profits, T_p = profits taxes, G = government purchases, and T_w = wage tax.

From equations (8.10) or (8.10'), we can see that the level of realized profits is determined by the interaction of the right-hand-side variables. Given the aggregate distribution factors, the level of national income is pushed up so that profits are realized according to equations (8.10) or (8.10'). The aggregate level of income is distributed to industries/jurisdictions in accordance with industrial/jurisdictional distribution factors. At this point, ignoring the re-distributional role of national and local governments, these industrial/jurisdictional distribution factors are reflected in the jurisdictional price/cost markups and in the jurisdictional ratios of the material bills to the wage bills.

3   A NUMERICAL EXAMPLE

We think that the regional and aggregate effects on national and local taxation
can best be illustrated by a numerical example. From this example, we go on
to consider extensions and further implications of the model. We consider an
economy with one industry and two jurisdictions with the following set of
initial variables (see Table 8.1).

Table 8.1   *Numerical example of a simple tax model*

	Symbol	Initial Value
Jurisdiction 1		
Parameters:		
Markup	k_1	2
(Materials Bill/Wage Bill)	j_1	2
Wage Share	α_1	0.25
Policy Variables:		
Profits Tax	T_{p1}	0
Wage Tax	Tw_1	0
Variables:		
Wage Bill	W_1	50
Materials Bill	M_1	100
Value-Added	Y_1	200
Post-Tax Profits	P_1	150
Rate of Profits	r_1	0.1
Jurisdiction 2		
Parameters:		
Markup	k_2	2
(Materials Bill/Wage Bill)	j_2	2
Wage Share	α_2	0.25
Policy Variables:		
Profits Tax	T_{p2}	0
Wage Tax	T_{w2}	0
Variables:		
Wage Bill	W_2	75
Materials Bill	M_2	150
Value Added	Y_2	300
Post Tax Profits	P_2	225
Rate of Profits	r_2	0.1

Table 8.1   continued

	Symbol	Initial Value
Macroeconomic Variables		
Parameters:		
Aggregate Profit Margin	$k-1$	1
Aggregate Materials Bill/Wage Bill	j	2
Aggregate Wage Share	α	0.25
Aggregate Income Multiplier	$1/(1-a)$	1.33
Policy Variables:		
National Profits Tax	Tpn	0
Aggregate Profits Tax	Tp	0
National Wage Tax	Twn	0
Aggregate Wage Tax	Tw	0
Variables:		
Aggregate Wage Bill	V	125
Aggregate Materials Bill	M	250
Aggregate Income	Y	500
Aggregate Pre-Tax Profits	$\Pi = I + G - Tw$	375
Aggregate Post-Tax Profits	$P = \Pi - Tp$	375

We now consider four cases: 1) where the national government sets a tax rate on wages equal to 25 per cent; 2) where the national government levies a lump sum tax on capital; 3) where jurisdiction 1 levies a tax rate on wages of 25 per cent; and 4) where jurisdiction 1 levies a lump sum capital tax.

1   A National Wage Tax of 25 per cent

Assuming that workers spend all their income and government purchases remain constant, this tax will reduce workers' consumption relative to the wage bill and reduce business profits. In other words, a national wage tax bears a double incidence. The wage tax reduces the disposable income of workers and capitalists simultaneously. Under the above assumptions, post-tax profits fall by the amount of the tax, while national income falls as a result of the operation of the basic income multiplier. Post-tax wages fall as a result of both the decline in national income and the increase in the wage tax. These two effects together cause post-tax wages to decline more than the tax increase and together create an excess tax burden. The excess tax burden is defined as a situation where the loss in private sector income is greater than the additional tax receipts. These results are summarized in Table 8.2, where the wage tax is written as:

$$Tw = t_w(W) \tag{8.11}$$

where $W = V$.

Assuming that overhead salaries equal zero, substitution of equation (8.11) into equation (8.10') and of equation (8.10') into equation (8.9) yields:

$$Y = (I + G)/(1 - \alpha)(1 - t_w) \tag{8.9'}$$

Assuming no short-period response to the tax change, that is where investment is fixed by past investment decisions and assuming that the capital stock remains constant, the wage tax has an equi-proportional impact on each of the jurisdictions. The rate of profit in each jurisdiction falls, but remains constant across jurisdictions. These results are presented in Table 8.2.

Table 8.2   Numerical example of the local tax model if the national government sets a wage tax equal to 25% (t_w = 0.25)

	Symbol	Initial Value
Jurisdiction 1		
Parameters:		
Markup	k_1	2
(Materials Bill/Wage Bill)	j_1	2
Wage Share	α_1	0.25
Policy Variables:		
Profits Tax	Tp_1	0
Wage Tax	Tw_1	0
Variables:		
Wage Bill	W_1	46.15
Materials Bill	M_1	92.3
Wage Bill + Material Bill	$W_1 + M_1$	138.46
Value-Added	Y_1	184.61
Post-Tax Profits	P_1	138.46
Rate of Profits	r_1	0.0923

Table 8.2   continued

	Symbol	Initial Value
Jurisdiction 2		
Parameters:		
Markup	k_2	2
(Materials Bill/Wage Bill)	j_2	2
Wage Share	α_2	0.25
Policy Variables:		
Profits Tax	Tp_2	0
Wage Tax	Tw_2	0
Variables:		
Wage Bill	W_2	69.23
Materials Bill	M_2	138.46
Wage Bill + Material Bill	$W_2 + M_2$	207.69
Value-Added	Y_2	276.92
Post Tax Profits	P_2	207.69
Rate of Profits	r_2	0.0923
Macroeconomic Variables		
Parameters:		
Aggregate Profit Margin	$k - 1$	1
Aggregate Materials Bill/Wage Bill	j	2
Aggregate Wage Share	α	0.25
Aggregate Income Multiplier	$1/(1 - \alpha)(1 - tw)$	1.23
Investment + Gov't Expenditures	$I + G$	375
Policy Variables:		
National Profits Tax	Tpn	0
Aggregate Profits Tax	Tp	0
National Wage Tax Rate	twn	0.25
National Wage Tax	Twn	28.846
Aggregate Wage Tax Rate	tw	0.25
Aggregate Wage Tax	Tw	28.846
Variables:		
Aggregate Wage Bill	W	115.38
Aggregate Materials Bill	M	230.76
Aggregate Income	Y	461.53
Aggregate Pre-Tax Profits	$\Pi = I + G - Tw$	346.15
Aggregate Post-Tax Profits	$P = \Pi - Tp$	346.15

Table 8.2   continued

Tax Burden Assessment

	Change	Percentage of Total Change
ΔPost-Tax Profits	−28.85	–
ΔPost-Tax Profits$_1$	−11.54	40
ΔPost-Tax Profit$_2$	−17.31	60
ΔPre-Tax Wage Bill	−9.62	–
ΔPre-Tax Wage Bill$_1$	−3.85	40
ΔPre-Tax Wage Bill$_2$	−5.77	60
ΔPost-Tax Wage Bill	−38.46	–
ΔPost-Tax Wage Bill$_1$	−15.38	40
ΔPost-Tax Wage Bill$_2$	−23.08	60

Tax Burden Ratio* = $[(28.85+38.46)/28.85] = 67.31/28.85 = 2.33$
Excess Tax Burden Ratio** = $(67.31 - 28.85)/28.85 = 1.33$

Notes:
* Tax Burden Ratio = The additional tax burden on wages and profits relative to the additional tax revenues raised. (The tax burden ratio is interpreted as the decline in private sector income as a result of a dollar increase in taxes.)
** Excess Tax Burden Ratio = The additional tax burden on wages and profits – the additional tax receipts/the additional tax receipts. (The excess tax burden ratio is interpreted as the decline in private sector income in excess of the tax receipts as a result of a dollar increase in taxes.)

To illustrate the impact on each of the jurisdictions of implementing a national wage tax, we now explain how the values of the various variables are derived. First, national income is derived using the basic formula as given in equation (8.9'). Second, the aggregate pre-tax wage bill is derived. Given that the wage share is 25 per cent of national income, the aggregate wage bill is 25 per cent of 461.53 or 115.38. Third, since J = 2, the materials bill is twice that of the wage bill, or 230.76. Fourth, now that the aggregate wage and materials bills are known, aggregate prime costs are also known, and we use the weights used to calculate the aggregate price/cost markup to disaggregate the prime costs over each jurisdiction. The weight applied to jurisdiction 1 to calculate the aggregate markup is $(W_1 + M_1)/(W + M) = 0.4$, and the weight applied to jurisdiction 2 to calculate the aggregate markup is $(W_2 + M_2)/(W + M) = 0.6$. Multiplying these weights by the aggregate materials bill shows that jurisdiction 1's prime costs equal 138.46 and jurisdiction 2's prime costs equal 207.69. Now that each of the industry's prime costs is determined, it is straightforward to derive the wage bill for each industry. Knowing that $M_j/W_j = 2$, $W_j + 2W_j = W_j + M_j$, or $W_j = (W_j + M_j)/3$. Again, once the industry wage bill is known, the industry material bill is given as two times the wage bill. Fifth, industry value added is derived as described in equation (8.1). Profits represent value added less the wage bill and overheads. Since overheads are assumed to be zero, profits represent value added less the wage bill. The rate of profit for each jurisdiction is simply the level of profits divided by the capital stock. Finally, the jurisdictional distribution of the tax burden is determined by the weights, $W_j + M_j/W + M$, used to derive the aggregate markup. Forty per cent of the aggregate decline in profits is distributed to jurisdiction 1 and sixty per cent of the decline is distributed to jurisdiction 2.

2 A Lump Sum Profits Tax

Here we suppose that the national government imposes a lump sum tax on the profits from capital. To contrast the effects of this tax with a national wage tax, we assume this tax is levied to raise the same amount of revenue as the wage tax, i.e. 28.846. As implied above, jurisdictions 1 and 2 have 1500 and 2250 units of capital respectively. Thus, the lump sum tax would amount to 0.00796 per unit of capital. As is evident in the model, this tax will simply redistribute profits to overheads, holding other things constant. National income, the wage share, the wage bill will all remain unchanged as long as business markups, government purchases, and investment remain unchanged in the short period. These results are reflected in the numerical example in Table 8.3.

Table 8.3 Numerical example of the local tax model if national lump sum tax per unit of capital = 0.00796 (or Tp = 28.846)

	Symbol	Initial Value
Jurisdiction 1		
Parameters:		
Markup	k_1	2
(Materials Bill/Wage Bill)	j_1	2
Wage Share	α_1	0.25
Policy Variables:		
Profits Tax	Tp_1	0
Wage Tax	$Tw1$	0
Variables:		
Wage Bill	W_1	50
Materials Bill	M_1	100
Wage Bill + Material Bill	$W_1 + M_1$	150
Value-Added	Y_1	200
Post-Tax Profits	P_1	138.46
Rate of Profits	r_1	0.0923

Table 8.3 continued

	Symbol	Initial Value
Jurisdiction 2		
Parameters:		
Markup	k_2	2
(Materials Bill/Wage Bill)	j_2	2
Wage Share	α_2	0.25
Policy Variables:		
Profits Tax	Tp_2	0
Wage Tax	Tw_2	0
Variables:		
Wage Bill	W_2	75
Materials Bill	M_2	150
Wage Bill + Material Bill	$W_2 + M_2$	225
Value-Added	Y_2	300
Post-Tax Profits	P_2	207.69
Rate of Profits	r_2	0.0923
Macroeconomic Variables		
Parameters:		
Aggregate Profit Margin	$k - 1$	1
Aggregate Materials Bill/Wage Bill	j	2
Aggregate Wage Share	α	0.25
Aggregate Income Multiplier	$1/(1 - \alpha)$	1.33
Investment + Gov't Expenditures	$I + G$	3.75
Policy Variables:		
National Profits Tax	Tpn	28.85
Aggregate Profits Tax	Tp	28.85
National Wage Tax Rate	twn	0
National Wage Tax	Twn	0
Aggregate Wage Tax Rate	tw	0
Aggregate Wage Tax	Tw	0
Variables:		
Aggregate Wage Bill	W	125
Aggregate Materials Bill	M	250
Aggregate Income	Y	500
Aggregate Pre-Tax Profits	$\Pi = I + G - Tw$	375
Aggregate Post-Tax Profits	$P = \Pi - Tp$	346.15

Table 8.3   continued

Tax Burden Assessment:

	Change	Percent of Total Change
ΔPost-Tax Profits	−28.85	–
ΔPost-Tax Profits$_1$	−11.54	40
ΔPost-Tax Profits$_2$	−17.31	60
ΔPre-Tax Wage	0	–
ΔPre-Tax Wage$_1$	0	–
ΔPre-Tax Wage$_2$	0	–
ΔPost-Tax Wage	0	–
ΔPost-Tax Wage$_1$	0	–
ΔPost-Tax Wage$_2$	0	–

Tax Burden Ratio = [(28.85/28.85] = 1.00
Excess Tax Burden Ratio = (28.85 − 28.85)/28.85 = 0

In comparing Table 8.2 with Table 8.3, under the assumptions of a fixed markup and investment determined by prior decisions, the profits tax appears to be superior to the wage tax. The profits tax results in no losses in national income, in wages or in employment, whereas the wage tax does. The excess burden of the tax is zero, compared to 1.33 in the previous case!

3   A Wage Tax of 25 per cent Levied by Jurisdiction 1

Now, we consider what happens if jurisdiction 1 raises its wage tax rate to 25 per cent. We continue to assume that business markups are constant and that the wage tax is not shifted through lower business markups (an increase in the unit costs of labour relative to the price of output). In this case, the introduction of the wage tax reduces workers' consumption relative to the wage bill and reduces the aggregate level of profits, national income and the wage and materials bills. The declines in national income, and in the wage and materials bills are then distributed over each of the jurisdictions based on the distribution or composition of industry in each jurisdiction. As a result, the non-taxing jurisdiction, jurisdiction 2, has to bear some of the burden, in terms of declining profits and wages, of the taxing jurisdiction's decision to tax.

To illustrate how this arises, we set the model up just as before with the same initial values for the variables. Jurisdiction 1 now levies a 25 per cent tax on wages. Since jurisdiction 1 has 40 per cent of the wage bill, its 25 per cent tax is equivalent to a 10 per cent tax on national wages ($0.25 \times 0.40 = 0.1$). Thus, the wage tax reduces the value of the income multiplier, $1/(1 - \alpha)(1 - t_w))$, from 1.33 to 1.29, which reduces national income to 483.87. Since the wage

Table 8.4   Numerical example of the local tax model if jurisdiction 1 sets a wage tax equal to 25% ($t_{w1} = 0.25$)

	Symbol	Initial Value
Jurisdiction 1		
Parameters:		
Markup	k_1	2
(Materials Bill/Wage Bill)	j_1	2
Wage Share	α_1	0.25
Policy Variables:		
Profits Tax	Tp_1	0
Wage Tax Rate	tw_1	0.25
Wage Tax	Tw_1	12.09
Variables:		
Wage Bill	W_1	48.38
Materials Bill	M_1	96.77
Wage Bill + Material Bill	$W_1 + M_1$	145.16
Value-Added	Y_1	193.54
Post-Tax Profits	P_1	145.16
Rate of Profits	r_1	0.0967
Jurisdiction 2		
Parameters:		
Markup	k_2	2
(Materials Bill/Wage Bill)	j_2	2
Wage Share	α_2	0.25
Policy Variables:		
Profits Tax	Tp_2	0
Wage Tax	Tw_2	0
Variables:		
Wage Bill	W_2	72.58
Materials Bill	M_2	145.16
Wage Bill + Material Bill	$W_2 + M_2$	217.74
Value-Added	Y_2	290.32
Post-Tax Profits	P_2	217.74
Rate of Profits	r_2	0.0967

Table 8.4   continued

	Symbol	Initial Value
Macroeconomic Variables		
Parameters:		
Aggregate Profit Margin	$k-1$	1
Aggregate Materials Bill/Wage Bill	j	2
Aggregate Wage Share	α	0.25
Aggregate Income Multiplier	$1/(1-\alpha)(1-tw)$	375
Investment + Gov't Expenditures	$I+G$	
Policy Variables:		
National Profits Tax	Tpn	0
Aggregate Profits Tax	Tp	0
National Wage Tax Rate	twn	0
National Wage Tax	Twn	0
Aggregate Wage Tax Rate	tw	0.10
Aggregate Wage Tax	Tw	12.09
Variables:		
Aggregate Wage Bill	W	120.96
Aggregate Materials Bill	M	241.93
Aggregate Income	Y	483.87
Aggregate Pre-Tax Profits	$\Pi = I + G - Tw$	375
Aggregate Post-Tax Profits	$P = \Pi - Tp$	362.90

Tax Burden Assessment:

		% of total change
ΔPost-Tax Profit	−12.097	–
ΔPost-Tax Profit$_1$	−4.84	40
ΔPost-Tax Profit$_2$	−7.26	60
ΔPre-Tax Wage	−4.02	–
ΔPre-Tax Wage$_1$	−1.61	40
ΔPre-Tax Wage$_2$	−2.42	60
ΔPost-Tax Wage	−16.13	–
ΔPost-Tax Wage$_1$	−13.71	85
ΔPost-Tax Wage$_2$	−2.42	15

Tax Burden Ratio = $[(12.097 + 16.13)/12.097] = 28.227/12.097 = 2.33$
Excess Tax Burden Ratio = $(28.227 − 12.097)/12.097 = 1.33$
Tax Burden Ratio$_1$ = $(4.84 + 13.71)/12.097 = 18.55/12.097 = 1.533$
Excess Tax Burden Ratio$_1$ = $(18.55−12.097)/12.097 = .533$

share is assumed to be constant, the wage bill declines to 120.96. Since the aggregate materials bill is assumed to be twice that of the wage bill, the materials bill declines to 241.93. Assuming that 40 per cent of the industry lies in jurisdiction 1 $((W_1 + M_1)/(W + M) = 0.40)$, and 60 per cent of the industry lies in jurisdiction 2, jurisdictions' 1 and 2 wage and materials bills are 145.16 and 217.74 respectively. The wage bill for each of the jurisdictions is given as: $W_j = (W_j + M_j)/(1 + j_j)$; and the materials bill is given as: $M_j = jW_j$. Profits and value-added for each of the jurisdictions are then derived as described above.

As in the case of a national wage tax, profits fall by the full amount of the increase in the wage tax levied by jurisdiction 1. The decline in profits is distributed to each jurisdiction according to the each sector's share of aggregate prime costs (the weights used to determine the aggregate markup). Again, as in the first case, pre-tax wages fall as a result of the decline in national income associated with the increase in the wage tax rate. The decline in pre-tax wages is distributed to each jurisdiction according to the aforementioned weights. It is the decline in national income that is distributed to jurisdiction 2 that causes jurisdiction 2's labour to bear some of the burden of jurisdiction 1's tax decision. (For this reason, labour in jurisdiction 2 should oppose an increase in the wage tax in jurisdiction 1!) In addition, labour in jurisdiction 1 has to bear an additional burden of paying the local wage tax rate of 25 per cent on its now lower pre-tax income. The wage tax burden in jurisdiction 1, and on labour in general, is greater than the wage tax revenues raised. The excess tax burden ratio for jurisdiction 1 is 0.533.

4   A Lump Sum Tax on Capital Levied by Jurisdiction 1.

We now assume that jurisdiction 1 levies a lump sum tax on capital equal to 12.09 (the tax revenues raised through the wage tax in the previous case). This amounts to a tax per unit of capital equal to 0.00806 (= 12.09/1500). This case is similar to case 2 above. In the short period, with a constant markup, the profits tax redistributes profits to overheads leaving national income, the wage bill and the materials bill unchanged. Jurisdiction 1's increase in the profits tax is ultimately borne by jurisdiction 1's capital and does not have an impact on jurisdiction 2's level of profits.

To consider this further, we develop Table 8.5 below. As we show, the decline in aggregate profits is solely the result of jurisdiction 1's loss in profits due to the lump sum tax. As evidenced in Table 8.5, the profits tax has an advantage over the wage tax, because the level of economic activity and the wage bill are unaffected by the tax. The excess burden of the tax, as we have defined it, is zero (unlike in the previous in the case of the wage tax where incomes declined by 33 per cent more than the tax revenue raised!).

Table 8.5 Numerical example of the local tax model if jurisdiction 1 sets a lump sum tax per unit of capital = 0.00806 (or Tp = 12.09)

	Symbol	Initial Value
Jurisdiction 1		
Parameters:		
Markup	k_1	2
(Materials Bill/Wage Bill)	j_1	2
Wage Share	α_1	0.25
Policy Variables:		
Profits Tax	Tp_1	12.097
Wage Tax Rate	tw_1	0
Wage Tax	Tw_1	0
Variables:		
Wage Bill	W_1	50
Materials Bill	M_1	100
Wage Bill + Material Bill	$W_1 + M_1$	150
Value-Added	Y_1	200
Post-Tax Profits	P_1	137.094
Rate of Profits	r_1	0.09194
Jurisdiction 2		
Parameters:		
Markup	k_2	2
(Materials Bill/Wage Bill)	j_2	2
Wage Share	α_2	0.25
Policy Variables:		
Profits Tax	Tp_2	0
Wage Tax	Tw_2	0
Variables:		
Wage Bill	W_2	75
Materials Bill	M_2	150
Wage Bill + Material Bill	$W_2 + M_2$	225
Value-Added	Y_2	300
Post-Tax Profits	P_2	225
Rate of Profits	r_2	0.10

Table 8.5   continued

	Symbol	Initial Value
Macroeconomic Variables		
Parameters:		
Aggregate Profit Margin	$k-1$	1
Aggregate Materials Bill/Wage Bill	j	2
Aggregate Wage Share	α	0.25
Aggregate Income Multiplier	$1/(1-a)$	1.33
Investment + Gov't Expenditures	$I+G$	375
Policy Variables:		
National Profits Tax	Tpn	0
Aggregate Profits Tax	Tp	12.097
National Wage Tax Rate	twn	0
National Wage Tax	Twn	0
Aggregate Wage Tax Rate	tw	0
Aggregate Wage Tax	Tw	0
Variables:		
Aggregate Wage Bill	W	125
Aggregate Materials Bill	M	250
Aggregate Income	Y	500
Aggregate Pre-Tax Profits	$\Pi = I + G - Tw$	375
Aggregate Post-Tax Profits	$P = \Pi - Tp$	362.90

Tax Burden Assessment		
		% of total change
ΔPost-Tax Profits	−12.097	–
ΔPost-Tax Profits$_1$	−12.097	100
ΔPost-Tax Profits$_2$	0	0
ΔPre-Tax Wage	0	–
ΔPre-Tax Wage$_1$	0	–
ΔPre-Tax Wage$_2$	0	–
ΔPost-Tax Wage	0	–
ΔPost-Tax Wage$_1$	0	–
ΔPost-Tax Wage$_2$	0	–

Tax Burden Ratio = $[(12.097)/12.097] = 1$
Excess Tax Burden Ratio = $(12.097 - 12.097)/12.097 = 0$
Tax Burden Ratio$_1$ = $[(12.097)/12.097] = 1$
Excess Tax Burden Ratio$_1$ = $(12.097 - 12.097)/12.097 = 0$

To sum up, in the simple numerical examples we present above, a national profits tax is preferred to a national wage tax. A national wage tax reduces the levels of national income, after-tax profits and wages, and imposes an excess tax burden. A national profits tax simply redistributes income from profits to overhead costs without affecting national income or the wage bill, imposes no excess burden, and leaves unchanged the relative rates of profits between jurisdictions. A local wage tax imposes an excess burden, reduces national income, the levels of profits and wages in all jurisdictions, and the rate of profits. A local profits tax, like before, generates no excess burden, but redistributes local profits to local overhead costs. This tax causes the local jurisdictions' rates of profits to fall in both absolute and relative firms. A fall in the rate of profits in a jurisdiction is one of the implications we now consider.

4   FURTHER IMPLICATIONS

As in any model, the assumptions play a pivotal role in determining the outcomes. We now begin to consider the results of relaxing our assumptions. In particular, we consider implications arising in the short period, implications arising in the long period, and other implications. The short-period implications arise as a result of two forces: 1) compensating changes in the government budget; and 2) workers having a non-zero propensity to save and capitalists having a non-zero propensity to consume. Other implications arise as a result of two forces: 1) changes in business markups in response to the tax change; and 2) changes in investment in response to changes in the rate of profit. Another implication arises, for example, in defining different tax bases, such as property or sales.

5   SHORT PERIOD IMPLICATIONS

In the examples above, we have assumed that the national and local governments raise tax revenues for the sake of doing so. Now we consider the incidence and effects of taxation when governments spends their taxes, i.e. when governments either use the tax receipts to purchase goods and services, transfer the tax receipts to workers, or transfer the tax receipts to capitalists. We consider in turn each of the four cases discussed above. In each of these cases for the sake of simplicity we assume that the national and local governments are operating with balanced budget constraints.

1   Short-period Implications Associated With a National Wage Tax

If the national government levies a tax on wage income to finance government purchases of goods and services, equation (8.10') reduces to:

$$P + Tp = \Pi = I \qquad (8.12)$$

and national income is rewritten as:

$$Y = I/(1 - \alpha) \qquad (8.13)$$

Maintaining the assumption that workers do not save, a wage tax has no impact on the pre- or post-tax levels of profits, the pre-tax wage bill and level of national income. The national government in this case simply takes disposable income from wage earners, which reduces their consumption relative to the wage bill, and substitutes its spending for that of wage earners, leaving the level of profits unaffected. In this case, capitalists in the wages-good industry lose profits to the gain of capitalists in the government-goods-and-service industry, but the overall rates of profits in each jurisdiction are unaffected.

As we show below, the tax burden ratio is one and the excess tax burden ratio is zero. If workers' marginal propensity to consume were less than one, workers would pay for some of the tax by reducing their savings and the tax would stimulate national income, profits and the pre-tax wage bill. Thus, the tax burden ratio would be less than one and the excess tax burden ratio would be negative.

If the wage tax receipts are used to transfer income to wage labour, the results are similar to those above, assuming that wage labour's marginal propensity to spend is one. The wage tax, on the one hand, reduces workers' consumption relative to the wage bill which reduces profits, but, on the other hand, the tax transfer to wage labour restores consumption back to its original level. This story may be further complicated if the tax distribution is other than a transfer distribution or if the marginal propensity to spend is less than one.

If the wage tax receipts are used to transfer income to capitalists, and capitalists' marginal propensity to consume is zero, then the result is the same as presented in Table 8.2. Workers' consumption falls relative to the wage bill, with no offset, and profits fall by the amount of the tax. The tax burden ratio is equal to one and the excess tax burden ratio is greater than one. In contrast, however, if capitalists' marginal propensity to consume is non-zero, then the falls in profits, the rate of profits, national income and the wage bill are offset to some degree, and the tax burden and excess tax burden ratios decline.

2   Short-period Implications Associated With a National Lump-sum Profits Tax

If the national lump sum profits tax is used to finance government purchases, then post-tax profits and the rate of profits across jurisdictions are unaffected by the tax, but national income and the wage bill rise, through the balanced budget income multiplier. The tax burden and excess tax burden ratios are negative, because the lump sum profits tax with a balanced budget causes the wage bill to increase without reducing profits. If the lump sum profits tax is transferred to workers, the results are the same if the marginal propensity to consume out of the transfers equals one. The results are dampened if the marginal propensity to consume is less than one. Finally, if the lump sum profits tax is transferred back to capitalists, the results are the same as in Table 8.3 above, if capitalists' marginal propensity to consume out of transfers equals zero. Again, these negative results are reduced insofar as capitalists have a non-zero marginal propensity to consume.

3   Short-period Implications Associated With a Local Wage Tax

Now we suppose that a jurisdiction increases its purchases/expenditures in response to an increase in its wage tax. In this case, the jurisdictional results depend upon how the government purchases/expenditures are distributed between the local jurisdictions, or, in other words, how the government purchases/expenditures affect the balance of trade between the jurisdictions. If, for example, the wage tax results in an increase in a jurisdiction's purchases from local contractors, without affecting the balance of trade between jurisdictions, then the wage tax has no impact on national income, value added in each jurisdiction, aggregate or jurisdictional pre-tax or post-tax profits, and the pre-tax wage bill in each jurisdiction. However, in the taxing jurisdiction, the post-tax wage bill falls by the full amount of wage tax, as jurisdiction purchases displace local workers' consumption.

The story gets more complicated if we allow for jurisdiction purchases to spill out of the local jurisdiction, or, more generally, if the additional government purchases upset the balance of trade between jurisdictions. If the taxing jurisdiction purchases goods and services from non-local contractors, exports increase in the non-taxing jurisdiction pushing up its value added, its wage bill and its level and rate of profits. At the same time, imports increase in the taxing and spending jurisdiction reducing its value added, wage bill and its level and rate of profits.

To illustrate, let us suppose that 60 per cent of jurisdiction 1's government purchases leak out to contractors in jurisdiction 2, (see Table 8.6). Recall that jurisdiction 1's economy comprises 40 per cent of the national economy. At the

Table 8.6   Numerical example of the local tax model if jurisdiction 1 sets a wage tax equal to 25% ($t_w = 0.25$) with a compensating change in government purchases, where 60% of the government purchases leak out to jurisdiction 2

	Symbol	Initial Value
Jurisdiction 1		
Parameters:		
Markup	k_1	2
(Materials Bill/Wage Bill)	j_1	2
Wage Share	α_1	0.25
Policy Variables:		
Profits Tax	Tp_1	0
Wage Tax Rate	tw_1	0.25
Wage Tax	Tw_1	12.10
Variables:		
Wage Bill	W_1	47.57
Materials Bill	M_1	95.15
Wage Bill + Material Bill	$W_1 + M_1$	142.73
Value-Added	Y_1	190.31
Post-Tax Profits	P_1	142.73
Rate of Profits	r_1	0.0951
Jurisdiction 2		
Parameters:		
Markup	k_2	2
(Materials Bill/Wage Bill)	j_2	2
Wage Share	α_2	0.25
Policy Variables:		
Profits Tax	Tp_2	0
Wage Tax	Tw_2	0
Variables:		
Wage Bill	W_2	77.41
Materials Bill	M_2	154.83
Wage Bill + Material Bill	$W_2 + M_2$	232.25
Value-Added	Y_2	309.66
Post-Tax Profits	P_2	232.25
Rate of Profits	r_2	0.103

Table 8.6   continued

	Symbol	Initial Value
Macroeconomic Variables		
Parameters:		
Aggregate Profit Margin	$k-1$	1
Aggregate Materials Bill/Wage Bill	j	2
Aggregate Wage Share	α	0.25
Aggregate Income Multiplier	$1/(1-a)(1-tw)$	1.29
Investment + Gov't Expenditures	$I+G$	387.10
Policy Variables:		
National Profits Tax	Tpn	0
Aggregate Profits Tax	Tp	0
National Wage Tax Rate	twn	0
National Wage Tax	Twn	0
Aggregate Wage Tax Rate	tw	0.10
Aggregate Wage Tax	Tw	12.10
Variables:		
Aggregate Wage Bill	W	125
Aggregate Materials Bill	M	250
Aggregate Income	Y	500
Aggregate Pre-Tax Profits	$\Pi = I + G - Tw$	375
Aggregate Post-Tax Profits	$P = \Pi - Tp$	375
Tax Burden Assessment		
ΔPost-Tax Profits	0	
ΔPost-Tax Profits$_1$	−7.26	
ΔPost-Tax Profits$_2$	7.26	
ΔPre-Tax Wage	0	
ΔPre-Tax Wage$_1$	−2.42	
ΔPre-Tax Wage$_2$	2.42	
ΔPost-Tax Wage	0	
ΔPost-Tax Wage$_1$	−14.53	
ΔPost-Tax Wage$_2$	2.42	

Tax Burden Ratio = $[(0)/12.1] = 0$
Excess Tax Burden Ratio = $(12.097 - 12.097)/12.097 = 0$
Tax Burden Ratio$_1$ = $[(14.53 + 7.26)/12.1] = 1.8$
Excess Tax Burden Ratio$_1$ = $(14.53+7.26 - 12.1)/12.1 = 9.69/12.1 = 0.8$

aggregate level, little has changed. The aggregate levels of pre- and post-tax profits, income, wage and material bills, profits and rate of profits are all unchanged. Since there are no profit taxes in this case, pre-tax and post-tax profits are equal. However, at the jurisdictional level, a redistribution of income from jurisdiction 1 to jurisdiction 2 has taken place. Jurisdiction 1's local purchases have increased by 40 per cent of the wage tax increase (12.10) or by 4.84 ($0.4 \times 12.10 = 4.84$). The net result is that pre- and post-tax profits decline by 7.26 ($-7.26 = 4.84 - 12.10$). Through the income multiplier, this reduction in profits pushes jurisdiction 1's value added down to 190.3, a change of -9.7 ($-7.26 \times 1.33 = -9.7$). Jurisdiction 1's wage and materials bills adjust accordingly. Likewise, jurisdiction 2's profits increase by the amount of jurisdiction 1's government purchases from jurisdiction 2 contractors, i.e. by 7.26. Value-added in jurisdiction 2 increases by 9.7 ($7.26 \times 1.33 = 9.7$) to 309.7. As a consequence, jurisdiction 1's rate of profit declines to 9.51 per cent while jurisdiction 2's rate of profit increases to 10.3 per cent. The loss in income in jurisdiction 1 relative to the wage tax receipts is 180 per cent, causing the excess tax burden ratio to be 80 per cent. Thus, the example shows that a jurisdiction has an incentive not to raise taxes, if others do not do the same, while at the same time, it is in the interest of non-taxing and spending jurisdictions to encourage others to spend and to tax.

If the taxing jurisdiction transfers the increase in the wage tax back to local workers, and if local workers spend all the tax transfers locally, the results are the same as if the government had not increased the wage tax at all. If the taxing jurisdiction transfers the wage tax increase to capitalists, and capitalists do not consume, then the result is the same as described in Table 8.4. But if capitalists do have a non-zero marginal propensity to consume out of transfer income, then the declines in the various incomes are offset according to the degree to which capitalists spend the transfer income. The decline in the local jurisdiction's income is offset according to the degree to which capitalists spend their income locally. If workers in the taxing jurisdiction pay for some of the tax by reducing their savings, then national income increases, and in each jurisdiction value-added increases, profits increase and the pre-tax wage bill increases relative to what is described in Table 8.6.

4   Short-period Implications Associated With a Local Lump-sum Profits Tax

Assuming that the receipts of the lump sum profits tax are used to finance local government purchases in jurisdiction 1, without affecting the balance of trade between jurisdictions, the taxing jurisdiction's pre-tax profits, value added and wage and material bills all increase without affecting the post-tax level of profits or rate of profit. The resulting increases at the aggregate level reflect the changes that have taken place in jurisdiction 1 without any changes having taken place in jurisdiction 2.

Again, the story is different if, as in Table 8.6, we allow for some of jurisdiction 1's government purchases to spill over into jurisdiction 2. As before we assume that 60 per cent of jurisdiction 1's tax receipts spill over to contractors in jurisdiction 2, since jurisdiction 1 represents 40 per cent of the economy. The results of imposing a lump sum profits tax are summarized in Table 8.7.

In Table 8.7, we assume that the lump sum profits tax is 12.1, the same as in Table 8.6, and is accompanied by an increase in government purchases of that amount. Pre-tax profits thus rise to 387.10, leaving post-tax profits unchanged. Through the income multiplier, aggregate income is pushed up to 516. As 25 per cent of aggregate income accrues to wages, the new wage bill is 129, and the new materials bill (twice that of the wage bill) is 258.

By disaggregating prime costs to the jurisdictional level, where 40 per cent of the prime costs is attributed to jurisdiction 1 and 60 per cent is attributed to jurisdiction 2, the wage bills in jurisdictions 1 and 2 have increase to 51.612 and 77.419 respectively. Given that profits are a markup of $(k - 1)$ over the wage and materials bills, then the new levels of profits of each of the jurisdictions are found. Pre-tax profits in jurisdictions 1 and 2 are pushed up to 154.84 and 232.25 respectively, but since capital in jurisdiction 1 bears the burden of paying for the profits tax, its after-tax profits fall to 142.74. In short, the imposition of the tax causes after-tax profits in the taxing jurisdiction to fall by 7.26, lowering the rate of profit to 0.095, and after-tax profits in the non-taxing jurisdiction to increase by 7.26, increasing the rate of profit to 0.103 (leaving aggregate profits unchanged).

In contrast to the local wage tax, this numerical example shows that both taxes produce the same decline in the rate of profits for jurisdiction 1, but nonetheless, the excess burden of the profits tax is much smaller than that of the wage tax. In fact, as we show below, the excess burden associated with the lump sum profits tax is negative, because the tax results in additional receipts, accompanied by a higher wage bill in jurisdiction 1.

Moreover, as before, this numerical example illustrates the incentive that jurisdictions have to encourage other jurisdictions to become taxing and spending jurisdictions. If the lump sum profits tax is distributed to wage earners and wage earners have a non-zero propensity to save, then the results summarized in Table 8.7 are dampened in positive relation to the propensity to save.

If the lump sum tax is redistributed to capitalists and capitalists' marginal propensity to consume is zero, then the results are the same as in Table 8.5. The results vary positively with capitalists' propensity to consume.

Table 8.7   The impact of jurisdiction 1 imposing a lump sum tax on capital with a compensating change in government purchases, where 60% of the jurisdiction 1 purchases leak out to jurisdiction 2

	Symbol	Initial Value
Jurisdiction 1		
Parameters:		
Markup	k_1	2
(Materials Bill/Wage Bill)	j_1	2
Wage Share	α_1	0.25
Policy Variables:		
Profits Tax	Tp_1	12.10
Wage Tax Rate	tw_1	0
Wage Tax	Tw_1	0
Variables:		
Wage Bill	W_1	51.61
Materials Bill	M_1	103.22
Wage Bill + Material Bill	$W_1 + M_1$	154.83
Value-Added	Y_1	206.45
Post-Tax Profits	P_1	142.74
Rate of Profits	r_1	0.0951
Jurisdiction 2		
Parameters:		
Markup	k_2	2
(Materials Bill/Wage Bill)	j_2	2
Wage Share	α_2	0.25
Policy Variables:		
Profits Tax	Tp_2	0
Wage Tax	Tw_2	0
Variables:		
Wage Bill	W_2	77.41
Materials Bill	M_2	154.83
Wage Bill + Material Bill	$W_2 + M_2$	232.25
Value-Added	Y_2	309.66
Post-Tax Profits	P_2	232.25
Rate of Profits	r_2	0.103

Table 8.7　continued

	Symbol	Initial Value
Macroeconomic Variables		
Parameters:		
Aggregate Profit Margin	$k-1$	1
Aggregate Materials Bill/Wage Bill	j	2
Aggregate Wage Share	α	0.25
Aggregate Income Multiplier	$1/(1-a)$	1.33
Investment + Gov't Expenditures	$I+G$	387.10
Policy Variables:		
National Profits Tax	Tpn	0
Aggregate Profits Tax	Tp	12.10
National Wage Tax Rate	twn	0
National Wage Tax	Twn	0
Aggregate Wage Tax Rate	tw	0
Aggregate Wage Tax	Tw	0
Variables:		
Aggregate Wage Bill	W	129.03
Aggregate Materials Bill	M	258.06
Aggregate Income	Y	516.12
Aggregate Pre-Tax Profits	$\Pi = I + G - Tw$	387.10
Aggregate Post-Tax Profits	$P = \Pi - Tp$	375

Tax burden of local lump sum profits tax

		% of total change
ΔProfit	0	–
ΔProfit$_1$	−7.257	–
ΔProfit$_2$	7.257	–
ΔPre-Tax Wage	4.032	–
ΔPre-Tax Wage$_1$	1.613	40
ΔPre-Tax Wage$_2$	2.42	60
ΔPost-Tax Wage$_1$	1.613	–
ΔPost-Tax Wage$_2$	2.42	–

Tax Burden Ratio $= [(-1.613 - 2.42)/12.097] = -0.33$
Excess Tax Burden Ratio $= (-1.613 - 2.42 - 12.097)/12.097 = -1.333$
Tax Burden Ratio$_1 = [(7.257 - 1.613)/12.097] = 0.467$
Excess Tax Burden Ratio$_1 = (7.257 - 1.613 - 12.097)/12.097 = -0.533$

In each of the previous scenarios, we have assumed that the national government evenly spends or distributes the tax receipts back to each of the jurisdictions according to the initial set of dis-aggregation weights. Also, we have assumed that each jurisdiction's spending is distributed over the national economy according to the relative size of each jurisdiction's economy. In an actual economy, of course, this might not be the case. The national government may play favourites or the state and local governments may attempt to direct their purchases to local contractors, as recipients of jurisdictions' transfers are generally likely to be local. In the US, for example, the existence of the US Senate, to some degree, allows smaller states to receive a larger share of the government expenditures than would have otherwise occurred. Or, in the United Kingdom, it has been argued that the application of the Barnett formula confers undue advantage on Scotland. Under this sort of scenario, the playing at favourites of the national or local governments could result in a change in the balance of economic power between jurisdictions. This scenario is more of a long-period story that we discuss further below.

6   FURTHER IMPLICATIONS

As we indicated above, we recognize at least two complications: 1) changes in the business price/cost markup with respect to a change in taxation; and 2) changes in investment with respect to changes in taxation.

1   Changes in the Business Price/Cost Markup

As shown in previous chapters, Laramie (1991) and Laramie and Mair (1996) have allowed for changes in the markup with respect to a change in taxation. Basically, a tax shift parameter is introduced into a markup function. Workers, for example, may attempt to shift the wage tax by squeezing or reducing the price/cost markup; businesses may attempt to shift the profits tax by increasing the price/cost markup. This sort of shifting may go on even when the aggregate levels of post-tax profits or post-tax wages are unaffected by taxation because of changes in the intra-industry distributions of profits and wages. The most that can be said at this point is that the precise nature of the dynamic process of tax shifting is unknown, but tax shifting may take place both over the short and long periods.

If the wage tax is shifted, then business markups are reduced, the pre-tax wage share increases, which in turn increases national income and the pre-tax and post-tax wage bills, and, holding government purchases constant, reduces the level of business profits. Again this story is further complicated by the savings behaviour of wage earners. For example, if wage earners are savers and have a non-zero propensity to save, then the shifting of the tax may further reduce business profits while increasing national income. In contrast, if the profits tax is shifted, business markups increase, the wage share falls, which in turn reduces the wage bill and national income. The fall in the wage bill reduces workers' savings which increases the level of profits.

We also have to consider changes in business markups at the jurisdictional level. In Table 8.3, we showed that jurisdiction 1's increase in the wage tax reduced not only the post-tax wage bill in jurisdiction 1 but also in jurisdiction 2. Worker groups in both jurisdictions may attempt to shift the wage tax but with the pressure to do so being greater in jurisdiction 1 than in jurisdiction 2, where the tax shifting in jurisdiction 1 may be constrained by the efforts of workers in jurisdiction 2. Likewise as we show in Table 8.5, following the introduction of a lump sum profits tax in jurisdiction 1, profits fall in jurisdiction 1 by the amount of the tax. Businesses in jurisdiction 1 may attempt to shift the tax, but again these attempts may be constrained by the pricing and production decisions in jurisdiction 2. In addition, businesses in jurisdiction1 may be able to shift the tax backwards through improved technology or innovations. Thus, when tax shifting enters the discussion, a Pandora's box of possibilities arises.

2 Changes in the Level and Patterns of Investment

As we show above, some circumstances exist where a change in tax policy affects the aggregate and jurisdictional levels and rates of profits. These changes may then have an impact on the aggregate and jurisdictional levels of investment, which, in turn, affects the aggregate growth rate and relative jurisdictional rates of growth. For example in Tables 8.2 and 8.3, we showed that increases in wage taxes or profits taxes reduce the aggregate level of profits and the rate of profits. Kalecki (1968, 1971) and Gomulka, et al (1992) have explained business fixed investment decision and aggregate investment decisions as a lagged function of business savings derived from profits and the rate of profits. Others such as Fazzari et al. (1988a, 1988b) have focused on net cash flow as a determinant of investment. As showed in Chapters 3 and 4, Laramie and Mair (1996, 1998) have connected these investment decisions to the structure of taxation via the level and rate of profits. Not surprisingly, Laramie and Mair have shown that taxation which depresses the level of profits and the rate of profits depresses economic growth, and, thus, the long-period incidence effects of taxation need to be considered.

One thing that has not been done yet in Kaleckian economics is to explain how the pattern of investment responds to inter-jurisdictional differentials in the rate of profits. As we show in Tables 8.5 and 8.6, differential tax policies produce differential rates of profit depending on the government budget stance (balanced or otherwise). We expect these differential rates of profits to set in

motion a redistribution of capital through dis-investment in the high tax jurisdiction and investment in the low tax jurisdiction. The impact of this process
on jurisdictional and aggregate growth rates has to be explored further.

3   Other Implications

In developing the model thus far, we have made a number of simplifying
assumptions. In particular, we have focused on only two types of taxes, wage
and profits taxation. The model could be easily refined to account for other
forms of taxation such as *ad valorem*, excise, property or corporate income.
Moreover, the model could be adjusted for the number of mechanisms available
to businesses to avoid local income taxation. For example, the model could be
adjusted to incorporate various forms of transfer pricing under which a business
shifts its costs to high taxing areas to avoid income taxes. Or the model could
be adjusted to incorporate the tax provision allowed by state governments in the
US that only tax profits derived from sales within the state. Profits derived
from sales to other jurisdictions are thus free of local income taxation. In
addition, in analysing the effects of local taxation, we have considered two
scenarios: 1) where the local jurisdiction maintains a trade balance and increases
in government purchases accrue to local contractors; and 2) where increases in
local government purchases spill over to the non-tax-increasing jurisdiction's
contractors. Clearly, we could consider any number of situations within the
framework of these two scenarios.

7   CONCLUSION

In this chapter, we have attempted to provide a new approach to the theory of
the incidence and effects of taxation. In particular, we have attempted to
consider how national taxation affects the performance of the economies of
local jurisdictions, and how local/jurisdictional taxation affects the local
economy, other local economies and the national economy. Essentially, we
have considered these effects when taxation changes independently of
government expenditures and when governments are constrained to maintain
balanced government budget stances. The short-period results show taxation of
profits taxation is preferable to taxation of wages, assuming that investment is
fixed by past decisions, and when business markups are fixed with respect to
the tax change. The results also show that national taxes, even with a balanced
budget constraint, are preferable to local taxes, because local tax policies tend
to drive a wedge between jurisdictional rates of profits. The exception to this
rule is if local government spending of its tax receipts does not create an
imbalance of trade between the jurisdictions.

These results have many policy implications. However, we must recognize that the model poses a paradox for policy makers. On the one hand, policy makers tend to want to extend the principle of subsidiarity and bring government closer to the people. In the US, this desire means more state and local autonomy. Granting states and localities more autonomy to raise taxes and giving these authorities more responsibilities to provide public expenditure may result in regressive tax policies and 'beggar thy neighbour' policies that will undercut national economic objectives of full employment, high incomes and high growth rates.

REFERENCES

Fazzari, S., Hubbard, G. and Petersen, B. (1988a), 'Financing constraints and corporate investment', *Brookings Papers on Economic Activity*, **1**, 141–206.

Fazzari, S., Hubbard, G. and Petersen, B. (1988b), 'Investment, financing decisions and tax policy', *American Economic Review*, **78** (2), 200–5.

Gomulka, S., Ostaszewski, A. and Davies, R.O. (1990), 'The innovation rate and Kalecki's theory of the trend, unemployment and business cycle', *Economica*, **57**, 525–40.

Kalecki, M. (1968), *Theory of Economic Dynamics*, New York, Monthly Review Press.

Kalecki, M. (1971), *Selected Essays on the Dynamics of the Capitalist Economy*, 1933–1970, Cambridge, Cambridge University Press.

Laramie, A.J. (1991), 'Taxation and Kalecki's distribution factors', *Journal of Post Keynesian Economics*, **4**, 583–94.

Laramie, A.J. and Mair, D. (1996), 'Taxation and Kalecki's theory of the business cycle', *Cambridge Journal of Economics*, **20** (4), 451–64.

Laramie, A.J. and Mair, D. (1998), 'The micro-macro dichotomy of public finance: a Kaleckian solution to the problem of growth and taxation', mimeo, Heriot-Watt University.

Sawyer, M.C. (1986), *The Economics of Michal Kalecki*, London, Macmillan.

9. Conclusion: policy implications

1 INTRODUCTION

In the preceding chapters we have set out the basic framework of the Kaleckian paradigm that we argue provides an alternative, and hitherto unexplored, avenue for the analysis of taxation. At various points we have identified certain policy implications which follow from our analysis. In this final chapter, we bring a number of themes together and consider in more detail the policy implications that follow from our analysis.

2 SUPPLY SIDE FISCAL POLICY

We claimed in the opening chapter that a potentially significant feature of this book is that it provides a challenge to the supply-side argument that economic growth can only be stimulated by cutting government spending and taxation. We now return to this issue. Knoester (1983, 1984, 1987, 1988, 1991) has published a number of papers analysing the effects of fiscal policy in Europe from a supply-side perspective. However, in a statement of disarming honesty, he writes (Knoester, 1988):

> the theoretical and empirical foundations of supply-side economics are rather weak. As a rule, the rationale for this new [supply-side] look on economic policy is based on fragmentary insights lacking a general framework.

A key message of supply-side economics is that tax cuts can be of major benefit in increasing economic growth and cutting unemployment. But, despite the increasing popularity of supply-side policies in Europe the transmission channels through which tax cuts can improve economic performance have not been properly developed. In the papers cited above, Knoester argues that the forward shifting of higher taxes and social security contributions into higher real wages can result in a negative instead of a positive balanced budget multiplier effect as a result of a simultaneous increase in public spending and taxation. This Knoester calls the *inverted Haavelmo effect*. Thus, a simultaneous decrease in taxation, financed by cutting public spending, will result in a substantial increase in economic performance. It is this inverted Haavelmo effect that Knoester argues provides the theoretical underpinning for supply-side fiscal policy.

The standard Keynesian view of the macroeconomic effects of simultaneous increases in public spending and taxation was formulated by Haavelmo (1945). The effect on the level of national income will be positive (the Haavelmo effect) and provides the rationale for higher public spending financed by higher taxation and/or higher social security contributions. But, as Knoester (1991) points out, Haavelmo qualified his conclusion with the statement: 'we only wanted to demonstrate that a "balanced budget" has a direct multiplier effect, with a multiplier equal to one, in addition to whatever (positive or negative) effects there might be from a redistribution of income'.

However, the phenomenon of the forward shifting of taxation into higher wages may have far-reaching consequences for income distribution. If higher taxes are shifted forward in full, each tax increase will lead to a corresponding higher real wage claim by employees, as a result of which income distribution deteriorates for employers, resulting in a fall in profits' share of national income. Thus, according to Knoester, higher taxation, in conjunction with forward tax shifting will alter the distribution of income in favour of employees and against employers. This, in turn, will depress investment and the rate of economic growth will fall. Simultaneously, the increase in real wages brought about by the forward shifting of taxes will push up the incidence of classical unemployment. Lower economic growth, combined with rising unemployment, will lead to an increase in public spending and social security benefits which, in turn, will lead to higher taxes and social security contributions. This will set in train a vicious spiral of rising taxation leading to further forward shifting into higher real wages and so on. A process will be established of increasing unemployment and taxation and falling economic growth. Thus, an inverted Haavelmo effect may result in which the negative effects of increasing taxation can outweigh the positive Keynesian effects on economic growth and unemployment of the increase in public spending.

As well as the effect on income distribution outlined above, Knoester (1991) identifies a second direct effect of higher real wages on a country's competitiveness and exports. Forward shifting of taxes will increase unit labour costs and cause competitiveness to deteriorate. As a result, exports fall which, in turn, causes a decrease in economic growth. For these two reasons, supply-side fiscal policy invokes the inverted Haavelmo effect to justify policies of reductions in taxation and public spending as a means of stimulating economic growth and reducing unemployment.

Knoester (1987, p. 167) claims that the introduction of the Haavelmo effect provides supply-side fiscal policy with the desired 'consistent theoretical framework'. This claim is based on what he describes as a 'synthesis of Keynesian income-expenditure analysis and neoclassical growth theory, i.e. ...

a mix of supply and demand'. His discovery of the inverse Haavelmo effect comes from recognizing that forward shifting of taxation results in a change in income distribution in favour of employees and away from employers.

We are not persuaded that Knoester has taken adequate account of the implications of tax-induced changes in income distribution. This is because his theory is based explicitly on the marginal productivity theory of income distribution where the economy is constrained by supply-side determinants. We have discussed above in Chapter 1 what we consider to be the restrictions which espousal of that theory implies for the theory of taxation. Our principal difference with Knoester is over what constitutes 'a consistent theoretical framework'. In our view, he falls into the same error as Burbidge (1976) identified in a number of studies of the incidence of the US corporation profits tax, namely, the juxtaposition of internally inconsistent pre-Keynesian microeconomic theory with Keynesian macroeconomic theory, and, therefore, allows for unemployment and surplus capacity as only special (short-run) cases with aggregate demand effects nullified in the long-run. This is the approach that permeates mainstream theory and, as we have seen, is recognized by certain leading public finance economists as a source of some concern.

In contrast to the marginal productivity based wage bargaining model in Knoester's approach, in which the real wage rate is determined in the labour market, a Kaleckian approach argues that the real wage is determined in the product market.[1] For a wage tax to be shifted, the markup, k, has to be inversely related to a change in the wage tax.

As we show in Chapter 2, under a balanced budget constraint, an increase in the wage tax increases the level of national income, and when the wage tax is shifted, via a reduction in the markup, the balanced budget effect on national income of the wage tax is heightened. In Chapter 3, we show that a balanced budget increase in the wage tax, through a reduction in worker savings, results in higher profits, assuming the wage tax is not shifted. However, we also show in Chapter 3 that the shifting of the wage tax, which increases the wage share and the wage bill, can result in an increase in worker savings and simultaneously dampen the balanced budget wage tax effect on the pre-tax and post-tax levels of profits. Thus, in the short period at least, shifting of the wage tax in a Kaleckian model results in exactly the opposite effects of those predicted by Koestner's neoclassical-Keynesian model. However, in the long period, where profits affect investment decisions, depending upon the parameters, we might find an inverted Haavelmo effect. The issue then becomes an empirical one.

1. Sawyer (1985) derives an expression for the real wage rate from the price markup equation: $w/p = (1/k)/(Q/N)$; where w = the money wage rate; p is the price level; k = the markup; Q = the level of output; and N = the level of employment.

3 KEYNESIAN VS KALECKIAN FISCAL POLICY

Clearly, we have reservations about the theoretical consistency of the supply-side approach to fiscal policy. Equally, we wish to demark ourselves from what has come to be known as orthodox Keynesian fiscal policy. There is a widespread tendency to give Keynes exclusive credit for 'discovering' macroeconomics. If Kalecki's contribution to the 'discovery' is recognized at all, it is generally parenthetical (Allsop, 1990, p. 181). This has given rise to a 'synecdochic fallacy', by which we mean there has been what we consider to be a fallacious identification of macroeconomic fiscal policy exclusively with Keynesian fiscal policy. Our objective in this book has been to attempt to establish a totally separate Kaleckian macroeconomic theory of taxation that has its own distinctive policy agenda.

As a consequence, we wish to stand aside from the debates over the efficacy of fiscal policy between monetarists and orthodox Keynesians or between orthodox Keynesians and post Keynesians. The mini-symposium on the viability of Keynesian demand management policy in the *Journal of Post Keynesian Economics*, 17, (2), *Winter* 1994–5, is, for example, a classic illustration of the disagreements which still rage over what Keynes did, or did not say, in the *General Theory*, and whether the macroeconomic policies which have been given the sobriquet 'Keynesian' are no more than a 'bastardization' of the term.

However, the one paper in that symposium which goes to what we consider to be the heart of the problem is by Epstein (1995). He argues that it is not enough for (post) Keynesians to expose the weaknesses or fallacies in the arguments of their critics. (Post) Keynesians have to recognize the extremely serious political and economic constraints on the ability of Keynesian demand management policy by itself to bring an economy to the level of full employment and keep it there. Chief among the political constraints that Epstein identifies is the one Kalecki (1971/1943) pointed out long ago, namely, the political power of rentiers and capitalists. We now consider this issue in more detail.

4 TAX SHIFTING, THE MARKUP AND THE DEGREE OF MONOPOLY

As we have demonstrated at a number of points in this book, and particularly in Chapter 3, the macroeconomic incidence and effects of taxation in a Kaleckian model depend critically on whether or not tax shifting occurs. Tax shifting occurs when either workers or capitalists are able to engineer a favourable shift in the markup in response to an increase in the taxation of wages or profits, in order to maintain or increase their share of national income. Indeed, as we demonstrate in Chapter 3, there will be no macroeconomic effects unless a change occurs in the distribution of income between wages and profits. Therefore, the markup, and its underlying theory of income distribution, play a pivotal role in determining the macroeconomic outcomes of fiscal policy.

1   Degree of Monopoly Theory of Income Distribution

Over the years, Kalecki's theory of income distribution has been the object of much confusion and misinterpretation. Much of this confusion stems from a failure to appreciate that his theory actually comprises two complementary theories. Nell (1972, p. 451) writes:

> Kalecki's [distribution] theory consists of two complementary parts: the degree of monopoly and the costs of materials determine costs and mark-ups on the one hand, and the pattern of consumption and investment spending determine output and employment on the other. Only by taking these two together do we get the complete theory.

Thus, there are two theories in Kalecki, the microeconomic theory based on the 'degree of monopoly' (and this is the one which has generated most of the controversy); and the macroeconomic theory based on Kalecki's aphorism that 'workers spend what they earn and capitalists earn what they spend'.

The version of Kalecki's distribution theory we employ here is the one that appeared in *Theory of Economic Dynamics* (Kalecki, 1954). This version provides an integrated treatment of Kalecki's theories of income determination and income distribution in which both microeconomic and macroeconomic forces act together. Direct labour's share of national income is determined by the process of firms marking up direct costs to obtain prices. The level of profits is determined by investment decisions taken in the past and (Kalecki, (1954), p. 47)

> the national output will be pushed up to the point where profits carved out of it in accordance with the 'distribution factors' are equal to the sum of capitalists' consumption and investment.

It is important to recognize that Kalecki's theory of income distribution is consistent with an approach to economics under which income and employment are determined, at least in part, by effective demand and where persistent unemployment is possible.

As Feiwel (1975, p. 87) observes, Kalecki's theory of distribution derives genealogically from the Ricardian tradition. Hahn (1972, p. 2) criticizes neo-classical distribution theory for its preoccupation with models of perfect competition in permanent equilibrium and its failure to recognize social class as an explanatory variable. He commends Kalecki's theoretical views as being important in their own right and because of their focus on an aspect of distribution theory hitherto neglected because of neoclassical preoccupations with the production function and perfect competition (Hahn (1972), p. 37). Hahn welcomes Kalecki's contribution too on the grounds of his rejection of perfect competition as being 'positively harmful' and his non-ideological use of social classes as the basis of analysis.

Kalecki's intention, according to Rothschild (1961, p. 180), was to develop a macroeconomic theory of income distribution. Like the marginal productivity school, he started at the microeconomic level with the single firm. But the categories Kalecki used did not lead him to the sort of adding-up problems which make the extension of marginal productivity theorizing to the entire economy such a doubtful procedure. Kalecki's categories of raw material prices and pricing policy do not become 'so irritatingly shiftable' (Rothschild, 1961, p. 180) when the *ceteris paribus* clause of sector analysis is dropped. Rothschild's view is that Kalecki's departure from neoclassical theory was not so much the result of a deliberate search for a macroeconomic theory as a macroeconomic theory developing out of his specific assumptions concerning the theory of the firm. This is also Feiwel's (1975, pp. 87–8) interpretation, that Kalecki's contribution to distribution theory lies in the integration of microeconomic and macroeconomic elements, in the building of a macroeconomic distribution theory on the stronger foundations of a more plausible theory of the firm and in bringing in the forces of market imperfection.

2   Microeconomic Dimension of Kalecki's Theory of Distribution

As we mention in Chapter 2, the precise nature of tax shifting is unknown since, as shown in other chapters, business and labour will probably attempt to shift taxes which may either counteract or intensify the effects of the tax policy depending upon the specific tax change and the government's budget stance. The extent to which a tax is shifted depends upon the specific determinants of business markups. As mentioned in Chapter 1, Laramie, Mair, Miller and Reynolds (1998) have estimated the degree of monopoly in the 'spirit' of Kalecki for a sample of UK manufacturing industries for the period 1985–90. We show that the markup, k and, therefore, its inverse, the share of wages in national income, can be estimated empirically from industry data. One of our main concerns is how tax shifting plays out in calendar time in environments where the distribution of income is determined by the 'degree of monopoly'. Future research on equation (1.4) will have to consider the relationship between tax shifting and business markups in order to understand more fully the micro and macroeconomic dimensions of tax policy.

3   Macroeconomic Dimension of Kalecki's Theory of Distribution

Kalecki's macroeconomic theory of income determination derives from his theory of the determination of profits (Kalecki, (1942, 1954)). Profits can be simply defined as the sum of investment and capitalist consumption. As we discussed in previous chapters, Kalecki posed the question – what is the significance of this identity? Does it mean that profits in a given period determine capitalists' consumption and investment, or vice versa? The answer, he argued, depends on which of these elements is subject to the decision of capitalists. Now, capitalists may decide to consume and to invest more in a given period than in the preceding one but they cannot decide to earn more. It is, therefore, the consumption and investment decisions of capitalists that determine profits and not vice versa. This very profound conclusion is central to Kalecki's entire schema.

This skeleton of Kalecki's theory of the determination of profits also provides his theory of effective demand. So why then would governments not use his theory to achieve full employment? Kalecki (1941/1943) concluded that the assumption that governments would maintain full employment if only they knew how to do so was fallacious for three reasons: 1) a dislike by 'industrial leaders' of government interference in the problem of employment as such; 2) a dislike by 'industrial leaders' of the direction of government spending, for example, public investment or subsidizing consumption; 3) a dislike by 'industrial leaders' of the social and political changes resulting from the maintenance of full employment.

The reasons behind these arguments for the rejection of full employment run as follows. First, while every extension of state activity is looked upon with suspicion by 'industrial leaders', the creation of employment is a particularly sensitive area. Under *laissez faire* capitalism, the level of employment depends largely on the state of confidence of businessmen. If this deteriorates, there will be a fall in private investment leading to falls in output and employment. This sensitivity of investment to the level of confidence gives capitalists a powerful indirect control over governments which must, therefore, avoid at all costs doing anything that might have adverse repercussions on the state of business confidence. Once governments learn the trick of increasing employment by their own purchases, Kalecki argued, this powerful controlling device that businessmen have over governments would lose much of its effectiveness.

Kalecki's second reason is a 'political' crowding out argument. Public investment is acceptable to 'industrial leaders' so long as it is restricted to activities such as roads, schools, hospitals etc. that do not compete with private investment. If the socialization of investment is carried too far this may result in nationalization of transport or public utilities so as to provide governments with new spheres in which to carry out investment (remember, Kalecki wrote this in 1943!). Businessmen would also be opposed to the subsidization of mass public consumption on the 'moral' grounds that it would violate the fundamental capitalist ethic 'You shall earn your bread in sweat'. (Kalecki (1943, p. 140) could not avoid adding 'unless you have private means'.)

Kalecki's third argument was that the maintenance of full employment would result in social and political changes that businessmen would find uncongenial. The 'sack' would cease to play its role as a disciplinary measure. As the self-assurance and the class-consciousness of the working class grew, the social position of businessmen would be undermined. Even though business profits would be higher under full employment than they were on average under *laissez faire*, Kalecki argued that businessmen would place greater value on 'industrial discipline' and 'political stability' than on profits.

> Their class instinct tells them that lasting full employment is unsound from their point of view and that unemployment is an integral part of the normal capitalist system. (Kalecki, (1943), p. 141)

5   INCOME DISTRIBUTION IN THE UNITED KINGDOM

In Kaleckian taxation theory, the macroeconomic outcomes hinge on what has been happening to the distribution of income. There is now a considerable body of evidence pointing to a significant shift in income distribution in the UK over the last two decades towards the higher income groups (Goodman and Webb, (1994), Jenkins, (1995), Jenkins and Cowell, (1994)). For example, Jenkins and Cowell estimate that 39 per cent of the growth in average income in the UK in the 1980s has been accounted for by the contribution of the richest tenth of the population. However, the discussion in the literature of the economic causes and consequences of this shift in income distribution has been anodyne.

Laramie, Mair and Toporowski (1999) have shown that Weintraub's (1979, 1981) consumption coefficient provides a useful technique for exploring the reasons for class-based changes in income distribution. The consumption coefficient, a, is defined simply as the ratio of total consumer expenditure (C) to income from employment, W, i.e. $a = C/W$. Weintraub (1979) showed how the consumption coefficient can simplify and generalize Kaleckian macroeconomics. He also showed (Weintraub, 1981) that the consumption coefficient can be decomposed into its determinants:

$$C = aW = c_w W + c_r \lambda \Pi + c_\theta \Theta \tag{9.1}$$

where c_w = average propensity to consume out of private sector income; c_r = average propensity to consume out of pre-tax distributed profits; Π = pre-tax profits; λ = corporate profit payout ratio; c_θ = average propensity to consume out of transfer payments (including government wages and salaries); and Θ = transfer payments (including government wages and salaries).

Dividing both sides of equation (9.1) by W yields:

$$a = c_w + c_r \lambda \Pi / W + c_\theta \Theta / W \qquad (9.2)$$

Analysis of the right-hand side of equation (9.2) allows us to consider the factors that have been affecting the consumption coefficient and the consequent economic implications. Over the period 1972–95, the consumption coefficient has risen more or less steadily. From a level of 1.33 in 1972, it dipped to 1.22 in 1975. Thereafter, it rose to a peak of 1.49 in 1988 before slipping to 1.39 in 1991 from which level it has risen again to 1.43 in the mid-1990s. The growth in the consumption coefficient has been driven entirely by: 1) an increase in P/W (the ratio of capitalist to wage income); and 2) by a growth in c_r (the average propensity to consume out of capitalist income). From a level of 0.34 in 1976, P/W has risen by 50 per cent to 0.51 in 1995. At the same time, c_r has risen by 85 per cent from a level of 0.35 in 1975 to 0.65 in 1994. The propensity to consume out of wage income, c_w, has remained static over the period and there has been no secular trend in the term $c_\theta \Theta / W$.

The consumption coefficient confirms the shift in income distribution in the UK but now analyses it in terms of social classes. Since the mid-1970s, 'capitalist income' (income from self-employment, rent, dividends and net interest) has risen significantly more rapidly than 'worker income' (total income from [private sector] employment). However, not only have capitalists in the UK increased their income share, they have also substantially increased their propensity to consume.

The behaviour of the consumption coefficient in the UK since the early 1970s reveals a Kaleckian story. At the microeconomic level, profits' share of income has risen or, conversely, the wage share has fallen. This change is confirmed by the behaviour of the aggregate markup (gross domestic product/income from employment) over the period. From a level of 1.4 in 1975 it has risen by 15 per cent to 1.6 in 1995. This confirms that there has been an increase in the 'degree of monopoly' in the UK economy over the last 20 years as a consequence of changes in the environmental and institutional factors of the kind we have discussed earlier in this chapter.

At the macroeconomic level, we observe an unbroken rising trend of 'capitalist' income in the UK since 1972 (Laramie, Mair and Toporowski, 1999). From 1972 to 1989, this has been tracked closely by investment, as we would expect in a Kaleckian world ('capitalists earn what they spend'). However, since 1989, investment in the UK has levelled off while capitalist income has continued to grow strongly. This supports the evidence from the consumption coefficient of the increasing scale of 'capitalists'' consumption. This suggests that capitalists' consumption is no longer the relatively unimportant and only slowly changing component of capitalists' expenditure that Kalecki originally thought it was. Capitalists, at least in the UK, no longer seem to be behaving in the traditional capitalist manner and are increasingly substituting consumption for investment.

This behaviour of the consumption coefficient has some rather worrying long-term implications for the UK. The fact that the consumption coefficient has been consistently greater than one and rising since the mid-1970s suggests that the levels of national income and profits in the UK have been pushed up. However, the rise in the coefficient has been accompanied by higher business markups and by a reduction in the national income share of income from (private sector) employment. With the consumption coefficient greater than one, these latter effects will have had a negative impact on current profits, with adverse longer-term effects on future investment. It seems to us that the redistribution of income that has occurred in recent years is potentially one of the most serious long-term issues facing the UK. Our concern is not simply over the equity issue this raises. It is the combination of the redistribution of income in association with the other changes revealed by the consumption coefficient that we think have potentially serious implications for the UK.

6   DEMOCRATIC IMPLICATIONS

The issue we have identified above poses a serious dilemma for British governments in the twenty-first century (Laramie and Mair, 1998). If governments seek to pursue fiscal objectives of stimulating investment and growth within a balanced budget framework by reducing the taxation of profits, they run the risk of achieving the exact opposite. This dilemma recalls a concern raised by Sir Samuel Brittan over quarter of a century ago (Brittan, 1975). Brittan's thesis was that liberal representative democracies suffer from internal contradictions that are likely to increase over time. The two endemic threats to liberal representative society that Brittan identified were: 1) the generation of excessive expectations; and 2) the disruptive effects of the pursuit of group self-interest in the market place.

Excessive expectations are generated by the democratic aspects of liberal democratic societies. The disruptive effects, Brittan argues, arise from elementary economic logic and are not directly connected with the political structure. The two are linked by a formula which Brittan, using a term suggested to him by Bertrand de Juvenel, describes as *the excessive burden placed on the 'sharing out' function of government* (emphasis in original). This function Brittan defines as the activities of the public authorities in influencing the allocation of resources, both through taxation and expenditure policies and through direct intervention in the market place. The growth of expectations imposes demands for different kinds of public spending and intervention that are incompatible both with each other and with the tax burden people are willing to bear. At the same time, in their pursuit of 'full employment' without currency collapse, governments have been tempted to intervene directly in the determination of pre-tax incomes. But, as Brittan warns, these attempts come to grief when they come up against the demands of different income groups for incompatible income shares.

Twenty-five years ago, when Brittan advanced this thesis, it could, with some justification, be argued that the UK was its best examplar. Indeed, its manifestations in other countries were usually described by the term 'English sickness'. Now, it may be argued that the policies of successive Conservative governments from 1979 to 1997, particularly those of Baroness Thatcher, have cured the UK of the 'English sickness'. A massive programme of privatization has rolled back 'the frontiers of the state', government spending as a percentage of GDP has levelled off since the early 1980s and Chancellors of the Exchequer have striven manfully, though not wholly successfully, to reduce the burden of taxation.

7 FISCAL STABILITY UNDER NEW LABOUR

It would appear that the Labour government in the UK is determined to carry on or, indeed, improve on, the good work of fiscal rectitude. The Pre-Budget Report of November 1997 (HM Treasury (1997), hereafter PBR) sets out the conditions under which the Labour government will seek to achieve its central economic objectives of high and stable levels of growth and employment. Low inflation and low government borrowing are seen to be the essential building blocks for long-term growth. Responsibility for the operation of monetary policy has been given to the Bank of England. The challenge now seen by the PBR is to apply a similar approach to fiscal policy in order to ensure that future governments will always set fiscal policy in ways that promote economic stability.

To this end, the government has published a Code for Fiscal Stability (HM Treasury (1998), hereafter CFS). The CFS enshrines the two cardinal rules that will henceforth determine fiscal policy in the UK. The first is the so-called 'golden rule' that over the economic cycle the government will only borrow to invest and not to fund current expenditure. The second is that public debt as a proportion of national income will be held over the cycle at a stable and prudent level.

These rules, linked to the government's plans for debt reduction, are intended to establish a sound long-term basis for fiscal policy. The application of these fiscal rules over the cycle will enable the automatic fiscal stabilizers to operate and contribute to economic stability. It is recognized that occasionally discretionary changes in fiscal policy may be necessary to provide a support for monetary policy, but always subject to the conditions of the CFS. These fiscal rules have been set out as an average over the cycle to recognize the significance of cyclical changes in the public finances. The government's intention is to enhance stability by allowing public borrowing to fluctuate due to cyclical changes in output, that is, by allowing the automatic stabilizers to operate. It is the government's clear intention that fiscal policy will play second fiddle to monetary policy. Any prospect of a return to the use of orthodox Keynesian fiscal stabilization policy of budget surpluses or deficits is clearly ruled out.

8   INCOME DISTRIBUTION AND FISCAL POLICY

Thus, it would appear that in the UK at least we are living in a fiscal world in which Dr Pangloss would feel comfortably at home. So, was Sir Samuel Brittan's warning premature or alarmist that the British liberal representative democratic system was in danger of collapse within the lifetimes of people then adult in the mid 1970s? A consequence of the effective disengagement by British governments over the last quarter of a century from responsibility for the 'sharing out' function has been a substantial shift in favour of 'capitalist' income. That in itself need not necessarily have been a bad thing if late twentieth-century British 'capitalists' had been behaving in the traditional capitalist manner. But it appears to us that they have not. The income gains of 'capitalists' have been used primarily to fund an increase in their consumption. Investment has declined relatively and with it prospects of faster long-term growth in the UK.

As we show in Chapter 3, cyclical stabilization of the economy around a zero trend rate of investment with a balanced budget constraint can be achieved in a Kaleckian schema by varying the structure of taxation. On the assumption of no tax shifting, greater stability over the cycle can be achieved in either of two ways. First, if investment is in an upswing, or at its peak, an *un-shifted* increase in the rate of taxation of wage income will reduce the impact of current investment on current profits and future investment. An *un-shifted* increase in the rate of taxation of wage income will dampen the upswing and reduce the peak of the cycle. Similarly, during the downswing and at the trough an *un-shifted* increase in the rate of taxation of wage income will again dampen the amplitude of the cycle. Second, the same stabilization objective can be achieved by an *un-shifted* reduction in the rate of profits tax during the upswing of the cycle and by an *un-shifted* reduction in the rate of profits tax during the downswing.

At a theoretical level, the stabilization policy choice facing a government would appear to be between raising the tax rate on wage income or cutting the tax rate on profits. The empirical evidence from the US we report in Chapter 6 suggests strongly that changes in tax rates on wage income have a much more potent effect on investment than changes in tax rates on profits. Thus, in practice, the fiscal burden of stabilization would be borne by the recipients of wage income but only if they are *unable* to shift their increased tax burden. Also, as we show in Chapter 3, assuming that savings out of wage income are non-zero, a balanced budget increase in the taxation of wage income will increase the trend level of investment. Thus, to achieve both stabilization and growth objectives in a balanced budget, no-tax-shifting scenario, our analysis suggests that the odds are heavily stacked in favour of increasing taxation of wage income relative to taxation of profits.

To ensure the success of such a stabilization and growth policy, a government would have to be satisfied that the strength of the 'degree of monopoly' was such as to preclude any tax shifting by earners of wage incomes. Thus, the success or failure of government fiscal policy will depend critically on the outcome of the class struggle over income shares. Success requires that the 'capitalists' are the winners.

Our analysis, which we discuss earlier in this chapter, of the 'degree of monopoly' forces at work in UK manufacturing suggests that entry barriers (particularly product differentiation as measured by the advertising:sales ratio), the degree of industry openness and the influence of changes in overhead costs in relation to prime costs (as measured by the growth rate of real industry output) all have a positive and statistically significant effect on the markup, k, and through k, inversely on the share of wages in national income. Whether a government would be prepared to allow the success of its fiscal policy to be determined by the vagaries of industrial markets or whether it would wish to be more confident of success by introducing an incomes policy which sought to ensure that wage earners bore the full burden of any increase in the taxation of their incomes is obviously an important issue that then arises.

Thus, Kaleckian analysis suggests that successful fiscal stabilization and growth policy is more than a matter of simply applying the 'cardinal rules' of fiscal prudence and waiting for the automatic stabilizers to kick in. Changes in income distribution are of critical importance. The discussion we have presented in this chapter suggests that strict control over the outcome of the class struggle over income shares to ensure 'capitalist' supremacy may be a necessary but not a sufficient condition for successful fiscal stabilization and growth policy in the UK. It will also require a fundamental switch in the pattern of capitalist expenditure away from consumption and back to investment which tax incentives may do little to stimulate.

REFERENCES

Allsopp, C. (1990), 'The macroeconomic role of the state', in Helm, D. (ed.), *The Economic Borders of the State*, Oxford, Oxford University Press.

Brittan, S. (1975), 'The economic consequences of democracy', *British Journal of Political Science*, **5**, 129–60.

Burbidge, J.B. (1976), 'Internally inconsistent mixtures of micro- and macro-theory in empirical studies of profits tax incidence', *Finanzarchiv*, **35**, 218–34.

Epstein, G. (1995), 'Keynesian demand management is alive and ill', *Journal of Post Keynesian Economics*, **17** (2), 307–10.

Feiwel, G. (1975), *The Intellectual Capital of Michal Kalecki*, Knoxville, University of Tennessee Press.

Goodman, A. and Webb, S. (1994), 'For richer, for poorer: the changing distribution of income in the UK, 1961–1991', *Fiscal Studies*, **15** (4), 29–62.

Haavelmo, T. (1945), 'Multiplier effects of a balanced budget', *Econometrica*, **13**, 311–18.

Hahn, F.H. (1972), *The Share of Wages in the National Income*, London, Weidenfeld and Nicolson.

Jenkins, S.P. (1995), 'Accounting for inequality trends: decomposition analyses for the UK, 1971–1986' *Economica*, **62**, 29–63.

Jenkins, S.P. and Cowell, F.A. (1994), 'Dwarfs and giants in the 1980s: trends in UK income distribution', *Fiscal Studies*, **15** (1), 99–118.

Kalecki, M. (1942), 'A theory of profits, *Economic Journal*, **52**, 258–67.

Kalecki, M. (1954), *Theory of Economic Dynamics*, London, Unwin University Books.

Kalecki, M. (1971/1943), 'Political aspects of full employment', *Political Quarterly*, **14**. Reprinted in *Selected Essays in the Dynamics of the Capitalist Economy*, Cambridge, Cambridge University Press.

Knoester, A. (1983), 'Stagnation and the inverted Haavelmo effect', *De Economist*, **131** (4), 548–84.

Knoester, A. (1984), 'Negative consequences of public sector expansion in the US and Europe', *Occasional Paper*, Washington, DC, American Enterprise Institute for Public Policy Research.

Knoester, A. (1987), 'Supply-side policies in four OECD countries', in Motamen, H. (ed.), *Economic Modeling in OECD Countries*, London, Chapman and Hall.

Knoester, A. (1988), 'Supply-side economics and the inverted Haavelmo effect', in Phelps, E.S. (ed.), *Recent Developments in Macroeconomics, Vol.II*, International Library of Critical Writings in Economics, Aldershot, Edward Elgar.

Knoester, A. (1991), 'The inverted Haavelmo effect and the effects of fiscal policies in the United States, the United Kingdom, Germany and the Netherlands', in Knoester, A. (ed), *Taxation in the United States and Europe*', New York, St. Martin's Press.

Laramie, A.J. and Mair, D. (1998), 'A reassessment of Schumpeter on fiscal policy from a dynamic tax incidence perspective', *Revista di Economia Contemporanea*, **4**, 7–42.

Laramie, A.J., Mair, D., Miller, A.G. and Reynolds, P.J. (1998), 'Kalecki's degree of monopoly theory of income distribution: the answer to a maiden's prayer?', mimeo, Heriot-Watt University, Edinburgh.

Laramie, A.J., Mair, D. and Toporowski, J. (1999), 'Weintraub's consumption coefficient: some economic evidence and implications for the UK, *Cambridge Journal of Economics*, forthcoming.

Nell, E.J. (1972), 'Two books on the theory of income distribution', *Journal of Economic Literature*, **10**, 442–53.

Rothschild, K.W. (1961), 'Some recent contributions to a macroeconomic theory of income distribution', *Scottish Journal of Political Economy*, 173–99.

Sawyer, M.C. (1985), *The Economics of Michal Kalecki*, London, Macmillan.

Weintraub, S. (1979), 'Generalizing Kalecki and simplifying macroeconomics', *Journal of Post Keynesian Economics*, **1** (3), 101–6.

Weintraub, S. (1981), 'An eclectic theory of income shares', *Journal of Post Keynesian Economics*, **4** (1), 10–24.

Index

Contractor's Principle 36
convergence criteria, Maastricht Treaty
    143
core assumptions, neoclassical theory
    112–13
corporate net interests, corporate profits
    tax incidence model 90
corporate profits
    corporate profits tax 93–7
    marginal propensity to save 98
    savings and investment identity 85
    state and local taxes, US 133–43
corporate profits identity 85, 100–8
corporate profits tax 82–108
    balanced budget constraint 92–3
    fixed government purchases 91–2
    framework for assessing incidence
        85–7
    Harberger-type models 83–4
    illustrating incidence of 87–8
    incidence model 88–91
    profit changes 93–7
    as revenue source 141–2
corporation tax 36
corrected growth equation 66–9, 75
Courvisanos, revision of investment
    theory 3–4
Crotty's criticisms, neoclassical theory
    114
cyclical component, of investment 54–8

degree of monopoly
    income distribution 12–17, 181–2
    output and employment 18–19
democratic implications, income distrib-
    ution 186–7
depreciation
    profits tax rate 56, 60–1
    taxation and 51–2
    wage tax rate 59, 60
direct labour, share of national income
    12, 14, 181
disruptive effects, group self interest
    186–7
distribution *see* income distribution
dividends, corporate profits tax incident
    model 90

economic effects, taxation 40

economic equilibrium, tax incidence
    theory 8
Economic Journal 1
economic policy, corporate profits tax
    98–100
Economic Recovery Act (1981),
    reduction in corporate profits tax 96
economic stability, taxation 69–70, 75–8
employment
    Kalecki's distribution theory 183–4
    see also unemployment
EMU
    fiscal policy 143–4
    Kaleckian theory 144–5
entrepreneurial savings, investment 49,
    88–9
equilibrium analysis
    Kalecki's hostility to 11
    tax incidence 7
equilibrium growth models 9
*Essays in the Theory of Economic
    Fluctuations* 18
Euro 143
European Monetary Union *see* EMU
European System of Central Banks 143
European Union, macroeconomic effects
    of fiscal policy 143–4
excessive expectations, liberal
    democratic societies 186
expenses, legitimation 39–40
exports, higher wages 178

Federal grants-in aid 137–8, 142
firms
    business property tax 36–8
    pricing behaviour 13, 30–1, 34–5
fiscal federalism 130, 137
fiscal policy
    business cycle theory 58–9
    EMU 143–4
    income distribution 188–90
    investment theory 117
    Keynesian vs. Kaleckian 180
    macro and micro aspects 8–10
    state and local taxes 130
    supply side 177–9
fiscal stability, New Labour 187–8

General Theory 1, 20, 25, 64, 111, 180
giant corporations 13